THE CORRESPONDENCE

between

PAUL CLAUDEL

AND

ANDRÉ GIDE

THE CORRESPONDENCE
1899-1926

between

PAUL CLAUDEL

AND

ANDRÉ GIDE

Introduction and Notes by Robert Mallet

PREFACED AND TRANSLATED BY
JOHN RUSSELL

PANTHEON

92
C57

121032

The publishers wish to thank Alfred A. Knopf,
Inc. for kind permission to quote passages from
The Journals of André Gide, Vols. I, II, III, translated by Justin O'Brien, copyrighted 1947, 1948,
1949 by Alfred A. Knopf, Inc.

Manufactured in the United States
Library of Congress catalog Card Number: 52-9674

PREFACE

By

JOHN RUSSELL

THE general course of this correspondence has been so carefully charted by Monsieur Robert Mallet that I need only refer the reader to his lengthy and illuminating Introduction. There are, however, certain aspects of the monumental exchange which may require some further elucidation for those whose first language is English. It is not only French literature, but French life, that is the enveloping subject of the book ; and letters which, in themselves, might seem trivial or otiose may acquire a new pungency if placed in their historical context.

The letters run from 1899 to 1926, but it is in the first fifteen years of this century that they are most momentous. It was at that time that the great generation of 1870 began to transform the appearance of French literature. The disciples of Mallarmé are now so much the Old Masters of the literary Louvre that it is difficult to recapture the sensations with which their works were originally received. In the case of Claudel, professional etiquette forbade him, as a diplomatist, to publish freely the enormous works of his youth. (Those who have read the early diaries of Paul Morand will realize how remote was Claudel from the ordinary climate of the Quai d'Orsay.) In the case of Gide, the books, though available to all, moved only at glacier-pace for the first years of their existence. The study of both writers, therefore, was invested with that element of conspiracy which so greatly enhances the pleasure of the discerning reader. Their books were awaited, when they were awaited at all, with an irresistible transport of sympathy to which the relaxed habits of our own era can offer no parallel. One has only to plunge one's thermometer, for instance, into that other great *Briefwechsel*, the correspondence of Alain Fournier and Jacques Rivière, to note how the mercury bursts from its container at the mention of Claudel or Gide. In French literary life, moreover, personalities are of great account. Social exchanges are accompanied by a degree of formality which, though sometimes ludicrous in the eyes of the blunt islander, is in fact merely a mark of respect for the rarity and complication of the spirit which is being addressed. (A shift of emphasis in a letter-ending may wound for twenty years—such are the hazards and advantages of ritual.) In these manœuvres, both Claudel and Gide were incomparably expert, and the Correspondence includes many letters which would lead one to believe that Gide was the professional diplomatist and Claudel, in comparison, a professional plain man. All these, however, are difficulties of manner, rather than of matter ; once launched, and once habituated to the obsolete upholstery, the many layers of velvet and plush which cover the simplest exchanges, the reader will be so possessed by a sense of sociable comfort that he will never again be able to end a letter with stubby little " Yours " ; older manners will prove contagious.

These, then, are polite letters. The matter may be savage enough—at one point it could hardly be more so—but the manner remains easy and distinguished. As the correspondence progresses we realize that the two combatants regarded themselves, almost consciously, as the plenipotentiaries of two great sections of the French people. If they address themselves to one another with such enormous gravity, it is because the outcome concerns many thousands of people beyond their immediate circle—many thousands, in fact, who may never have heard of either Claudel or Gide, and many thousands who were not even born at the time the letters went back and forth between France and China and Japan. Claudel's letters are astir to the last with the conviction that Gide will one day be converted to Catholicism, and Gide has saluted in Claudel one of the most immovable spirits that ever held a pen. The conflict is one that will never grow obsolete : that between authority and the individual. There was really no chance that this conflict would be resolved within the present correspondence. Formal hopes and formal admirations are one thing, and the hazards of true intimacy quite another. There is no true intimacy in this correspondence, though a great many intimate things are said. Only in its opening years does the struggle contain some slight element of inconclusiveness. Gide's conversion at that point would have changed the course of French literature ; *Strait is the Gate*, *The Vatican Cellars*, *The Coiners*, and many other important books would have been written differently, or not at all. His gifts were by no means fully developed, and it must naturally have seemed to Claudel that here, as in so many other cases, a new and valuable human being could be refashioned in accordance with the precepts of the Church. In the event, as everyone knows, Gide was to display supreme powers of non-allegiance ; but to assume that this was inevitable is to ignore the personal authority of Claudel in the first decade of this century.

We in England have had famous proselytes, but we have had nothing quite like Claudel. The young men of forty years old were convinced that the universal disturbances of adolescence could be taken in hand, if they so chose, by a personality of overwhelming power. Here, for instance, is a story told by Jacques Rivière in 1907 :

" L. L., who knew Jammes, went to stay with him, and there met Claudel. Claudel tackled him about religion, took him up to his room for an hour, and gave him a most appalling talking-to. L. L. came out in tears, a broken man, and left the house at once, saying to Jammes that his friend was really too cruel. Since then he has written to Claudel to ask for further information. . . ."

A month later Rivière was himself appealing to Claudel in terms which, extravagant as they may now seem, were then the almost daily pabulum of this great proselyte.

" For more than a year (he wrote) I have lived by you and in you ; my support, my faith, my perpetual preoccupation—you are all of these. I have adored you as Simon adored Cébès, I have bowed down before you, I have sought out your soul with the hands of a supplicant. . . . I want you to be brutal, to throw me to the ground, to insult me. . . ."

Rivière was not a hysterical boy, but a man of profound, though not lively, intelligence. His own long exchanges with Claudel display to perfection the majestic assurance with which he has been brought round to Rome. A rich if inflexible humanity marked Claudel's letters. Tears flowed (" Not vainly ", said Claudel, " are they given the name of *aquae scaturientis*.") as Rivière was brought into the company of " Patmore, Péguy, Chesterton, and, if I may say so, myself—the writers whose role is to re-establish a Catholic sensibility and a Catholic imagination after four centuries of progressive desiccation ". Rivière was no match for Claudel, of course. Indeed, he never wanted to be a match for him, but merely to be drawn towards God in harmony with the man he admired above all others. With Gide, equal was matched with equal. The Correspondence does not in itself give the full measure of Gide's resistance to Claudel. His large and heterogeneous *œuvre* is in very great part a sustained rejoinder to the affirmations of a mind which had been made up, once and for all, upon every important question. What must have seemed in 1900 the grotesque presumption of an isolated dilettante has since been consecrated by the gratitude of that vast number of readers whom Gide has endowed with the image of a world in which Man will have been perfected by his own efforts. For those, therefore, who may question the stature of Gide as a purely creative writer, or who may regard Claudel merely as an irritable old image-factory, these letters will not come as a conclusive rebuttal ; but for those whose interest is in the movement of thought, or in the struggle between sacred and secular wisdom, or in the organization of literature, or in the professional reflections of two great artists at the height of their powers, the Correspondence will certainly be one of the most curious books to have come out of France since the end of the war.

CONTENTS

INTRODUCTION

By

ROBERT MALLET

THIS is doubtless the first occasion on which two writers—and, what is more, two writers of quite exceptional standing—have agreed to the publication in their lifetime of the letters which have passed between them. Certain critics might see in this decision the triumph of unrestrained impatience over modesty ; but this would be a frivolous interpretation. If this grave confrontation is to be really understood, we must study it with the weightiest and most objective attention.

We are not concerned here simply with a long exchange of letters in which the two correspondents have noted all the fluctuations of their material and moral existence. Every correspondence has its mirror-letters. Those which are published here have more to offer : milestone-letters, letters which mark out an itinerary and give exact details of places and distances, letters which need to be read not merely " between the lines " but also between the intervals which separate them, letters which illuminate as much by what is said as by what is left unsaid, and letters in which, thanks to the continual play of opposition and attraction, reticence and candour, we can discern how two consciences moved steadily away from each other towards what each considered to be his appointed goal.

We are concerned, in fact, with a dialogue that cannot be kept within the limits of a correspondence, any more than it can be bounded by the personalities of the two correspondents. That is why Paul Claudel and André Gide, convinced that they have both played symbolic rôles in which many contradictory aspirations are fused and summarized, have consented to hand over these letters ; they have generously understood that already it is for others to interpret their transcendent significance.

The correspondence lasted for just over a quarter of a century, and it is now twenty-five years since it came to an end. The publication of this book may thus be said to celebrate the jubilee of the inaugural letters. Old age has procured for Claudel and

Gide the privilege of looking back upon these two long, and very
different, phases in their relationship—the one marked by the
elaboration of friendly ties, the other by their gradual dissolution.
It has allowed them, too, to consider twenty years of hostile dis-
affection as quite long enough for any deadlock ; and they have
broken this deadlock in recognition of a lapse of time which
permits of the unembarrassed disclosure of all the arguments on
both sides.

Both one and the other have given over all the letters which they
had kept. The question then arose : was it better to publish a
selection of letters, and thus to print only those which had some
spiritual or literary interest that derived directly from the essential
problems of the relationship, or should the public be apprised of
even its most insignificant aspects ? We decided on the second
solution. It may result in a less lively or a less direct account of
the fundamental debate, but it has the advantage of revealing the
general and circulatory aspect of the exchanges. It may seem
tedious to those readers who are in a hurry, or have formed the
habit of the " literary digest " ; but it will satisfy those who like
to explore a subject by themselves, and who appreciate those
texts which derive a real documentary value from the distinction
of their signatories. As for the danger of dispersing the interest of
the volume, we have tried to avoid this, in the *Introduction*, by
underlining the principal phases of a correspondence which resolves
itself into a series of passages of arms with intermediary breathing-
spaces.

We have therefore the satisfaction of publishing 171 letters—all
those, that is to say, which have survived. The reader will notice
that there are 125 letters from Paul Claudel as against only 46
from André Gide. This regrettable difference is due in part to the
fact that Gide was a less assiduous correspondent than Claudel.
But it must be explained primarily by the loss of a section of Paul
Claudel's archives at the time when the French Embassy in Tokyo
was burnt down during the earthquake of 1923.

In order to offset this inferiority of numbers, we thought it
opportune to interpolate into the Correspondence all those passages
in the Journal of André Gide which concern Paul Claudel. André
Gide scrupled to give immediate assent to this idea, because the
passages in question had been written for the most part under the
stress of the moment ; they rarely spared Paul Claudel and at

times manhandled him rather roughly. We informed Paul Claudel of this scruple, and he unhesitatingly declared that he wished the extracts to appear in full, or not at all : " it would be too easy," he added, " to accuse me of having wanted to shorten them to my own advantage."

There then arose a second problem of equilibrium—not, this time, of quantity, but of tone. And so we suggested to André Gide that we should publish an interview in the course of which Paul Claudel had maltreated him pretty severely. This interview, in itself, would counterbalance all the extracts from Gide's *Journal*, for it made up in virulence for what it lacked in length. André Gide was delighted to be able to return Paul Claudel's courtesy and at once gave his approval. Thus we can say that both correspondents have put their cards on the table with an identical straightforwardness that redoubles the value of this publication.

From 1890 to 1894 Mallarmé's " evening classes ", as Paul Claudel has called them, attracted a large number of studious disciples. Among them were two young men who had already made themselves felt, the one by his violence, the other by his subtlety ; both listened with an identical fervour to the master's teaching. The first had already conquered the truth ; the second was still searching for it. Mallarmé's conversation had the miraculous effect of providing these two very divergent natures with something that sent both of them, at the same moment, into the wildest exaltation. Chance decreed that André Gide and Paul Claudel should never come face to face in the little *salon* in the rue de Rome ; but this common devotion to Mallarmé had its part in the initial encounter of the two writers. They first met at the apartment of Marcel Schwob who, with his usual sureness of judgment, had discerned the germs of genius in the earliest writings [1] of the two young men who, for their part, were each quick to discover and appreciate the other ; fired by an identical veneration for Mallarmé, they instantly struck up a friendly acquaintance.

In 1893 Paul Claudel went into professional exile—an exile to which his temperament, ill-suited to the literary intrigues of Paris, was well able to adapt itself ; and in fact he profited by it to preserve intact an intransigent originality of mind which would

[1] For instance, Claudel's *Tête d'Or* (1889) and Gide's *Cahiers d'André Walter* (1891).

elsewhere have inevitably been modified. André Gide also went on his travels, but these, in his case, were in the service—for such he conceived it to be—of nothing but his own longing for knowledge. He did not lose track of Claudel, who was successively Vice-Consul in Boston, Vice-Consul in New York and (from 1896 onwards) Consul in Foochow. He sent him all his books as and when they appeared. It was on receiving *Le Prométhée mal enchaîné* and *Philoctète*, in 1899, that Paul Claudel began the correspondence that was to last for thirty years.

In 1900 the Consul profited by a long spell of home leave to strengthen the literary ties which bound him to his correspondent ; Gide for his part was drawn in curiosity towards Claudel, but some secret intuition discouraged him from concluding any formal pact of friendship. His tormented spirituality attracted Claudel. Claudel's proselytical self-assurance disturbed Gide. Gide was apparently more interested in Claudel's work than in the man himself, whereas for Claudel the secrets of the heart were more important than those of any book—though both of course knew that the one cannot be separated from the other, and that they must rather be sought out reciprocally. " I had a sort of presentiment ", Gide said later, " of the trouble which Claudel would give me later, and of the stifling effect that he might have upon me. An instinct of preservation told me to be on my guard. I didn't listen to it."

If in 1900 André Gide allowed himself, despite his reticences, to become a friend of Claudel, it was because in the end the chances of profit seemed to him greater than the chances of loss. But he behaved, in this nascent friendship, with a discretion which would have allowed him, with his natural taste for liberty, to end it as he pleased. He didn't burn his bridges (for he still sent Claudel all his books) but he never made a definitive crossing. He simply omitted to write. Claudel, himself less complex, and guided only by the wish to guide others, went on writing until one day, " weary of discharging his letters into a void ", he complains of the silence which greets his remarks and asks for a reply—which never comes.

When Claudel again had leave, in 1905, the two writers resumed their acquaintance. André Gide, in his own words, had been " bowled over " by one of Claudel's recent works, the *Ode aux Muses*, and in one of his letters he thanks him for " providing such a feast ". Claudel, encouraged by this gesture, wrote by return of post to say how much he would like to see Gide again, and undertook, even before he had seen him again, to prove to him, in a further letter, that " there is no truth elsewhere than in Christ ". This expansiveness did not provoke any visible reaction from Gide ; and Gide's silence corresponds to what, in another man, would be signified by a definite withdrawal.

They met on 30th November 1905 at the house of Arthur Fontaine, a great friend of Francis Jammes', who had organized a literary party at which Gide was to read aloud from Jammes' latest work—*L'Eglise habillée de Feuilles*. No doubt Claudel inferred, from the fact that Gide, a Protestant, was prepared to read so profoundly Catholic a poem, that he really understood Catholicism ; and perhaps—why not ?—he saw in it the presage of a conversion which it was his duty to accelerate. So he made haste to give animated (or, if you prefer, whole-hearted) expression to religious opinions so categorical that Gide, still reeling from the sledge-hammer blow, remarked the next day in his *Journal* (1st December 1905) on the extent to which " genuine passion is unfavourable to eloquence ". Five days later, Claudel lunched with Gide and did not hesitate to make a frontal attack on the problem of faith. His host had also faced it, but without, as yet, finding any solution. He asked Gide, with a coldness that made the question the more scorching : " Why do you not become a convert ? " André Gide could reply only by expressing his confusion in the face of so exact and so urgent an interrogation. And Claudel, before leaving, left him the address of his confessor. But on the morrow, he realized that he must have seemed brutal in his exhortations—and also that his eloquence had failed of its effect. So he wrote to Gide, excused himself for talking like " a zealot and a fanatic ", and asked him none the less to accept him for what he was. With his letter he sent a notebook of Biblical quotations and advised his friend to look into them. In his *Journal* for 6th December 1905, Gide gives a full account of the conversation of the previous day, and of his disquiet at the thought of it. On the 8th he confessed to this disquiet in a letter to Claudel, but did it with a subtlety that, without actually distorting the truth, yet gave it a more agreeable appearance. There were two more meetings in Paris before Claudel left to be married and to embark, a few days later, for the Far East. The consul had prepared, and had had printed, a résumé of Christian doctrine in which he gave methodical expression

to his efforts as a proselyte, and which he meant to complement—
or to compensate for—the effect of his " heated letters ". He made
sure that Gide had a copy, and in a last letter before leaving he
made a critical analysis of his own missionary violence ; and he
gave Gide, whom he longed to win over and dreaded to offend,
a piece of advice which, on his lips, could not assume the air of a
command : " open your heart to the inrush of truth, and make
way in your intelligence for enormous deserted spaces ".

Many months went by, and neither of the correspondents felt
disposed to re-open the vital question. Perhaps they were embarrassed at the idea of resuming, at so great a distance, their
vehement discussions. Gide was the first to refer to them, but he
only excused himself for not wishing to resume them. Claudel
seized the chance of reopening the struggle, but he in his turn
reproached himself for his " awkwardness and indiscretion ",
despite the fact that he had acted from " conviction and the desire
to do good ". Time and distance made it plain to him that he had
intervened too soon, too brusquely, and without regard for an
exceptionally delicate sensibility which needed to be won over by
some refinement of strategy, even if it were naturally inclined to
the course which Claudel was urging upon it. The one felt that he
had been brutalized, the other that he had been brutal ; both felt
that the intimacy of their intelligence had far outstripped the
intimacy of their hearts ; and so there ensued a mutual stiffening
which caused their letters, in 1907, to be numerous, but concerned
only with literary matters. Claudel's *Art poétique* was about to be
published by the *Mercure de France* ; Gide had agreed to read the
proofs, and the two friends found in this a subject for several
exchanges of letters. They also discussed the merits of André
Suarès, whose tumultuous inspiration they found by turns repellent
and magnetic. In February 1908 Claudel, at Foochow, received
Gide's *Le Retour de l'Enfant prodigue*, which the author had not sent
to him without some apprehension. The reactions of Francis
Jammes had seemed to justify this ; for he had sent Gide a lengthy
reprimand after reading the final scene, in which the Prodigal
encourages his younger brother to follow his example and says
to him : " Come, kiss me, my young brother. All my hopes go
with you. Be strong, forget us, forget me. May you not come
back. . . ." A few days after he received Jammes' letter Gide
wrote as follows to Christian Beck :

" Perhaps you may not know that Claudel, after finding in Jammes a lamb who could easily be led back to the Lord, decided to take me on in my turn ? That is called ' conversion ', is it not ? No doubt he realized that with my Protestant heredity and education he had not an easy task before him. He persevered, none the less, encouraged to the point of excess by my very lively sympathy for his work and the immense respect with which, in consequence, I listened to everything he said. In letters and conversations alike, we went in very deep. . . . Jammes then gave me to understand he was preparing an article, a dithyrambic ' study ', to celebrate my conversion. I realized that there was some risk of a misunderstanding and, being determined not to owe Jammes' praises to an (involuntary but evident) moral compromise, I wrote him a long letter of explanation. After that he suddenly cooled off ; he felt that I was ' escaping '. All the same, I understood with every fibre of my being both the *interest* of what Claudel and he wanted me to do, and the reasons why I wasn't going to do it. And I understood how, if I had done it, it could only have been after the fashion of my Prodigal Son who returned home in order to help his younger brother to run away. I therefore wrote this little ' occasional piece ', and put into it all my heart, and all my reason too. I dedicated it to Arthur Fontaine, a friend of Jammes and of myself, who was deeply interested in the ' religious question ', and to whom Jammes dedicated his *Pensées des Jardins* before he went back to Catholicism ; I meant it as a kind of pendant to Jammes' book."

It is plain that Gide wished to place himself squarely in opposition to Claudel ; and indeed the book itself is proof enough of this. Jammes was not mistaken, but his rebuke, so far from bringing him nearer to Gide, had the opposite effect. Claudel for his part knew quite well that too impetuous a campaign would not merely fail, but might actually do harm to his cause ; he therefore made a show of subtlety. He complimented Gide on his style, expressed surprise that Gide had feared to shock him, and was full of understanding for Gide's unquiet frame of mind : such was the trend of his cordial reply. And though he made his opinion clear, he did so in such a way that even the most timid of readers could not suppose that he was being laid siege to.

A few months later Gide published an article on Dostoevsky, and Claudel once again reopened the religious question and expressed his regret that he had acted so hastily : " I am always afraid that you may break off our correspondence. I can no longer take up a sheet of writing-paper without falling a victim to a sort of lyrical intoxication which puts me to shame as soon as I have stuck on the stamp ; and if my letters were not so long, I should then begin them all over again. . . ."

Gide was not a good correspondent. He admits to it himself and adds in explanation that : " If I am not a better correspondent, it is because each of your letters causes a great commotion within me, and it would be a considerable business for me to reply to it ". But his interest in Claudel is greater than his fear of being encircled, and he goes on to say : " Do not imitate my long silence ". He is evidently possessed by a two-edged desire : not to sacrifice his freedom of mind for the sake of his friend, and not to sacrifice his friend for the sake of his freedom of mind. On 9th January 1909 he wrote to Claudel to explain the underlying reasons for the formation of *La Nouvelle Revue Française,* to which he asks him to contribute. It is a very long letter, but only in one short passage does the vital thread of the correspondence show through. " I often think of you, dear friend, for the memory of you is allied to certain grave preoccupations towards which I am ceaselessly impelled by the natural bent of my mind and the hideous pressure of the external world. I am extraordinarily anxious to read your new works." And he offers to watch over the various publications which Claudel himself is prevented, by absence, from supervising effectively. In this way the two writers remain in contact without having to refer to the problems which preoccupy them.

When *La Porte étroite* appeared in the spring of 1909, Claudel did not fail to comment upon it. His comments were very reserved, and he was obviously straining to remain perfectly objective. His courteous comments upon Protestantism are in the same tone as Gide's comments upon Catholicism ; he could not help remarking, however, that Alissa's renunciation of happiness was as gratuitously good as Lafcadio's experiments in *Les Caves du Vatican* were to be gratuitously evil. Claudel thought that such sacrifices (and the obstinacy of a piety that refused all thought of reward) were of doubtful utility. He seems to long to say that, if Alissa had been a Catholic, and guided by her sense of abnegation, she would have entered a convent and her sacrifice would have served some purpose. But he avoids saying anything aggressive, and this time it is Gide who provokes him by criticizing the " state of repose " to which

Catholicism inclines. Claudel's answer is prompt and passionate, but there is no harm in this, because it is more likely to seduce André Gide than to shock him. To say that Catholicism is a continual struggle, that the Catholic is constantly on trial in the most thoughtful and sensitive parts of his nature, and that truth is the surest spur to self-improvement—all this could not but appeal to somebody for whom stability, however based, would always amount in the end to a state of anguish.

In autumn 1909 Claudel left China for ever, returned to France, and was appointed to the French Consulate in Prague. In November he invited Gide to dinner with Charles-Louis Philippe. The author of *Bubu de Montparnasse* interested Claudel, who was often led by his evangelical turn of mind to essay the most unlikely encounters. Philippe was a man tormented by doubt and disquiet, and he hoped to find a new security in the wake of Claudel. After the meal, Gide noted in his diary : " much to say, but no time ". One can readily imagine the conversation in which the great proselyte was faced by two men who longed to drink from the same source, and yet feared that they might drown where they had merely wished to drink. Philippe died hardly a month later, and before he had had time to resolve his doubts. Claudel bitterly regretted that he had not been more ardent in his approaches : " I blame myself ", he wrote to Gide, " for not having been enough of a preacher, enough of a fanatic. But well-being makes us drowsy, and art makes us insensitive to the pathetic reality of things." These remarks, when addressed to Gide, were meant to remind him of his precarious state—to preach a sermon, in fact, on the necessity of not acting as if he were to be on the earth for ever. But André Gide, who was deeply affected by the death of Philippe, interpreted it as an impulse of fraternal charity. He replied at once, with a quotation from a letter which Philippe had written to him after reading *Le Retour de l'Enfant prodigue*. Philippe had squarely reproached him for having devoted so much talent to the specious doctrine of escape, when so many dependable joys were in store for the man who knew how to stay at home—or who, after having run away, had the courage to go back.

Such a letter was tantamount to putting a fresh weapon into Claudel's hands ; but Gide did not envisage any renewal of combat. He simply added the words : " I don't doubt that this letter will make you the more sorry that you did not pursue your conversations further "—a remark so objective as to indicate an obstinate coolness which was more redoubtable than any open hostility.

A few days later, and without mentioning Philippe's letter, Claudel congratulated Gide on having so bravely protested against the concept of *Realpolitik*, in the name of which the monarchist press was trying to excuse or, what was worse, to justify the massacres of St Bartholomew's Eve. In fact the Catholic writer took up the defence of the persecuted Protestants and succeeded in touching Gide's heart ; for this defence—far more than any of Claudel's proselytical outbursts—revealed the cement which bound the two Churches together, like neighbouring stones in the edifice of Christianity. In March 1910 Claudel again congratulated Gide —this time on the article in which Gide, in *La Nouvelle Revue Française*, had attacked the sterile scepticism of Remy de Gourmont : " I find in M. de Gourmont ", Gide had said, " that fatal propensity (which Voltaire also had) to regard as stupid or hypocritical everything which betokens lofty aspirations, reverence, or piety. . . . Like the Encyclopaedists, M. de Gourmont does not understand or admit, or want to admit, that free-thinking has not a monopoly of intelligence, or religion a monopoly of stupidity." [1]

Of course this article could only encourage Claudel to hope for the conversion of his friend ; and, a few days before Christmas 1910, he decided that the conditions were favourable to a fresh attempt. " I am going to communion to-morrow ", he wrote. " Ah ! my dear friend, what immense joys you forego—joys beside which all others are as nothing. . . . How I should like to share with my friends a little of the joy which fills me to overflowing." It is not difficult to read between the lines of this letter, and the brevity of Gide's answer must not be mistaken for indifference : " What am I to say about the end of your letter ? It moved what is deepest in me ; and I can remember well enough the ardent piety of my adolescence to understand the felicity which you describe to me to-day." Gide pretends not to have read between the lines, and not to have understood that, if Claudel paraded his happiness, it was in the hope that Gide would soon come to share it. Gide, for his part, wanted to make it clear that, for him, the Faith was not to be conceived in terms of the present or the future, but in terms of a past which, though it remained an affecting memory, could not be resuscitated.

[1] Further extracts from this article may be found in the Notes to Letter 70.

Claudel took the point. For the moment he did not persist. His many letters during the year 1911 kept strictly to literature and politics. He sent Gide his *Le Chemin de la Croix*, but without any commentary ; and the only answer he received was this : " Thank you very much for your book which I received safely the day before yesterday ". Perhaps Gide was the first to weary of a correspondence in which nothing was discussed but the merits of d'Ablancourt's version of Tacitus or the typography of *L'Otage* ; anyway, on 7th December 1911 he seemed to turn back to the subject of religion by telling Claudel of his sister-in-law's conversion. Claudel was quick to respond : " I was greatly moved by the news of a conversion in your family. When shall I learn of your own, my dear friend ? "

Six years earlier, he had put the same question by word of mouth. For someone who does not want to answer, correspondence is, of course, much more convenient than the cut-and-thrust of conversation. But if it is easier to evade the point in a letter, the effect of the written word is sometimes more direct ; it lacks, after all, the softening accompaniment of an accommodating glance or tone of voice. Claudel's question, so solemn and so concise, had the effect of an impeachment—and all the more so as, remembering his remorse after Philippe's death, he went on to say : " I am much less shy of these questions than I used to be. Religion seems to me something so enormous, so monumental, like the works of Nature. Not to acknowledge this great truth of Nature can only be a mutilation and an artificiality. . . ." And Claudel went on to show that, so far from mutilating himself man is enlarged by his adherence to " something as vast as the starry vault, where the ocean itself can move at ease, and one can breathe to the limit of one's lungs ". It is the unbeliever who, in Claudel's eyes, is diminished and enjoys only " a shrunken, amputated world ".

By return of post—contrary to his usual custom—André Gide acknowledges receipt of this letter, whose impassioned tone must certainly have moved him. He is almost afraid, as he admits, to say to what extent he was " touché ". The use of this word, with its overtones from duelling, must have greatly encouraged Claudel. But the next phrase erected a new barrier. Gide revealed the secret of his inhibition : " the fidelity which I owe to those relations and elders who lived in such constant, noble, and radiant communion with God, and who gave me my noblest images of

abnegation ". As if to make up for this avowal (whose effect upon
Claudel Gide was well able to imagine) he went on to speak of his
sister-in-law's conversion, and to insist upon his own part in it :
" I had previously had long conversations with her on the subject
of the Catholic religion which I defended (eloquently, it seems)
against her scorn ". It would seem as if he wanted to show that,
though his thoughts were still submissive to Protestantism, he had
none the less once thrown in his weight on the other side. He is
as anxious to show himself objective as he is to affirm himself
inaccessible to Claudel's proselytism.

But Claudel decided to carry on with his campaign. No convinced Catholic would shrink before the possibility of a rebuff,
when the salvation of a soul was in question. He wrote in answer :
" One of these days we must talk together like those characters in
Dostoevsky's novels who tell each other things so confidential that
on the morrow they no longer dare to look at one another and are
seized with a mortal and mutual hatred ". And he tries to prove
that Gide would not be in any way unfaithful to the memory of
his parents if he were to enter the Catholic fold. Gide did not
reply at once. A month later he wrote : " How could I leave
your last letter so long unanswered ? Was I afraid of being led on
to reply in too intimate a manner ? " He himself answers this
question with a courteous " No " that did not at all deceive Claudel.
He went on to speak of a controversy in which he was attacking a
certain Catholic (but un-Christian) review ; he himself, he said,
preferred his lonely situation and could never side with those who
used the crucifix as a bludgeon ; and if he listened so attentively
to Claudel, it was because Claudel was so different from those who
lowered the credit of Catholicism.

This is a defensive, second-line argument. Gide knew very
well that a religion is not really contaminated by a minority of
undesirables ; and " even to-day ", Claudel answered, " the true
visage of our Saviour is most hideously defamed and spat upon ".
In a later letter, which is now unfortunately lost, Gide must have
returned to the theme of the " bad Catholic ", for in his reply
Claudel agrees with all that Gide has said against the " profiteers
of Christ " ; but he ends, with irrepressible frankness, by saying :
" the House of God is not built with the motes that one takes out
of one's neighbour's eye, but with the beams that one takes out of
one's own ". After reading this admonition, Gide must have

thought it was undeserved. His *Journal*, in any case, reflects an impatience that he had kept out of his letters. " I wish I had never known Claudel. His friendship lies heavy upon my thoughts. I can't bring myself to offend him, but my way of thinking is antagonistic to his."

Some weeks later, Claudel received what seems to have been an enigmatical letter which filled him with disquiet and perplexity. We do not know what Gide said in this letter, but we may imagine that he tried to explain the necessities° of a religious-minded man who was torn between his longing for God and his hatred of dogma, between his taste for self-discipline and his horror of any discipline imposed by others. For the first time Claudel spoke of " the Devil "—using the word in its philosophical sense as symbolizing the power of evil. He felt that Gide's supersensitive temperament leaves him peculiarly open to this sinister influence, and he hastened to add : " in any case, do rid yourself of the idea that whatever you say or do or believe could discourage or disconcert or scandalize me ". And he ended : " nobody can say that you are an easy man to know ". Gide's answer, which has since been lost, must have shown a readiness to be known better—for we next see Claudel congratulating himself on not having given offence by his candour, sympathizing with Gide's tormented state. " What pathos there is ", he went on, " in the spectacle of a soul in search of the light ! What drama can compare with that ! " It is a drama at which Claudel can no longer remain seated in his stall. Rather does he rise, mount the stage, and intervene in the action, which does not seem to him to be in accord with the Truth of tragedy. No matter what the hazards may be, he now sees himself as the humble delegate of the Supreme Dramatist. " Courage, Gide ! My heart and my prayers are with you during these sacred days " : such, in brief, is the tone of his intervention.

He believed that he had shattered the defences of his opponent, who for some weeks past had been brought to combat, after noting in his *Journal* : " How easily at this moment I could throw myself into the confessional ! How difficult it is to be at one and the same time, from one's own point of view, he who commands and he who obeys ! But where is the director of conscience who would be subtle enough to understand this floating, this passionate indecision that possesses my whole being, this equal aptitude for contrary extremes ? "

Only if he knew these thoughts could Claudel realize that Gide is at once near and far, and that, though the south face of the peach may seem ripe as it hangs on the wall, the other side may yet be as green as can be. As it was, Gide executed a strategic retreat and remained under cover for some considerable time. In September 1912 Claudel complained that he had been for a long time without news of Gide, and three weeks later he wrote to ask : " Why this delay ? Why go on living in that terrifying void ? "

In the autumn of 1912 they met once more in Paris. Gide was disappointed by the encounter, for he had the feeling that Claudel's flood of rhetoric had never left him the chance of saying so much as one word. Claudel, who still did not realize the strength of Gide's resistance and thought that he was merely hesitating over the final step, discussed him with the Abbé Fontaine, his director of conscience, and was rash enough to tell Gide about the discussion, and to urge him to go and see the Abbé Fontaine.

Once again Gide closed up completely on the religious issue, but Claudel continued to allude directly to it and to say, for instance, that " it is simply appalling to let oneself die of hunger when there is bread enough for all ". And then, remembering that Gide might well be offended, he added : " Don't bear me any grudge ".

At the end of 1913 Claudel displayed some anxiety about Gide's new book, *Les Caves du Vatican*, which was to include an epigraph from Claudel's *L'Annonce faite à Marie*. The title had made Claudel apprehensive lest his name should be associated with a book in which the person of the Sovereign Pontiff was not treated with the respect which all Catholics owed to him. The book began serial publication in the *N.R.F.* for 1st January 1914, and Gide, who did not feel that he had endangered the dignity of the Pope, saw no reason to expunge the epigraph. But, although Claudel's original fears were unfounded, he detected in the *Caves* certain allusions to forbidden habits ; and these he could not but condemn unreservedly. He at once wrote off what Gide later described as a letter of " commination ". He did not mince his words. It was at once a cry of alarm (" Don't you see that you, and those who are near to you, will be lost ? " and a summons to explain himself : " Answer me. You owe me an answer. If you remain silent, or if you are not absolutely frank, I shall know where I stand." Gide turned at bay, like an animal caught in his lair, but he knew that

he was caught. " Whether I answer, or whether I don't, I sense
that you are going to misjudge me."

He chose to answer, making it clear that he replied to his friend
as he would reply to a priest. But if his answer corresponded to
what is generally called a confession, his tone was not that of a
penitent. He was asked, " Is it true ? " and he replied, " Yes, it
is true ", with the merest sketch of an " Alas ! " If he has regrets,
they are more for the reprobation which his attitude will inspire,
than for the added attitude itself. No sooner has he revealed the
truth than he added a commentary to it and tried to prove that
books full of " lying conventions " are stifling the younger generation. Sincerity, however abandoned, seemed to him preferable to
hypocrisy, however well-intentioned. He knew quite well that
such remarks would vex Claudel, who was more likely to welcome
an act of contrition than an attempt at self-justification. So he
added : " I expect nothing but anger from you ". In a second
letter, written almost immediately afterwards, he attempted to
modify the impression of intransigence which, if taken at its face
value, might have robbed him of his last hope of being understood.
And yet, no sooner had he done so than he felt oppressed by the
prospect of unending discussions ; for these, after all, could only
hinder the free development of his true nature. And so he finished
on yet another note : " Sometimes I end by wishing that you would
betray me, for then I should feel delivered of my regard for you and
for all that you represent in my eyes—a regard which so often
halts and embarrasses me ".

This impulsive letter, so free from circumspection, is the exact
reflection of a truthful nature which is determined to preserve
itself from outside interference. Gide is at once hopeful of being
given Claudel's advice, and anxious lest he should be unable to
follow it. The letter ends with the words : " Farewell. You can
now do me great harm, and I am at your mercy."

Claudel, on the contrary, thought that he could still do his friend
a great deal of good. There is no weakness in his long reply, but
there is a certain indulgence. He too is glad to be rid of doubts
that had weighed heavily on him ; but the new lack of doubt is
also a grave source of anxiety. He deplores Gide's presumption
in claiming to act as both judge and defendant in his own case ; it
is to God, above all, that the case must be referred. He exerts
himself to show that the first essential is to avoid a scandal ; and

it can best be avoided by the suppression of the fatal passage in the *Caves*. He encourages Gide to hope that the long process of his spiritual evolution may even now be approaching a happy conclusion ; " little by little ", he urges, " people will forget ".

Gide was touched by these proofs of Claudel's affection, but he was far from accepting such advice. " No," he replied, " do not ask me either to whitewash or to compromise ; or it will be I who will think less of you."

But he wished to show that he was well disposed towards Claudel, even if he was not prepared to give up the integrity of his own thoughts ; and so he asked for the address of the Abbé Fontaine.

Gide's letter crossed with another from Claudel, in which Gide was again asked to suppress the offending passage in the *Caves* and to remove the quotation from *L'Annonce faite à Marie*. By return of post, Gide agreed to the excision of the phrase from *L'Annonce*, but declared that he could not but retain his own passage, which had been dictated by an irrepressible instinct of sincerity. Till that moment Claudel had believed that Gide was weakening ; disabused, he made no secret of his anger and wrote back that to retain " that abominable and scandalous passage " was contrary to " the most strict of duties ". " May God, whom you mock, be with you " was the phrase with which he ended his letter.

Gide never went to call on the Abbé Fontaine, and the *Caves du Vatican* was never expurgated. For many months the correspondence lay dormant ; neither party could overcome the inevitable stiffness that followed so grave a dispute. The war of 1914-1918, with its complement of new duties and new preoccupations, was a further cause of involuntary estrangement ; but contact was not altogether lost. In 1916, for instance, Gide tried, without success, to persuade Claudel to write a preface for a translation of Miguel de Unamuno. After Claudel had denounced Unamuno for his " modernism ", Gide noted in his *Journal* that " Decidedly, all roads do not lead to Rome. Only by saying nothing at all can one be sure of being orthodox. Not to go in is still the best way of not going out."

These apparent flippancies were written at the moment of Gide's gravest spiritual crisis—a crisis reflected in his *Numquid et tu . . . ?* ; ready as he was to decry the interpreters of religion, he never wavered in his attitude towards religion itself. This is very well shown by many entries in his *Journal*—notably in that invoca-

tion which would have delighted Claudel, had he but seen it :
" O Lord, I come to you like a child ; like the child whom you
wish me to become—for he who abandons himself to you becomes
a child. I renounce all those things that were once my pride, and
which in your presence would be my shame. I hearken to you,
and I offer you my heart."

But these notes were not published until 1922, and then only in
an edition of seventy copies. By then, Gide's point of view had
changed ; but Claudel had been favourably impressed by the
Christian overtones of *La Symphonie Pastorale* and *Dostoevsky*, and
when he was sent one of the few copies of *Numquid et tu . . . ?* he
replied with a long and friendly letter that began : " My Dear
Gide,—I have just received your book, which makes it possible for
me to resume our conversation. Despite its ten years' interruption,
you may be sure that I have never ceased to think of you and to
pray that you will be enlightened once and for all. I feel that in
these ten years your path has, all the same, drawn nearer to the
humble highway which I am treading" (Tokyo, 12th January 1924).
This estimate of Gide's position was already two years out of date,
but Claudel envisaged Gide as a man " at grips with Grace " and
urged him to adopt the " prayer of annihilation ", in which his
whole self could be offered to God. Gide preferred to remain silent,
rather than to explain he is no longer in that particular frame of
mind.

A year later Claudel left Tokyo and spent some weeks in France
before leaving for Washington, where he had been appointed
French Ambassador. He took the opportunity of asking for an
interview with Gide, who wrote in answer : " I should like to see
you again . . . and I am afraid of you, Claudel. . . . Our
conversation cannot but be a grave matter, and I am always
terribly shaken by what you say. . . . All our conversations remain
vivid in my mind."

On 14th May 1925 the two writers met, after an interval of
thirteen years. Gide was on the point of starting on a long journey
into Equatorial Africa, and Claudel thought to himself—" I was so
naive ", he said later—that in planning this journey Gide appre-
hended, and confusedly wished, that it might mean the end of him.
He therefore thought that the moment had come for a new and
decisive attempt at conversion.

After the interview he made some notes at the foot of the last letter that he had then received from Gide : " A long and solemn talk. He told me that his religious disquietude is at an end, that he enjoys a sort of *felicity*, founded on work and human sympathy. The *Goethean* side of his character has got the better of the Christian side." And he noted, too, that Gide had seemed " deeply interested and deeply shaken " by his arguments.

If we consult Gide's *Journal*, however, we find that irony, not emotion, is the dominant reaction. After a minute description of the scene of their encounter, and a half-humorous portrait of Claudel, Gide ends by saying : " In the presence of Claudel I am aware only of what I lack ; he dominates me ; he overhangs me ; he has more base and surface, more health, money, genius, power, children, faith, etc., than I. I think only of obeying without a word."

But Claudel had no idea of the immense and insuperable distances which now separated him from Gide. His conscience as a Christian prompted him to make one more effort—to write to Madame André Gide, and to ask for an interview at which they could discuss the best way of saving her husband. In a reply which was well worthy of her noble nature, Madame Gide delicately rejected Claudel's proposal, and suggested that it was in their prayers that they could most profitably meet.

On his return from Africa, Gide learned of Claudel's letter to Madame Gide and wrote to thank him for his solicitude. His distress at having to disappoint Claudel was, he assured him, the measure of his affection for his old adversary. The last letter of this twenty-seven-years' correspondence is from Claudel. Hope and anxiety dispute for mastery in his final message, and he ends by saying that Gide is " the stake, the protagonist, and the cockpit of a great struggle whose conclusion I cannot forecast ".

Since 1926, the play has still been going on, but Claudel has never again mounted the stage. He no longer plays his missionary rôle, although he remembers how powerful, when he first met André Gide, were his hopes of converting him. The works of this youthful Protestant were instinct, after all, with the signs of a Christian ideal that remained intact even after many spectacular attempts to get away from it. Certain natures are obviously lost to God, by reason of a coarseness of fibre which makes them impervious to the vibrations of the spirit ; but Claudel recognized in

Gide a man impregnated with spirituality. He believed, too, in Pascal's maxim : " You would not seek me if you had not already found me "—even if the seeking sometimes (Gide's was a case in point) involved sudden revulsions such as that implied in the proposition : " To know God is to seek Him ". He knew well that the road which leads to, or leads back to, God is often a mazy road that winds through country that is sometimes chaotic. Impassioned sinners never frighten Claudel—whose own heroes, like Mesa in *Partage de Midi* and Rodrigue in *Le Soulier de Satin*, often find their way to God as a consequence of some culpable passion ; and there is even a certain parallelism between Gide's position, as a young man, and Claudel's. Gide's Prodigal (" It was not a lodging that I looked for, on my travels, but my own hunger ") is of the same race as Claudel's Simon Agnel, in *Tête d'Or*, who, when asked why he left home, replied : " I remember that I was rebellious by nature. I wanted to get to the end of the road. I wanted to go over there, where the plains stretch into infinity. . . . And so I went away from home." Simon Agnel came to a bad end because he had not the sense to return home, but Gide's Prodigal came back from his escapade and resumed his place under the family roof. Was he really blameworthy for inspiring his young brother with the taste for escape ? Flight is unimportant if the fugitive can eventually find his way back. Hungry travellers make the best guests—such was Claudel's train of thought ; and Gide, he knew, hungered after the truth. Gide would make a great believer, if he could only once be brought to the point of believing ; and Claudel bent to the task all the missionary energies which resound, for instance, throughout his *Magnificat*. (As he said in 1930, " I have always wanted one thing only, and all my books are directed towards it : to be a road that people can use, and then forget ".)

Gide liked and appreciated the element of fervour in Claudel's nature, but the mere fact of being the object of a campaign was enough to drive him in upon himself. And there was one supreme obstacle to his becoming a Catholic : he considered that Catholicism had forfeited the purity of the evangelical spirit by according to the decisions of the Councils and the Popes an importance equivalent to that of the Word of Christ. He also accused Catholicism of having neglected the study of the Scriptures, and of under-estimating their institutional character. The divinity of Papal pronouncements was a point on which it was really impossible for Gide to debate. Claudel was, however, admirably qualified to expound the Biblical foundations of Catholicism ; and rarely did he advance an argument without giving chapter and verse. Claudel was also supremely well able to combat Gide's conviction that Catholicism was a religion of comfort and repose. " Not peace, but the sword " was the very essence of Claudel's proselytism ; and certainly his own sword was never in its scabbard. But Gide continued to believe that Protestantism offered the truer school of heroism. Moreover, he was determined that any change of position he might make should be arrived at of his own free choice. Another's arguments, however persuasive and well-founded, would never suffice. And the final obstacle to his conversion was that he always set a higher value upon the desire than upon its satisfaction ; expectation, for him, was more important than the event itself.

The composition of *Numquid et tu . . . ?* corresponds to one of those ' mystical deviations ' which have occurred from time to time throughout Gide's life. Characteristically, he only allowed it to be printed at a time when it no longer represented his current point of view, and when he had become " neither Protestant, nor Catholic, but quite simply a Christian ". The problem was one of universality : Claudel regarded his Church as the one universal element in a world of unsatisfying particulars, and Gide, in his own search for universality, had rejected the Catholic Church on the grounds that it expressed only one particular aspect of spirituality. As the differences between them grew greater and more obvious, Claudel seems to have decided that the case called for violent action. As he had said in his *Le Soulier de Satin* : " It is time to wake all these sleepers. If they get a bit hurt—well, that can't be helped ! We've never pampered ourselves—why should we pamper them ? " Perhaps Gide could hardly have been described as asleep. In any case, the treatment had the opposite effect from that which Claudel intended. By 1926 Claudel had come to regard Gide as the personification of that culpable pride which prevents men from bowing the knee and admitting their own weakness. Gide, on his side, saw Claudel as the incarnation of the infatuated convert. In his last letter, Claudel spoke of that blend of horror and affection with which he and all his Catholic friends were following Gide's career ; but in the next twenty-five years, his own affection for Gide would seem to have given place almost entirely to sensations of righteous disgust. The formula " *damnare errorem non errantem* " no longer

seems to have applied, and Claudel condemned Gide not merely
as a sinner, but as the cause of sin in others. His influence throughout the world was nothing less than the premonitory flickering of
the fires of hell. Gide's personal damnation was perhaps no more
than his involuntary contribution to the harmony of God's universe ;
but the damnation of his disciples was something that Claudel felt
called upon to prevent to the limit of his powers. This was an
attitude that Gide found quite congenial. He was gratified, in
fact, to find that, like Goethe, he was detested by the Catholics.
He did not return their feelings. Like Goethe, again, he regarded
Catholicism as " a fruitful stage in the evolution of that Humanism
which religion is in duty bound to oppose ". Not for nothing, in
fact, did Claudel note, after his last interview with Gide, that " the
Christian side of his character has given in to the Goethean side ".
There is nothing in Gide more Goethean than the passage from
his *Journal* for December 1931 which concludes his contribution to
his book : " Claudel . . . I like him and want him thus. . . .
We can admit him, admire him, he owes it to himself to vomit us.
As for me, I would rather be vomited, than vomit."

With such an adversary, Claudel could not but bring to bear
every weapon in his armoury. " What would you ? " as he wrote
to Jacques Rivière, " It's yes *or* it's no ". And Rivière himself, who
hesitated all his life between the influence of Gide and the influence
of Claudel, said : " To refuse Claudel's Christianity is to leave
oneself with no resource but the void ". Claudel's great strength
as a proselyte lay in his power of presenting the Either/Or as an
alternative of real, terrifying, and implacable significance. Gide
was quite ready to accept it ; and in 1948 we find him still convinced that man " should learn to demand from himself, for virtue's
sake, what he now believes to be demanded by God ". Unconvinced
of the possibility of any future life, and assured as ever of the
supreme importance of personal liberty of thought, Gide is nevertheless far from being a traditional " free-thinker ". The transcendental element in religion still seems to him of value in human
affairs ; he has long ceased to wish either to convince or to be
convinced, and the Christian overtones of his position are something that he would not wish either to forego or to justify. As for
Claudel, he no longer concerns himself with nuances. It is " Yea "
or " Nay " with him, and his " Nay " has the old sledge-hammer
force.

And so these two famous writers rise above the torrent of contemporary thought, and divide it like the two cut-waters of a venerable bridge. A common arch unites them, whether they admit it or not. During the preparation of this book they have both given unsparing assistance to its editor ; without any concern as to how it might affect their individual reputations, they have striven to create a book which can stand above all considerations of personality. They began as partners, and they ended as adversaries. Claudel's prediction (that they would one day resemble those characters in Dostoevsky who have spoken of matters so intimate that they can no longer look one another in the face)—that prediction has been fulfilled. It is towards the horizon that their gaze is now turned—towards that extremest point on the horizon at which every wanderer comes finally face to face with the truth.

ROBERT MALLET.

THE CORRESPONDENCE

1.—*Paul Claudel to André Gide*

French Consulate, Kuliang,
28th August 1899.

Dear Sir,

I feel honoured that you should have written to me, and I am greatly enjoying the two books you were good enough to send me. I liked especially the three pieces which follow your *Philoctète*, and most particularly *El Hadj* and the *Narcisse*. The quality of your mind is as rare as its movement is particular to yourself. You seem to " draw off " the subject by draining away a part of that belt of liquid in which ideas are suspended, and you illuminate and clarify them in the process—though not so much as to spoil the play of refraction or to take away from the charm of your ideas. Your mind has no slope. And I greatly enjoyed studying your style, in which words and phrases come together not so much in logical concert or from some secret harmonic necessity, as from a sort of humid attraction or clandestine circulation which animates the whole book and makes it all seem to be metamorphosed from one and the same word.

Had I not once the pleasure of meeting you at Mallarmé's or somewhere ? I feel sure I did.

Believe me,
Yours most sincerely,

PAUL CLAUDEL.

2.—*Paul Claudel to André Gide*

Saturday [postmarked 12th May 1900].

Dear Sir,

I read with great interest and pleasure the book which I took away from our interview the other day. Your way of writing is one of the most interesting and original that can be studied by

a writer who habitually meditates upon his art. What struck me
above all, this time, was the *unity of movement*, the mellow coherence
of the phrases which revert to, and prolong, a single line of thought,
and the generous, easy way in which those phrases open and shut
on your ideas. There seems to be something liquid and previously-
existing which comes to life as your thought passes over it—much
as a lake merges imperceptibly with the air and yet, as a swan
moves across it, restores progressively the whole landscape in its
steely mirror. I shall put it in another way if I say that your
ideas come to us in a sort of secret serum which gives them their
lustre and their life.

I shall say nothing of the way in which your two books have
made clear to me the character of your mind. That is too delicate
a subject, and rather than say something idiotic I prefer to read
over again the recitatives of *Paludes*, which are like those little
phials of translucent agate in which the Chinese bottle samples of
all known varieties of fog—river-mist, sea-mist, and early morning
fogs half-broken through by the sun.

Paludes is the fullest account which we possess of that peculiar,
stifled and stagnant atmosphere that we breathed from 1885 to
1890. The question is—does the stagnation derive from the outlet,
or from the source ? Is it the slope that is lacking, or just that the
water won't flow ?

A cordial handshake,

Paul Claudel.

3.—*Paul Claudel to André Gide*

37 Quai d'Anjou,
11th July [1900].

My dear Gide,

On returning here I found on my table, and read with much
interest, your Brussels lecture. The whole thing is summarized,
is it not, in that phrase on page 33 : " The true artist, in his search
for the deepest influences, will hover above the work of art, trying
to forget it and to rise further away from it. He will see it as a
staging-point, a *frontier*." You put it very well when you say that
the person who talks is not the one best placed to hear what he is

saying ; only another purer ear can distinguish all the resonancy
of the sounds he gives forth. The pasticheur, for his part, stupidly
copies *its method* (free verse, alexandrines, pointillism, etc.).

Are you in Paris at the moment ? I should like to go on with our
conversation because, in view of what is happening in China, I
may have to go back at 24 hours' notice.

Your devoted,

P. CLAUDEL.

4.—*Paul Claudel to André Gide*

Kuliang, 7th August [1903].
the day of the typhoon.

My dear Gide,

I used to write to my friends, but as I never got an answer,
I became tired of firing into space my " Epistles " which had not
even the merit of being in verse. At distances like these one can
only " correspond " independently.

Your *Pretexts*, which I took with me into the mountains, provide
me with a pretext—that of resuming with you that sort of mortuary,
theoretical and telepathic acquaintance. I am delighted to note,
on every page, that we are of the same generation, and that you
have expressed, in your charming and distinguished way, the
feelings and opinions that we, as a generation, have been allotted.
I am particularly grateful for what you say about Life, about the
mob, about literary theories, and about Villiers, whom you appraise
with particular skill. On the other hand I don't understand your
admiration for the flatulent Verhaeren—or for Nietzsche, although
your pages on this agitated being are very interesting. For my part
I have the deepest horror of such supersensitive " lyrical " writers.
They have the same effect on me as those horrible little terriers who
put their paws on one and make one feel the convulsive shivering
which animates their wretched bodies. Besides, I've never felt
strong enough to get to grips with any of the books you praise so
highly. A quotation like the one you give is quite enough for
me : " I want man to be proud, alive, affirmative in the greatest
possible degree ; I want the world, and I want it *for what it is*.
I still want it. I want it for all eternity." Don't you feel the horror
and the platitude of these *repetitions* (which are the basis of Nietzsche's

style, as they are of his philosophy) ? Aren't they the mark of a
man who wants to say something, can't manage to bring it off and
gets carried away by his appalling volubility ? How can one care
for so anti-musical a theory ? No man is great in himself, but
rather by the way in which he harmonizes with his environment
and the degree to which this harmony enriches and instructs the
rest of mankind.

Why don't you take up criticism deliberately and of your own
preference ? It seems to me that you have a very acute critical
sense—something that is as rare as the sense of poetry, and perhaps
rarer. It's not everybody who knows what a man, or a tree, is
trying to say. At any rate I only know of two critics who really
deserve the name—Baudelaire and Poe.

Speaking of Poe, do you know his *Eureka* ? It's magnificent. It
annoys me that modern superstitions prevent the poets of our time
from writing large-scale works on the lines of the " περι φύσεως "
of Heraclitus or Empedocles. A poet has a quite special sense of
construction, proportion, and what I shall call " creative harmony ",
which has no counterpart in science proper, and would find its
natural expression in speculations of this cosmological sort. At the
very least it would provide the immense backgrounds and the rich
perspectives which are lacking in the miserable little poetry of our
times.

My great joy lies in the thought that we are watching the twilight
of nineteenth-century Science. All the abominable theories which
oppressed us in our youth, the theories of Laplace, evolution, and
" power-equivalents " are tumbling down one after the other. At
last we shall be able to take deep breaths of holy darkness and thrice-
happy ignorance. What a deliverance for the savant himself—
henceforth he can give himself in complete freedom to the contemplation of things without the nightmare of some " explanation "
to be proven ! How absurd it is, when one thinks of it, ever to
claim to explain anything, or to exhaust it as a source of knowledge,
when this knowledge is itself based on an infinite number of reper-
cussions ! I am writing at present a kind of dialectical poem to
celebrate the advent of new times and of that state of delectable
ignorance which is predicted by one of the characters in a play of
mine which you may have read.

What rubbish I am writing ! Being imprisoned by a typhoon
plays these bad jokes on me !

Thank you again for your remembrances and for the pleasure I had in reading your book.

PAUL CLAUDEL.

5.—*Paul Claudel to André Gide*

[Paris] Thursday [Spring 1905].

My dear Friend,

Here is *Léonainie*. My rôle as translator is too inconsiderable for you to put anything more than my initials.

Won't you come to see me one of these days—or one of these evenings ? I have a service to ask of you.

I grasp your hand with affection,

PAUL CLAUDEL.

Gide : *Journal*

Tuesday, 16 May 1905.

" Quiet dinner. I read the admirable first act of *Tête d'or* to Em."

Auteuil, Wednesday, 17 May 1905.

" I stop at the office of the *Occident* to get Claudel's *The Muses*. The few lines that I read while walking seize hold of my thought at once. It is a shock to my whole being and, as it were, the *warning* that I have been waiting for almost a month now."

6.—*Paul Claudel to André Gide*

Villeneuve-sur-Fère (Aisne),
22nd September [1905].

My dear Gide,

A certain Franz Blei has written to ask for permission to translate my works into German, and even to have them acted in the theatres

of that country. He gives you as a reference and assures me that
he has already translated your *Roi Candaule* and put it on the stage.
Can you tell me if this gentleman is reliable and what were the
terms of your agreement with him ? Did Vallette want to intervene
in the arrangements ? Also I don't know enough German to
supervise the translation, and I'd like to know if you were satisfied
with what he did.

You are one of the people I should have liked to see when I was
in Paris, but you seem to be very difficult to get hold of. Couldn't
we arrange a meeting in October, when I shall be back in Paris ?

Cordially yours,

P. CLAUDEL.

———

7.—*André Gide to Paul Claudel*

Cuverville par Criquetot-l'Esneval
(Seine Inferieure),
25th September 1905.

My dear Claudel,

I do not know Franz Blei personally, but as correspondents
we are on the best of terms. He seems to me an excellent person,
and as zealous as he is devoted. It's quite true that he translated
my *Roi Candaule* and that he is making it his business to have it
acted (contracts have even been signed with theatres in Berlin,
Vienna, etc.). I wish I could say he was a good translator, but I'm
bound to say that his translation of my play is still sadly out of key
and *de-stylized*, although I myself took it in hand and suggested or
imposed many corrections and revisions, etc. I must add, though,
that the Germans think him a good translator ; and perhaps I
should think the same if I had not a standard of comparison in the
remarkable translations which another, less-known translator has
just made of certain other books of mine. I have just recommended
to him (the other translator) Jammes' three short novels, and would
gladly recommend your plays—but for reasons of a sadly material
sort he certainly would not undertake any work that does not offer
certain success (by which I mean success in selling to the widest
possible public). With Franz Blei you have every chance of being
acted, because he is on excellent terms with more than one theatrical

manager. (I delight in the idea of seeing *L'Échange* on the German stage !) And although the translation may be rather colourless (colourless but certainly not bad) I should accept, if I were you.

Once you have any prospect of being acted, you must join the Société des Auteurs Dramatiques. It's their job to defend your rights and to secure for you the proper percentage of the receipts.

As for the publication of the translation in book form, get Vallette to intervene on your behalf from the beginning. He will claim for you (while allowing the translator his rights) the derisory sum to which you will be entitled (200 or 300 francs a volume !).

If I had thought it wouldn't bore you to see me again, I should have hurried to see you as soon as I knew you were back in France. I longed to see you, but at the same time I dreaded being a nuisance. At the slightest word from you. . . .

Thank you, Claudel, for writing the *Ode aux Muses*. It really did me a great service last winter. I gave it, together with *L'Arbre*, to several Germans (among others) and made them all read it, and I am very glad to see that my modest sowing is beginning to yield a harvest.

Au revoir, my dear Claudel. What I have said of Franz Blei is between ourselves. I am most cordially

Yours,

ANDRÉ GIDE.

Need I say again with what pleasure *L'Hermitage* would welcome something of yours ?

——— —

8.—*Paul Claudel to André Gide*

Villeneuve-sur-Fère (Aisne),
27th September [1905].

Thank you, my dear Gide, for the information which you so kindly give me. It will be most useful.

We might have looked at one another for a long while, like china dogs on a mantelshelf. You are certainly one of the men whom I most esteem and whom I most wanted to see when I returned to France. But I didn't want to be a nuisance, and as you had never answered my letters I wondered if the acquaintance was one which you would renew with pleasure. Now all my doubts are removed.

Let us try to arrange a meeting.   I shall be back in Paris on 2nd October and shall be there throughout the winter.

All yours,

P. CLAUDEL.

———

9.—*Paul Claudel to André Gide*

7th November 1905,
The Feast of the Immaculate Conception.

My dear Friend,

As for what people call " Art " and " Beauty ", I had rather that they perished a thousand times over than that we should prefer such creatures to their Creator and the futile constructions of our imagination to the reality in which alone we may find delight. What is it that St. John condemns, under the name of the three Concupiscences,—the preferring of things for their own sake, and the considering of them as nothing more than that, and the liking of them for what they are not, that is to say, for what is no part of the Eternal Being, instead of for what makes them eternally the creatures of their Creator, sustained by the working of this glorious goodness ?   Can't you see the basis of a whole art, brilliant and generous, in that chapter in *Proverbs* when the Spirit of God moves over chaos in sublime liberty ?   What is art, if not an exclamation and an acclamation, a counting and a conferring of Graces, like the Canticle of the young men in the fiery furnace, like St. Francis of Assisi's Canticle of the Sun ?   More than that—a sort of mimicry of the Word that creates, the Word that is " poetry ", a repeating of the *Fiat* which brought everything about ?   What sort of a thing is modern art, from which everything of real substance has been taken away, and with it that powerful source of youth inherent only in the heavenly *naturalness* that animates Homeric poetry, for example ?   How should we prefer these enormous gardens which we work with our hands, like Cain the first of all farmers, to the Paradise which Our Lord has bounded by four rivers ?

We cannot all become Saints, but it is our duty to do what we can, in all honesty, every moment of our lives ; and, to speak the truth, it is in this alone that sanctity consists—in a filial submission of our will to the Will of our heavenly father.   How then can you speak of a pagan sanctity,—that is to say, of an execrable pride, of the spiritual gormandizing of a creation that has turned in upon itself and revels in its strength and beauty, as if it were itself responsible for their creation ? All that comes not from the source is corruption and uncleanliness. It is for you, my dear Gide, to realize the stage which you have reached in your life, to have no illusions as to the demands of the voice which summons you, to gauge the obstacles which stand in your way, and to see whether, in respect of absolute Truth, you are still in that state of *invincible ignorance* which alone excuses the schismatic and the procrastinator. It is before God that you have to examine yourself in the sincerity of your own conscience.

I read yesterday a book which made me shudder—Philippe's *Bubu de Montparnasse.* What a hell it is that surrounds us ! Evil has always the same face, and as I followed this coarse and touching story there came to my mind memories of that hideous Paganism, as the black historians of Rome describe it—Sejanus' daughter, of whom I spoke to you yesterday, that beast Nero, an " artist " after the heart of the iniquitous Renan, slavering over the victims of the arena, Batavia slavered over by Germanicus, and children and young girls sent by the hundreds to the brothels of Rome.— What a responsibility for us ! You know that there are two sorts of duties—the duties of charity and the duties of justice. The duties of charity are to intervene to the limits of our strength in the necessities of our neighbour (*prochain, proximus :* he who is nearest). The duties of justice, which are still more binding, are founded on that great truth of the division of labour, which obtains throughout the whole of Christian society. Others have to bake our bread, slaughter beasts for us, and so on. And we also—it is of supreme importance—we also must shoulder, as good founders of families, the burden which is laid upon us of being such-and-such a flower or fruit. When we appear before God's tribunal, let us hope not to hear the appalling clamour of those unhappy multitudes, those submerged myriads who will give evidence against us and say : " O Lord, we others were born to ignorance, poverty, crime, and servitude. But look at those who were rich, whose parents were people of honesty and good character, who enjoyed leisure, education, and wide knowledge. We do not reproach them for not coming to our aid, for having left us, their brothers and Thy children, in our ghastly twilight. But let them be judged. What have they done with the rare and exceptional gifts which were accorded to them ? Were these simply given in order that they could have a more amusing time ? Or become artists and dilettantes ? How have they fulfilled the mission which was given them before Thee, in our name and in our stead,—in the name of ourselves, the miserable legion of the lost and the drowned ? " What a responsibility for us writers, above all, who are the leaders of men and the directors of their souls ! The mere fact of our enlightenment makes us spread light all about us. We are delegated by the rest of the world to the way of knowledge and truth, and there is no other truth but Christ, who is the Way and the Life, and the duty of knowing and serving Him lies more heavily on us than upon others, and lies upon us with a terrible urgency. May you grasp all this in a generous spirit, my dear Gide, and may this festival of Christmas, which once witnessed the great compassion of God towards myself when in the half-darkness of Notre-Dame He came and took a poor child by the hand—may this festival not pass without giving me the joy of breaking the bread of the Saints and the Strong with a brother.

P. CLAUDEL.

Gide : Journal

1 December 1905.

Yesterday I read *L'Église habillée de feuilles* at the Arthur Fontaines' to Raymond Bonheur, Paul Claudel, and the Mithouards. . . . Paul Claudel, whom I have not seen for more than three years, was there. As a young man he looked like a nail ; now he looks like a sledge-hammer. Not very high forehead, but rather wide ; face without subtlety as if chiselled out ; bull neck continued by the straight line of the head, through which passion can rush to flood the brain. Yes, I think this is the dominating impression : the head is of one piece with the body. I shall study him more fully next Tuesday (when he comes to lunch with us) ; I was a bit too concerned with defending myself and only half responded to his advances. He gives me the impression of a solidified cyclone. When he talks, it is as if something were released within him ; he proceeds by sudden affirmations and maintains a hostile tone even when you share his opinion.

While I am talking with Fontaine, out of the corner of my ear

I hear him proclaiming his admiration for Baudelaire. Mithouard, tactlessly taking up the subject, speaks of Baudelaire's " health ", seeing in him above all a " healthy " genius. Must he for this reason give himself permission to admire him ?

" Poe and Baudelaire," declares Paul Claudel with a sort of stifled rage, " are the only two modern critics." Then he praises, most intelligently, the critical intelligence of Baudelaire and Poe, but in terms so close to those recently used, on this very same subject, by Rémy de Gourmont that I can hardly keep myself from pointing this out. But I am afraid, at the mere name of Gourmont, of provoking an explosion.

Claudel is wearing a little jacket that is too short and that makes him look even more thickset and lumpish. One's eyes are constantly drawn to and shocked by his necktie, a four-in-hand the colour of a locust-bean. After reading, as I compare Francis Jammes' series of poems with Verlaine's *Sagesse*, Claudel at once declares that *L'Église habillée de feuilles* is a much finer work, that he for one has " never liked *Sagesse* very much, in which Verlaine's juggling is always apparent and spoils even the best poems ".

He talks in a not very loud voice, like a man very much in earnest ; I notice once more how unsuitable real passion is to eloquence.

———

10.—*Paul Claudel to André Gide*

[Paris] Tuesday evening,
[5th December 1905.]

My dear Friend,

What would you ? You must take me as I am, and a Claudel who was not a zealot and fanatic would no longer be Claudel. How I should like to be more eloquent ! But alas—it is at such moments that I see how terrible it is not to have obeyed that absolute duty which commands one to be a saint !

I am sending you a notebook of quotations from the Scriptures and the Fathers of the Church. I made this collection at the time of my greatest moral distress, and I am sure it will interest you.

Although it has not pleased God to make me one of His priests,

I have a profound love of souls. Yours is very dear to me. Why
can I not help you a little ? It is terrible to know what I know
and to put it so badly. We must see each other again ; I have
many things to say to you and I am afraid I have scandalized you
by speaking rather abruptly of certain matters. But then I could
not have borne for you to take me for what I am not. May God
bless you.

P. CLAUDEL.

Gide :   Journal

5 December 1905.

Paul Claudel came to lunch. Too short a jacket, aniline-coloured
necktie ; his face still more square than the day before yesterday ;
his speech both precise and full of images ; his voice staccato,
clipped, and authoritative.

His conversation, very rich and alive, does not improvise anything, you feel. He recites truths that he has patiently worked out.
Yet he knows how to joke and, if he only let himself go a bit more
on the spur of the moment, would not be without charm. I try to
discover what is lacking in that voice. . . . A little human warmth ?
. . . No, not even that ; he has something much better. It is, I
believe, the most *gripping* voice I have ever heard. No, he doesn't
charm ; he does not want to charm ; he convinces—or impresses.
I didn't even seek to protect myself from him, and when, after the
meal, speaking of God, of Catholicism, of his faith, of his happiness,
he added as I said that I understood him :

" But, Gide, then why don't you become converted ? . . . "
(this without any brutality, without even a smile). I let it be
apparent how his words had upset my mind.

I should attempt to set them down here if I were not to find
them in his *Traité de la Co-naissance du monde et de soi-même* that he
has just finished. Likewise I should write down the few details he
gave about his life if I did not think that life were to become famous.

L'Ode aux Muses, he tells us, begun in 1900, hung for a long time
interrupted. He didn't know " how to finish it ". It was only in
1904 that he added the invocation to Erato and the end.

" For a long time, for two years, I went without writing ; I
thought I must sacrifice art to religion. My art ! God alone could

know the value of this sacrifice. I was saved when I understood
that art and religion must not be set in antagonism within us.
That they must not be confused either. That they must remain,
so to speak, perpendicular to each other ; and that their very
struggle nourishes our life. One must recall here the words of
Christ : ' Not peace, but a sword '. That's what Christ means.
We must not seek happiness in peace, but in conflict. The life of
a saint is a struggle from one end to the other ; the greatest saint
is the one who at the end is the most vanquished."

He speaks during the lunch of a certain " frontal sense " that
allows us, without reading them, to recognize in advance a good or
a bad book, and always warned him against Auguste Comte. I
should be more amused to hear him execute Bernardin, if he did
not at the same time demolish Rousseau. He demolishes many
others ! Beating about him with a monstrance, he devastates our
literature.

(I remember my consternation, at Cuverville, when, pruning
and cleaning out a peony plant, I noticed that a branch I had just
removed because it seemed to me dead was still full of sap.)

He speaks with the greatest respect of Thomas Hardy and
Joseph Conrad, and with the greatest scorn of English writers in
general " who have never learned that the rule of ' nothing un-
essential ' is the first condition of art ".

He talks a great deal ; you are aware of the pressure of ideas
and images within him. As, apropos of I don't remember what or
whom, I spoke of the weakening memory : " Memory doesn't
weaken," he immediately exclaimed. " None of man's faculties
weakens with age. That is a gross error. All man's faculties
develop continuously from birth to death."

He talks endlessly ; someone else's thought does not stop his
for an instant ; even a cannon could not divert him. In talking
with him, in trying to talk with him, one is forced to interrupt
him. He waits politely until you have finished your sentence,
then resumes where he had stopped, at the very word, as if you
had said nothing.

He shocked Francis Jammes some time ago (in 1900) when he
replied to Jammes's anguish with " I have my God ".

(The greatest advantage of religious faith for the artist is that it
permits him a *limitless* pride.)

Upon leaving me he gives me the address of his confessor.

He also said :

" I attach absolutely no value to the literary quality of my work. Frizeau was the first one who, brought back to God by my drama*t* because he saw religion dominating everything in them, made me think : then I haven't written in vain. The literary beauty of my work has no other significance for me than that found by a workman who is aware of having performed his task well ; I simply did my best ; but had I been a carpenter, I should have been just a*s* conscientious in planing a plank properly as I have been in writing properly."

11.—*André Gide to Paul Claudel*

Thursday [8th December 1905].

My dear Friend,

I am deeply touched by your letter and by the loan of your most precious notebook. I see you took my confused questions quite seriously . . . thank you.

No, I did not understand—how could I understand ?—That you had " a profound love of souls " ? That was what I needed you to tell me—and that my own soul was dear to you. You mustn't see it as a matter of pride—but a hideous need of affection, of love, so great a thirst for sympathy that I feared I was deceiving myself, and was only trying to draw near to God in order to draw near to you—near enough, at any rate, to hear you better.

But since you love souls you will understand that there are some to whom nothing is more repellent than a temperate and business-like religion ; and that after having at the beginning of my life drawn daily nourishment from the Bible, and found in prayer the first of necessities, I have since preferred—finding, as it seemed, more illumination in what the Christian calls " the false gods "— I have since preferred to break abruptly with my first beliefs rather than to arrive at some lukewarm compromise between art and religion. Perhaps Catholicism would have offered a less strenuous opposition within me—not so much to two beliefs as to two systems of ethics. . . . *For the first time* the day before yesterday (but I could glimpse it already in your books) I could see by the light of

your mind, not so much a solution—it would be absurd to hope
for that—as a new and acceptable battle-ground.

And do you know what was tormenting me at this time—the
difficulty, the impossibility perhaps, of reaching sanctity by the
road of paganism ; and when you spoke to me, Claudel, of one's
" absolute duty to be a saint ", did you guess that you could not
have said anything to which I should react more violently ? Ah !
How right I was to be apprehensive of meeting you ! And how
frightened I am of your violence at this moment !

I may keep the notebook for a few days, mayn't I ? It's only
right that, after making me hungry, you should satisfy my hunger.

I am,

Affectionately yours,

ANDRÉ GIDE.

I was astonished to find in your notebook the death-mask of
Keats. . . .

12.—*Paul Claudel to André Gide*

Paris, Saturday
[postmarked 16th December 1905].

My dear Friend,

Well, is there a new silence between us ? Do not consider my
last letter as indiscreet—it isn't. I spoke to you *directly*—something
that does not happen often in this world—like brother to brother,
like soul to soul, irrespective of any consideration of time, or place,
or physical personality. But I understand your distress, my poor
friend. Everything *in tempore suo*. And it would have been very
unbecoming in me to have demanded of you, immediately, what it
took me four years to decide for myself. Something has to die
inside one. How deeply I feel that, and how I wish I could help
you more ! I shall not be in France for ever ; while I am here,
do not scruple to profit by what lies near at hand. Consider me as
a nameless, impersonal thing—a sort of vegetable substance with
whom you have no need to be embarrassed.

If you no longer need my Biblical notebook, be kind and send it
back to me. I have other souls in anguish who have asked for my

help, and I should like to lend it to them. They offer me a degree
of confidence which I find both frightening and humbling. But in
any case they will later see for themselves the grotesque insufficiency
of the helpmeet whom they have chosen. A plank of fir is no great
matter, but at least it can sometimes help somebody to cross a
ditch, and even an abyss.

I grasp your hand, my dear Gide. Don't think ill of me, don't
sulk with me, don't feel awkward with me—and above all don't
think of me as a man of letters.

P. CLAUDEL.

———

13.—*André Gide to Paul Claudel*

Sunday morning [17th December 1905].

My dear Claudel,

Every day I mean to write to you, and then I draw back
before the enormity of all that I could tell you. . . . Your letter
that came this morning encourages me to send you a very simple
note—for the time being.

Let me know if I can come and talk to you one evening—Wednesday or Thursday or Friday. I should have liked to make it sooner,
but since I saw you I have been harassed all the time by one small
vexation after another. Forgive me for keeping your notebook so
long ; I am still struggling with it—or I should already have
returned it to you. Please let me have it till to-morrow evening.
I will leave it at your flat.

Yours,

ANDRÉ GIDE.

Gide : *Journal*

18 December 1905.

What especially shocked Paul Claudel when, after several years
in the Orient, he returned to modern civilization, was the waste.

" What ! " he exclaimed, " when St. Francis of Assisi found in
the mud of a path a bit of crumpled parchment, he picked it up in
his hand, smoothed it out, because he had seen writing on it—

writing, that sacred thing—and look at us, what we do with it to-day ! It really pains me to think of that enormous mass of paper which is covered with printing for one day and then thrown into the garbage-pail. . . . We have not only no more respect for the writing of others, but not even for our own. . . ." ·

14.—*Paul Claudel to André Gide*

[Paris, December 1905.]

My dear Gide,

Here is the manuscript of a most admirable book which my friend Suarès has entrusted to me. You will find that it echoes many of the conversations that I have had, during the last eight months, with this lonely being. Do go through it. I shall come and fetch it on Saturday morning, in order to take it to the *Mercure* —I am asking them to print it.

I grasp your hand most cordially,

P. CLAUDEL.

15.—*Paul Claudel to André Gide*

Friday [postmarked January 1906].

Dear Gide,

Would you, to save yourself bothér, be good enough to leave Suarès' manuscript with your concierge, and I will fetch it at about half-past ten ? I hope that it will have interested you.

I leave on Monday morning for Lyons and shall stay there for a fortnight. In fact I must tell you that I am engaged to a young lady of that city—Mademoiselle Reine Sainte-Marie-Perrin, the daughter of the architect of Fourvières—and am to marry her in a few weeks' time.

I grasp your hand with affection,

P. CLAUDEL.

16.—*Paul Claudel to André Gide*

Saturday [postmarked January 1906].

My dear Gide,

Your concierge told me to-day that you were away and would only come back this evening. I myself have to go to Lyons on Monday morning and cannot call on you again. Would you be good enough to give Suarès' manuscript to Vallette, who is expecting it? Forgive me for causing you—quite involuntarily—this trouble, and believe me to be most affectionately yours.

P. CLAUDEL.

17.—*Paul Claudel to André Gide*

37 Quai d'Anjou, Thursday,
[January 1906].

My dear Gide,

Are you in Paris, and would you come and dine here informally at 8.15, and bring Madame Gide with you? I should like you to meet my friends the Berthelots. Be assured that nothing will be said about the forbidden subjects.

I grasp your hand,

P. CLAUDEL.

18.—*Paul Claudel to André Gide*

[Paris], Friday
[postmarked 9th March 1906].

I must tell you that I leave for Pekin on 1st April. I hope that you will think of me and remain my friend, and that you will forgive the heated letter I wrote to you some weeks ago. I am sending you a list of propositions which I drew up at the request of a friend, and in which I have tried to summarize the ensemble of my beliefs.

Do not regard it as an attempt at an apologia for your personal instruction, but simply as a small remembrance—like those simple pictures which the devout send to one another at certain solemn moments in life.

I grasp your hand with affection,

P. CLAUDEL.

My respectful greetings to Madame Gide.

———

Summary of all Christian doctrine

1. God is the perfect Being, in whom all potency is act. He is inaccessible to our senses, and we can assert of him only that He *is* and what He *is not*.

2. By what do we recognize a living creature that we cannot see ? By the movement to which he gives rise. The mole beneath the earth, the hare in the hedge, the heart beneath our fingers. But we see that the whole universe is never still for a moment. In this world everything is movement ; everything bears witness to the holy commotion of all living creatures, for they are always in a state of creation ; they cannot exist by themselves ; nor can they *subsist* in the presence of the motionless Creator. The afflux is everywhere evident.

3. Our faith allows us to penetrate further into the mystery of divine physiology, and to distinguish within it three relations— functions, or rôles, or persons : the *Father*, who engenders ; the *Son*, or the Word, or Reason, who by the fact of his existence tells the Father, unto all eternity, that He Is ; the *Spirit*, or Emanation, or Love, which flows out equally from the one to the other and vice versa, and is the Breath exhaled and inhaled.

4. God, being all-powerful, has created only those things which are good. We call " good " something that is exactly adapted to its purpose ; a good pen, a good horse ; more or less good according to whether it is more or less well adapted. God has created only things which are *very good*—perfectly adapted in their appointed way, that is to say, to bear explicit witness to Him and make Him better understood. And, of course, any imperfection in the product can only be the result of an obstacle foreign to the will of Him who made it.

5. But we can see that to-day, in point of fact, things are no longer very good, that is to say, perfectly adapted in our sight to bear unambiguous witness to their Creator. We no longer understand their language. What are we to say, if we look into ourselves ?—That we live in a state of disorder. The original *order* of things has been corrupted, and with it the Commandment which enjoins all things to appear as they are ; there is a mechanical defect which disturbs the smooth running of the entire engine.

6. This disorder cannot, by definition, be the work of the Creator, because all things which are his work are necessarily good. Therefore it can only be the work of the free creature—free, that is to say, to set himself up as the end instead of God. A difference of direction, a wrong preference. This corrupted preference is what we call *original sin,* and its root cause is that it is in himself, rather than in God, that the creature chooses to seek his satisfaction.

7. The consequence of original sin, by which the finite creature chooses himself as his end, is the *End,* or death, or separation. The separation of the rebel angels who would never be reintegrated into life ; and, for man, the loss of that essential state in which he had found his satisfaction.

8. By the fact of his sin, Man withdraws from God his body and the service of his body, with which the whole natural order is securely united. He is no longer adapted to his purpose. That which he has thrown away as an innocent, he cannot restore as a sinner. God alone can give God (or the work of God) back to God, by a kind of new creation or regeneration. *Fiat,* says the Father, *voluntas mea. Fiat voluntas tua,* the Son replies.

9. After his fall, man hides, confesses, rediscovers, and buries away in the womb of woman both his origin and his crime : and God comes forth again after many generations from the breast of Mary Immaculate.

10. By the fact of his fall, man has consented to the End, or death, or limitation, or separation : by the Cross, the Son of man has consented to the End, or death, or annihilation of that limitation and that separation.

11. By our union with Christ, the head of the race, in the visible unity of the Church, the totality of the faithful are restored to God.

12. We must be in union with Christ. If we are to be attached to the head, we must also be part of the body. We form the body of the Church by our submission to its outward forms—that is to

say, to its lawful shepherds—and by our participation in its life—
that is to say, in the sacraments which are its arteries.

13. Christ is with us. He is ever-present to his Church—as a
law-giver, through the Pope and his hierarchy, as a doctor through
the sacrament of penitence, and as nourishment through the
Eucharist.

14. Thus we are never far from eternal joy. It is not a dream
or a morbid appetite ; it is an organic and rightful need of our
nature, the most essential of its needs. " The Kingdom of Heaven
is within us." It resides in a free act of our will, in an act of consent
to that Grace which is there for our acceptance. To enter the
Kingdom, we must submit to an " order " which we accept as an
accepted order. It consists in the restoration of that orderly state
of things in which creature submits to his Creator and takes part,
in his appointed place, in the life of his Creator. *Fiat voluntas tua.*

15. That is why Catholic Truth is best learnt not in theory, by
a mere nod of the listening mind, but in practice—by placing our
whole being in its true setting, like a *mot juste* : by taking up our
allotted position : and by participation in the rites of the Church.

19.—*Paul Claudel to André Gide*

Hôtel de l'Europe [Lyons],
14th March 1906.

Too late, my dear Gide, adieu !

Yes, I have the feeling that many things remain unsaid between
us. What I did say, I don't regret, all things considered. I may
be this or that, and my remarks may please or displease, but they
do at least bear witness to the truth which resides uniquely and
exclusively in the teaching of the Catholic Church, and nowhere
else. Open your heart to this inrush of the truth, make way in
your intelligence for the immense deserted spaces.

What comfort was mine that June morning in the Church of
Fourvières ! With God one is never lonely, despite the most
atrocious of separations. One acts in accord with an enormous,
sweet, and noble harmony. What dignity it gives to the least of
our actions.

I very much liked your *Amyntas*, especially the page on habits
and the roots that one takes everywhere with one. . . . What an

excellent writer you are, your mind is as graceful as the most supple of bodies, and what a fine use of syntax ! I remember a page where there were two imperfect subjunctives that I very much admired.

Forgive this hasty letter. A last handshake, and I shall once again be swallowed up for several long years. I take the boat at 11 a.m. on the 18th. As you know, I am to be married to-morrow.

P. CLAUDEL.

Gide :   Journal

Tuesday morning.

" . . . This morning a very fine letter from Claudel."

20.—Paul Claudel to André Gide

Tientsin, 21st August 1906.
[postcard of Chinese children.]

My dear Friend,

I no longer receive L'Ermitage, and I am sorry, because I liked it very much and still consider myself as one of its contributors. Could you ask them to resume sending it to me ? Thank you in advance. And send me your news. My respects to Madame Gide.

PAUL CLAUDEL.

21.—André Gide to Paul Claudel

Villa Montmorency,
18 Avenue des Sycomores,
7th November 1906.

My dear Claudel,

I was so sorry not to receive your play—Fontaine and several others had told me about it. Ducoté's faithless secretary was keeping back at the office of l'Ermitage the three copies which you kindly put down in my name ; I happened to pass by there the other day ;—I at once gave one copy to my friend, your admirer Jacques

Copeau, another to my friend your admirer Henri Ghéon, and began to read the third copy myself.

It would be better for me to write a long article on *Partage de Midi* than to speak to you about it in these few lines. There are certain pages before which I tremble, as Moses trembled when he saw the burning bush, and I experience that secret enthusiasm, of which our literature seems to want to disabuse us, but which ought to be our normal condition. That is why we owe you our gratitude. But I expected to prefer the *Cantique de Mésa* to the admirable love-duet in the second act.

I shall re-read your play, and more than once ; perhaps I shall one day speak of it at greater length. As soon as I had read it for the first time I lent it to my friend Marcel Drouin (Michel Arnauld) who would be more than pleased if you would allow Chapon to put aside a copy for him. Perhaps you have already read something by him in *l'Ermitage* or the *Revue Blanche*, when he took over from me when I gave up my position as critic ; he follows all that you write with the liveliest interest. He was my friend for a long time before he became my brother-in-law.

I have asked Ducoté to send your *l'Ermitage* ; but alas ! not for long ; *l'Ermitage* is coming to an end. The plausible machinations of one of the secretaries (which Ducoté was too indolent to put a stop to) have got the better of all our good intentions. For a time I thought of taking it in hand again (I'd almost given it up, I admit), but the burdens are decidedly too heavy, as are the expenditures of energy, money, self-respect—and copy. Also, I should have to be more certain of being able to write more often for it myself. This summer I have had to interrupt all my work—all my reading, even—because I have been reduced to imbecility by my bouts of all too frequent insomnia ; I had to try to recover my youth on the beaches of Brittany, where I lived a primitive life, far from everything and everybody. I often thought of you there.

Believe me—after my imaginary conversations with you, a letter like this one gives me no satisfaction at all. But no matter ! Better even this than that you should be left to think of me as silent.

My wife also remembers you often and sends you her affectionate regards. And now that you are no longer alone, I send my respects, along with my greetings.

Au revoir,

ANDRÉ GIDE

22.—*Paul Claudel to André Gide*

Tientsin, Christmas 1906.

My dear Friend,

Thank you for your letter and your affectionate remembrances, which I fully return. I have often been on the point of writing to you. But what am I to say ? I am only too ashamed already of my awkwardness and indiscretion. Still, we all express ourselves as best we can. I don't lack either conviction or goodwill. But, at the same time, it's not with big words and involved ideas that souls are won over. You are an upright man, and sooner or later you will meet the person whom you need.

No, Gide, it's not the wretched farrago of poor Claudel that has won your affection, but what you somehow manage to read between the lines.

These are bad times ! Never was there greater need of God—or greater determination to repulse Him. The lips reject what the stomach cries out for. . . . Thus are the words of Amos confirmed : " In these times I shall send down hunger upon the earth —not hunger for bread, but hunger for the word of God ". In the *Concordance*, the word " hunger " is referred back to the maledictions of *Deuteronomy*.

What a wretched business it is—all these books and magazines which come to hand ! It shows to what a degree of debility and fatuity their " intelligence " has fallen—which is yet so proud of itself and its distractions. Somebody—anybody—without virtue, talent or intelligence (a Russian, one might say, or a Rémy de Gourmont—and for my part I would just as soon say a Kant or a Renan), thinks up an idea, just one poor little idea as absurd as you please, as repellent as you please, and feels nothing but disgust and despair at the thought of it ; yet people will flock to follow him. The doctrine of Christ, which is all peace, all joy, all order, promise, light, enhancement of character and reason, is being abandoned by them all, just as He had foreseen. " I come in the name of my father and you have not welcomed me : If another comes in my name you will make him welcome." It is easier to renounce one's joy than to renounce one's pride.

I still work to a certain extent. This great luminous cold is very stimulating. I haven't got a play in mind, and besides I am tired of the conventional, fictitious side of the drama. For the moment

I prefer the ode, which is poetry in its pure and single state, with nothing but movement and proportion to be considered. I've written two of them. I also expect to become a father in January. You can see that I'm not losing such time as is left me by the tramways, the drains, and the accounts of the Concession which I administer.

My respects and best remembrances to Madame Gide, and for yourself an affectionate handshake.

P. Claudel.

23.—*Paul Claudel to André Gide*

French Consulate, Tientsin,
31st January 1907.

Dear Friend,

I have a favour to ask you, as one colleague, or rather one friend, to another. You know that I am printing—or rather, alas, that the *Mercure* is printing—two books for me at this moment : *Connaissance de l'Est* and *l'Art poétique*. I corrected the first proofs of the *Connaissance*, and I am wondering if you would consent to go through the second set ? Do this kindness to a friend and an exile. The parcel of *l'Art poétique* will go off shortly.

I need not tell you that in its new form the book is quite unworthily printed. What I should like, at the least, is :—

that the titles should be set in strong black characters ;

that they should be separated from the text by several blank lines ;

that each poem should begin on a fresh page.

All my blessings go with you !

Have you read Suarès' *Voici l'Homme* ?

You will know that I am the father of a very pretty little girl—at least, she seems so to me. It is a completely new experience and it has affected me in a quite new and very powerful way. I was present throughout the accouchement, which is a most beautiful and moving affair, and not at all the thing of filth and horror which that *disgusting* Zola makes it out to be.

I grasp your hand most affectionately.
Remember me to Madame Gide.

P. Claudel.

Gide :   *Journal*

6 February 1907.

Have forsaken this notebook the last few days, but for the sake of work.   I am composing an *Enfant prodigue*, in which I am trying to make a dialogue of my spiritual reticences and impulses.

This morning, from Claudel, a letter full of a sacred wrath, against the epoch, against Gourmont, Rousseau, Kant, Renan. . . . Holy wrath no doubt, but wrath all the same, and just as painful to my mind as the barking of a dog is to my ear.   I cannot endure it and cover my ears at once.   But I hear it nevertheless and then have trouble getting back to work.

———

24.—*Paul Claudel to André Gide*

French Consulate, Tientsin,
9th February 1907.

Dear Gide,

I am sending to-day to the *Mercure* a parcel with the proofs of *l'Art poétique*.   I hardly like to ask if you would be good enough to read the next set.   Who else could do it ?   The text is so very difficult and needs to be exactly right.   I should have liked to use a lay-out which I tried, I think with success, in *Partage de Midi*.   It comprises a *pause*—that is to say, a blank space of two or three letters.   Commas and full-stops only indicate a rough and purely logical articulation of the phrase.   Yet there are pauses and halts in my text which owe nothing to grammar and are yet absolutely indispensable to the verse.   But how can one try to get the type-setters to see the point of them ?

The *Mercure* quite forgot to send me the proof of the third fragment which completes the volume *Développement de l'Église* (published in the *Mercure* in 1903).   Would you yourself take care to see that this gap is made good, and go through the proofs.   I've nothing to alter in the text.   You need only add at the end the date 1900.

I sent Vallette a sketch of the title-page, with this epigram from St. Augustine : *Sicut creator, ita moderator, Donec universi seculi pulcritudo . . . velut magnum carmen ineffabilis modulatoris* (St. Augustine.

Fifth Epistle to Marcellinus). As Vallette has already lost the instructions I sent him, you will be able to supervise in this respect.

I thank you a thousand times and shake your hand affectionately.

PAUL CLAUDEL.

25.—André Gide to Paul Claudel

14th March [1907].

My dear Claudel,

I shall write you a long letter in a few days' time. Meanwhile here is a hasty note to say how happy I am to render you the service for which you ask. I immediately got into touch with Vallette about it ; so I hope that it will be merely a question of patience ; you know that I shall take the greatest possible pains with the work.

I was greatly moved by the news of the birth of your daughter. Who was the first to tell me of it ? I forget. Perhaps Philippe Berthelot, whom I met by chance, and who also told me that you were " putting on weight ". You explained to me, one day, how a man's faculties must go on developing continuously till the day of his death.

I've begun work again, after a long interruption due to senile exhaustion, and have finished an *Enfant prodigue,* which I should have dedicated to you if I hadn't dedicated it to Fontaine.

I was so anxious to like Suarès that I sent for two copies of *Voici l'Homme*—one of them on *Hollande* paper—in order to put a finer edge on my enjoyment. The book for me was rich in exasperation —and in almost nothing else. The best phrases are those which most resemble your own : " but you would not be the person you are if we had not *enough* of you (I mean : enough *with* you) ". I stand before that, as if before a sheep with six feet or a two-headed calf, and painfully ask myself : " how does he manage to breathe ? " And it grieves me to think that this very *formlessness* passes, in Mauclair's eyes, for the purest mark of genius. And then what repels me most of all is the sort of religious puffery which is found in its most astonishing form in the proclamation on the final page. How can he say, of a book which is no more than a sheaf of paper, that it was *finished* on Good Friday? What does it mean? It's grotesque.

Au revoir. Perhaps, although I have not been presented to Madame Paul Claudel, I may ask you to give her my regards. My wife and I smile tenderly upon little Marie.

I am,
Yours,
ANDRÉ GIDE.

Could you, in return for the zeal which I shall bring to the correction of your proofs,—could you let me have two copies of *Partage de Midi*, if you still have any? You would give great pleasure to me, and great pleasure to two of your most fervent admirers—one of them being the critic Michel Arnauld, who is my brother-in-law.

Gide :   *Journal*
22 April 1907.

Now I am correcting for Claudel the proofs of *Connaissance de l'Est*.

24 April 1907.

I go to consult Marcel Drouin about the Claudel proofs I am correcting. Wonderful *Connaissance de l'Est*, which I am rereading with close attention. Certain less ample, less inspired chapters still do not mar the book ; a large number of them are of the loftiest beauty.

————

26.—*Paul Claudel to André Gide*

French Consulate, Tientsin,
29th April 1907.

Dear Friend,

Thank you for your kindness in taking upon yourself that heavy burden. I have every confidence in you. I thought I had asked the *Occident*, a long time ago, to send you the two copies for which you ask. To make up for my negligence I am writing to them to-day and asking them to send you three copies. You can pick them up at Chapon's.

I am saddened that you should think so severely of Suarès' book.

You seem to me to judge it too objectively. This journal is the work of a sick man and a prisoner. There is a soul in the book, and that's quite enough to make us forgive all his poor poses and affectations! When a bird dashes itself a hundred times running against a window or a barbed-wire fence, it distresses us, but it distresses the bird still more, and not its nerves only. Suarès is one of the victims of that abominable idol of *Art* to which so many poor wretches have sacrificed their lives. It's neither an end of life, nor a way of life, but a way of existing.

Berthelot tells me I may be sent to Calcutta. I should love it. Tientsin is really a little austere. Still, I've done some work here —I've just finished my *Troisième Ode* and am about to start the *Quatrième*.

I grasp your hand with affection. My respects to Madame Gide. Don't forget to send me the *Enfant prodigue*.

PAUL CLAUDEL.

Gide : *Journal*

16 May 1907.

Perplexities as I correct for Claudel the proofs of *Co-naissance du monde et de soi-même* : so often grammar and syntax are intentionally outraged that I fear, at times, taking for an error some deliberate anomaly. But what is one to think of " *plus ou moindre ?* " Religious certainty gives this robust mind a deplorable infatuation. Perhaps it is impossible to write quite correctly without some fear of making a mistake.

27.—*André Gide to Paul Claudel*

Cuverville (Seine-Inférieure),
20th June 1907.

My dear Claudel,

I have received the three copies of *Partage de Midi* which you were good enough to send me by way of Chapon, and I thank you most warmly on behalf of the three readers whose happiness I have secured.

The correction of *Connaissance de l'Est* has offered no difficulty. I very much enjoyed doing it, and this minute scrutiny of the little book redoubled my admiration for it. As for the *Co-naissance*, I had a great deal of trouble with it. Sometimes I didn't know whether the negligence of the printers or your own decision was responsible for the unusual orthography of certain phrases. (There were in any case a considerable number of errors.) Fortunately your typescript got me out of the difficulty and I was able in the end to resolve all my doubts. I took my task to heart and was *determined* that you should be satisfied. Alas! as for the word " *rhythme* ", like Verlaine and like myself, you must give it up. It occurs often in your book, spelt now in one way and now in another, and only at the end of the volume did I learn from your handwritten correction that you prefer the authentic Greek spelling. I had already corrected the few instances in which " h " appeared as the second letter, and I was afraid that the printer would panic if I went back on it, and that you would be left with a hybrid formation, or with some deplorable errors. I hope you won't be too upset. I think that in all other respects the text is as you would wish it.

What you say of Suarès moves me, makes me perhaps understand a little better what lies behind his book—or, at any rate, reveals its origin to me—but it doesn't make me like it more. There is nothing there but intellectual gossip and rough sketches for master-pieces ; perhaps this agitation is a necessary preliminary to any well-nourished work of art, but the work of art only begins when all that has been pared away. I fear that Suarès is satisfied by this first immature state. The equivalent of that in painting or sculpture would horrify you, and in any period less sadly decadent than our own the publication, even the idea of such a book, would be impossible . . . during the author's lifetime, at any rate. For the rest, as I expected, the nebula-fanciers see it as a work of genius and Mauclair did not fail to write an article about it. I am delighted (1) for Suarès—and I say it in all sincerity, because I hold him in high esteem, despite my opinion of his book ; (2) because I like well-defined positions, and the fact of knowing exactly what one dislikes is a step towards a better understanding of *who one is*. It is certain that, in comparison with Suarès' book, purity of form seems thin, the *ne quid nimis* (which, as you were saying, should be found at the entrance to every work of art) seems a mark of penury, and choice a mark of parsimony, etc. Forgive me for insisting, where insistence is painful to you ; it hurts me also to say this to you and it hurts me to think it, because I have the liveliest regard for you.

What! You may be going to Calcutta! This news has had a great effect on me—I fear I shan't know how to resist the longing to visit you there . . . yes, I shan't even try . . . I am already dreaming of it. And when I write " au revoir " in this letter, it is with Calcutta in mind. I think of you, of the two of you, of the three of you already! My wife joins me in sending our greetings and I am very affectionately yours,

A. GIDE.

I think that you are being sent *Vers et Prose* in which my *Enfant prodigue* appears.

I read in Verlaine's letter " I certainly put ' *rhythme* ' and now they have printed it wrongly ".

28.—*Paul Claudel to André Gide*

French Consulate, Tientsin,
22nd July 1907.

Dear Friend,

Your letter gave me great pleasure. I was beginning to be a little anxious about my two children, of whom I no longer had any news. I see that thanks to you they are going to make a decent entry into the world. You could see, when you read the purified text of *Connaissance de l'Est*, how bad I am at correcting. I had written only yesterday to the *Mercure* to ask for news.

Alas, I no longer receive *Vers et Prose*. After *Connaissance de l'Est* had been printed with a great many of the vilest misprints I wrote Paul Fort an extremely severe letter. (" The nation of Spain " instead of " Space ", " *mer* " instead of the sea-word " *amer* ", etc.) This deprives me of *L'Enfant prodigue*, eager as I am to read it. I hope you will send it to me.

Leaving Suarès himself on one side, I quite agree with you on the question of *mesure*. The farther I go, and the more I think about my art, the more I recognize that *mesure* is not only the supreme test of finish and ornament, but, in point of fact, the prime engine of creative activity. Just as the whole nature of a number is altered if one adds or subtracts a single unit, so all artistic forms are not only enfeebled, but deformed and destroyed if one's hand is too

heavy. Only a perfect balance is creative. This ancient truth has
been obscured by that inrush of savagery, the Romantic Movement.
Alas, no, I'm not going to Calcutta, for the moment at any rate.
Later I probably shall. My life here is one of continual combat.
It is always difficult to administer men, even in the smallest area.

My respectful greetings to Madame Gide. An affectionate
handshake for yourself.

P. CLAUDEL.

29.—*André Gide to Paul Claudel*

[Paris], 24th October 1907.

A hasty note (I've just left the *Mercure*) in the hope that it
may catch up with the letter that Vallette wrote to you three days
ago. Do not become involved with this Parisian *Société d'Auteurs
Dramatiques*. Unless your plays have first been acted in Paris,
these Gentlemen pay no attention to you and merely make a
semblance of looking after your interests. I couldn't get anything
out of them (though I was fully entitled to do so, having been acted
once in Paris). In Berlin you will have an " agent ", no doubt the
same as mine, whose job it is to defend *your* interests at the same
time as your translator's. The ensuing calculations are perfectly
easy. The agent pays himself out of your royalties, at a rate which
is always the same, and is settled by agreement, and fixed, and
then you divide the rest with the translator in equal shares. Really
it's not easy for them to do us down—I've gone into the whole
question ; after having been suspicious from every point of view,
I'm now quite confident that the organization works well.

This *agent* has got money back from Cracow for me ! Percentages
from performances from which I hardly expected anything—and
last year, when the theatrical manager who is putting my play on
at this moment broke his word to me, the agent managed to make
him pay me substantial compensation and sign a new contract,
more binding than the first. Even if I'd been there myself I could
never have secured that alone—or with the help of the *Société* in
Paris. Moreover, Blei seems to me very honest, and not at all a
Jew, either in fact or in character. He has very great admiration
for you which it was easy for me to inculcate. The annoying thing
is that he doesn't know French well and his translations are far

from perfect ; but he has always been so zealous, so complaisant, and so " straight " that I think you can congratulate yourself on having him as your translator. (All this between ourselves of course.)

To put on your play (it's not *L'Échange* any longer, but *Partage de Midi*, he tells me) seems to me very hazardous ; it's true that in Berlin they are so glad to swallow anything " new " that I am ready for everything and nothing. We shall see. Please hope for the success of my *Roi Candaule* ; Blei's prestige with the managers may be greatly enhanced by it. Au revoir, my dear Claudel ! I am only now going back to Paris. That's why I haven't sent you my *Enfant prodigue* before now. Here it is.

Don't be too forgetful of me, for I am your friend,

ANDRÉ GIDE.

Gide : *Journal*

13 December 1907.

I find and reread a letter from Paul Claudel (1899) : " Your mind has no slope ", he said to me. That is just what is needed. No praise is more precious to me.

30.—*Paul Claudel to André Gide*

French Consulate, Tientsin,
16th December 1907.

Best Christmas wishes, my dear Gide, to you and Madame Gide. I kept putting off my answer till I had received your *Enfant prodigue*, but so far nothing has arrived. Have I thanked you properly for the admirable care with which you corrected my two books ? It was terribly difficult work. The text of the first book is now perfect. In the second there are still a few mistakes, of which only one really distresses me, " *bourse* " instead of " *bouse* " as it should have been.

I was very happy to hear of Jammes' marriage. Do you know somebody called Ruyters who sent me an abominable book called *Le Mauvais Riche*, and who no doubt expected compliments from me because he seemed angry when I told him what I thought of such filth. I saw that he had dedicated the book to you,—but you can't like it any better than I do.

I am not working much just now, except on the *Odes,* which give me a lòt of trouble, for it is the first time that I have attempted *la parole dure* and the pure movement of thought, unsustained by any story or objective theory.

I grasp your hand. My respectful regards to Madame Gide.

P. CLAUDEL.

31.—*André Gide to Paul Claudel*

17th January 1908.

My dear Friend,

I am ashamed, distressed, and furious with myself for passing the gross blunder which you point out to me, and I send you my most abject apologies ! It's no good saying that I took all possible pains over the corrections—I should only embarrass myself the more !

I was going to send you my *Enfant prodigue* when Jammes discovered that it contained elements of Jansenism, and Frizeau (it comes back to me now), that it was a work of bad faith. They made me doubtful—not by any means of the sincerity of the book, or of its profound piety—but of the welcome which you might perhaps accord to it. Still, since you ask for it, here it is.

As for Ruyters, I thought you knew him already, for he once wrote an essay on you. It was well written, insufficiently penetrating perhaps, but revealing the most cordial and lively admiration for your work. He would not have turned towards it if he had not recognized in you a number of his ideas (or if you prefer, in himself a number of your ideas)—putting aside all question of faith. You may say that that is the only question of any importance—but, because of Paul of Tarsus, I'm not quite convinced of it. Don't suppose, if I say that I hold in high esteem his character, his honesty, and his intellectual probity—don't suppose that because of this I applaud what shocked you in *Le Mauvais Riche* ; but I see that Jammes is still a friend of Gourmont's, and consequently tolerates in Gourmont blasphemies which seem to me to bespeak a quite different opacity of mind and in fact cause me positive distress. As for the dedication, it's true that Ruyters had sounded me about it and that, fearing to disoblige me, he had made his offer by letter —and I must own that I accepted it. He is my Philippe Berthelot.

Yes, Jammes is married. For him, for his mother, and for his wife, I am extremely happy. Nothing is so noble and so touching as that ceremony, so simple and so pure, in a little village church that you must surely know, since Fontaine, or Jammes, was telling me that your family comes from a neighbouring parish. A few special friends, no display of any sort . . . and complete liberty to join with all one's heart in this holy celebration.

I have seen Jammes since, at Orthez, whither I was summoned by a sad bereavement—but that in passing. I know he is working (if the word has still some meaning for him) on a sequel to *Jean de Norrieu*. But no doubt I am telling you nothing that he has not already told you himself.

I read (or saw, at any rate) in an important German Review which is directed by our translator Franz Blei, an article on *Partage de Midi*. Blei tells me that he had begun negotiations for a possible performance of your play, but that the managers want it to be cut. He has replied in magnificent style—*All* or nothing. But *la Presse* has just given my *Roi Candaule* such a terrible wigging (it was revived on the 9th in Berlin) that Blei must be cured for some time to come of any ambition to put on anything.

I am happy to learn that you are writing *Odes* and you have made me hope for a great deal from them. In the Review *Antée*, of which Griffin and I have more or less taken over the direction, and which, moribund a few months ago, has come to life again— if *Antée* does not seem to you unworthy—we should be more than happy to publish a new work of yours.

If you'd rather have the *Grande Revue* . . . make use of me as you please.

Au revoir. All my respects to Madame Claudel, please. As you know, I am affectionately yours,

ANDRÉ GIDE.

32.—*Paul Claudel to André Gide*

French Consulate, Tientsin,
6th February 1908.

My dear Friend,

Forgive me for having distressed you by the way in which I spoke of Ruyters. You must understand the position of a Catholic, in this happy epoch of ours, when all the books, papers, Reviews that he receives from France, bring him bundles and cartloads of nothing but insults, mockery, attacks of every sort and from every side upon all that he reveres in the world, and news of ruin, persecution and apostacy. For me, if anyone attacks the Church, it is as if he had struck my father or my mother, and when I was sent those pretty speeches as if they were something that I should be delighted to read and to admire, then I admit that I saw red. It's perfectly useless, of course ; I don't doubt that Ruyters is a man of honour according to his lights, and he has been very civil to me in his time. But how can he believe that those insipid problems have the smallest importance for me beside the only things which I really have at heart, or that I can in the least degree enjoy reading the horrors which he sent me ? I could say the same and more of Gourmont, who at least doesn't send me his books. That doesn't stop me having excellent friends among Jews, Protestants, and atheists, such as Schwob, Suarès, and Berthelot, but these are simply passive unbelievers, not personal enemies of Christ. I own that I cannot listen in cold blood to these insults ; my whole heart rises against them. A little more charity would be an improvement, of course. Of course I shouldn't reproach you, even had I the right to do so, for accepting the dedication of that book. After all, for you Christ is no more than any other figure from History or Legend. But for me he is something quite other.

As for Berthelot, he is the only man to whom I ever dedicated a book, in order to acknowledge in however small a way my immense obligations to him, for it was he who saved me from the abyss of sorrow, passion, and madness into which I had fallen.

I've been carrying on for some time a most interesting correspondence with a professor of philosophy of the University of Grenoble, M. Georges Dumesnil, whose reply to the *Mercure* questionnaire had very much impressed me. He has read very widely and has reflected in a most interesting way on his reading. As we are both Christians, that is to say that we have got beyond first principles and the B-A, BA, and are like two astronomers or geographers who compare their conclusions and correlations and are delighted to find themselves in perfect agreement. He taught me an admirable phrase of Aristotle which I did not know and which sums up all my convictions at this moment : " In everything, begin with the best ".

Perhaps you have read in *l'Occident* a series of articles about me by Jacques Rivière. This young man has a remarkably penetrating intelligence. But (by expounding them in didactic style) he has, of course, transformed into set doctrines a great many things which for me are only *propositions*, or landmarks which point the way to further reflexion. Consequently he has given my lucubrations a mystagogic and vaguely heretical character which rather frightens me. In fact I should have prefaced even my *Art poétique* with the foreword which Poe wrote for his masterpiece *Eureka*.

I haven't much news of Jammes, but I am content to know that he is happy, as he deserves to be.

I am writing philosophically for my play to be put on in Berlin. Fundamentally the attempt seems to me simply a bad joke. A play of mine in translation is like an opera without music. Anyway it seems that in Belgium my works are read aloud to groups of miners and metallurgists who enjoy them as much as anything else.

I have also heard from somebody called R. Monfort, 98 rue Truffaut, who asks for leave to set *Le Repos du Septième Jour* to music. I gave it, with my blessing and general permission to tinker about with it as much as he likes. I don't really see that play as an opera. As the second act takes place in complete darkness, a stretch of the Underground Railway could be hired for the occasion. Do you know anything of Monfort?

Forgive this overlong letter. I have taken advantage of the Chinese national holiday to bore you. Please give my respectful regards to Madame Gide. I grip your hand affectionately.

P. Claudel.

33.—*Paul Claudel to André Gide*

French Consulate, Tientsin,
3rd March 1908.

My dearest Friend,

I have just received your *Enfant prodigue* and I need not say that I read it with great interest. It reveals more of your soul, more of your thoughts, than any other book of yours that I know. And what a pleasure it is to savour that noble style of yours—so flexible and so distinguished, above all (I would say) so easy, and so homogeneous that it unrolls the narrative from beginning to end without a moment's loss of continuity! For my private satisfaction I noted certain piquant Germanisms and the use of " *distingués* " with the infinitive which gave me just the sense of how the poor mother, grown old and stout, appeared to the son whom she had borne late in life. It was one of those audacities which you alone can permit yourself.

I don't know anything about your past life, but it's easy to see that you were unhappy and suppressed as a child, and that your heart overflowed with affection which was neither understood nor satisfied. To this I trace the chief of your talent, which is what I shall call a modest shyness, with all the sense of almost exaggerated elegance, of modesty, of social incompatibility, of fundamental curiosity and reserve, which we associate with the shyness of the hart or the deer. I know for myself the battles and the uneasiness which arise when a child is not understood by his family and his elders. It is perfectly true that each generation brings something new which its seniors are incompetent to judge. Thence comes a rebellion which is almost legitimate, in a certain degree.

So you see that you were quite wrong to be afraid I should be shocked by these pages. On the contrary, I was much moved by them. Of course, I don't share the sentiments of your prodigal. The wise course is not to run away from the disagreeable side of life, but to conquer it. And if you must have adventure, what could be more surprising and audacious than the practical acceptance of a supernatural and invisible world, beside which the world which we know is as nothing? What kingdoms are richer and more mysterious than those of Grace? Those who know nothing of such things are like a man who has never seen the Tropics, or a eunuch who speaks of love. What is the wind on one's face compared with the winds of the spirit? Besides, you who are so fine an artist—surely you can't deny the importance, in any domain, of choice, of sacrifice, and of self-imposed limits? For every phrase you write, you throw away twenty—of which several are very good. You can't write as you want to, any more than you can think or act as you want to. What is the point of running away and cursing the *house*? There is one house that it is sometimes healthy and necessary to leave, as was shown by these texts : " A man shall leave his father and mother "—" Who is my mother ? And who are my brethren ? "—" Let the dead bury their dead "— " The foxes have their holes but the Son of Man hath nowhere to lay his head ", etc. But that house is not the Church, which is the Word made visible : " The first commandment is to love God with all one's soul ; and the second, *which is like to this,* is to love one's neighbour as oneself." The Church is only exclusive because she is Catholic, and therefore universal, and leaves absolutely nothing outside herself. Whatever is not within God's edifice is shut in the hideously narrow limits of self-esteem, which are like the tiny dungeon to which Sainte Thérèse likened hell. There is most religion where there is most love, and there is most love where there is most unity. Those who resemble Christ resemble one another with a magnificent diversity. Revelation did not come to us as a poetic or philosophical inspiration. Christ came among us in flesh and blood, and he has not left us without a guide and a shepherd. The Church is a sort of eucharistic corporation. Finally—*and this is where I reproach you most*—no, it is not from laziness that we draw near to God. Terrible struggles and un-relenting energy are needed if we are to return to the faith and keep to it. The Catholic's life is one long scandal, one long contra-diction. Every conversation, every book, every newspaper is the negation of all that he loves and believes. He is alone with the word of God, in whom he believes. There is an admirable text of St. Paul on the subject.

Those are all the mental notes I made about your book, which I like because it makes me know you better. But how am I to interpret the younger son whom you accompany as far as the front gate ? He could be given other advice than to *run away,* and there are other ways of saving himself than by flight. The joy of this fortieth year which we are both traversing is precisely what I call the *happiness of responsibility,* the profound satisfaction of knowing that so many hearts are resting upon our own, that so many hands are clasping ours, and the sense that we shan't let them down, that we are in possession of the truth and are contributing to the solidarity of the universe. None of the intoxications of passion can replace this deep feeling of brotherhood.

I grasp your hand affectionately. My respectful regards to Madame Gide.

P. CLAUDEL.

34.—*Paul Claudel to André Gide*

French Consulate, Tientsin,
30th July 1908.

My dear Friend,

I am so happy to be able to tell you that my son Pierre was born on the 23rd. It all went off perfectly.

I was absolutely delighted to read the long article on Dostoevsky which you sent me—it is a magnificent piece of criticism. I am so glad to see you do homage to this great writer. Hitherto, the success of that noisy and intrusive Tolstoy has fortunately made Dostoevsky the preserve of a small number of readers. Dostoevsky is one of the men whom I studied most at the time of the crisis in my development, and one of those who most sustained and consoled me.

Why do you believe that a Catholic cannot comfortably share the religious transports of this great-hearted man ? His attacks on the Church are of no importance and spring merely from the naive enthusiasm of an ignorant recluse. We can smile upon his attempts to reveal to the world a Russian Christ, of whom the world knows nothing, but whose principles are included in our orthodoxy— *Christus heri et hodie. Si quis dixerit : Ecce* hic *est Christus non* illic *notite credere.*

There is no Russian or English or German Christ, but a *Catholic* Christ, in a church which is only exclusive because it is universal, and in a truth which is only intransigent because it contains *all* truth.

Besides, Dostoevsky has felt the greatness of the Church in the dialogue in the *Brothers Karamazov*, though he was so petty as to deny all faith to the Grand Inquisitor. The Inquisitor is absolutely right to oppose the false Christ whose ignorant and hubristic intervention disturb the magnificent order of Redemption. *Church* means union. " He who is not with me is against me." He who does not act as a member of the Church can only act in his own name ; he is a pseudo-Christ and a *wastrel*. It is amusing to see a Russian reproach the Catholic Church with its hunger for temporal domination. Think of that—several years after the horrors committed in Poland by the Orthodox clergy—the appalling story, for instance, of the nuns of Minsk. For lack of precise tenets and an authority to uphold them, we end up in France with the fatuous religiosity of Lamartine, and in Russia with the rank socialism of Gorky or the daydreams of Merejkovsky. (Have you read his article on Dostoevsky when he claims that Dostoevsky was fundamentally ill-natured ? It's very unfair, but also a very profound point of view.)

I grasp your hand with affection,

P. CLAUDEL.

35.—*André Gide to Paul Claudel* [1]

July 1908.

. . . After what I last wrote to you about Suarès, I wonder if I dare tell you what has happened ? Seeing that he had written a long essay on Ibsen, I got hold of the two numbers of the *Revue des Deux Mondes* which continued it. A new Suarès was revealed to me, still un-ordered, of course, diffuse and vaguely grandiloquent in certain places, but so noble in his carriage, so lofty in the cast of his thought, so proud and strong in his intellectual self-assurance that I was quite abashed and considered it my duty to bring this masterly study to the notice of all those who might have heard me criticize Suarès. Since then I have read his *Visite à Pascal* with even greater admiration ; from the very beginning one feels oneself in the presence of a master of the art of writing ; and my admiration is now as great as—in fact is greater than—my former irritation—I might also say as my hatred. (I remember that Jammes was so enraged by *Tête d'Or* that he threw Rouart's (?) copy in the fire and asked him never again to speak of its author !) Finally, may I say that I now long to know your friend (the only writer who has been of some assistance to me these last months—I speak of the " moderns ", because for several months now I have lived almost continuously with Pascal—do you know his letters to Mlle de Roannez ?), but I should like to know him THROUGH YOU.

Au revoir, my dear Claudel. Imperfect as this letter may be, I am sending it to you, rather than not write to you at all.

You can be sure that you are no farther at Tientsin than I feel myself to be from all the contemporary " Literary movement ".

[1] This extract from a letter was found among the papers of André Suarès, to whom Paul Claudel had sent it.

(Excellent, what Suarès has just written about Porto-Riche ! He purifies the literary air all round him !)   Au revoir !   Once I begin to talk of books this letter won't go off to-day.

All my respects to Madame Claudel ;   my wife's best remembrances.

Most affectionately yours,

ANDRÉ GIDE.

36.—Paul Claudel to André Gide

Tientsin, 4th August 1908.

My dear Friend,

I am using these big ugly sheets of paper because it is summer-time (40° in the shade) and one has to take one's ease on a large and very hard bed which one has all to oneself.   I am replying, as usual, immediately after reading your letter.   I never see your handwriting (or that of Jammes or Frizeau) without a quickening of my heartbeats.   I am always afraid you will stop writing.   For myself, my psychology as a correspondent could be the subject of a novel à la Dostoevsky.   I can't take hold of a piece of writing-paper without falling a victim to a sort of lyrical intoxication which puts me to shame as soon as I've stuck on the stamp. If my letters weren't so long I'd begin them all over again !   Well, anyway, please endure this lunatic side of me in a philosophical spirit (like all *theorists* I have to have it), and answer from time to time. . . .

You have grasped just what I meant when I quoted from Merejkovsky at the end of my last letter.   It was simply the exaggeration of one specific trait in his complex and endearing character.   The taste for suffering (and for making others suffer) is found in all Dostoevsky books.   It must be a Slav characteristic. I must say though, that among all the many Russians whom I have known I have only found one really remarkable trait, and that is their love of drink.   In other respects they are much like other men. They play bridge very well, but then so do the Belgians.

I am delighted with what you say about Suarès and am going to write to him.   He is really a masterly writer and I was sure that eventually you would like him.   Moreover, he is a large-hearted

man with a great capacity for suffering, and I must own that that
is what I find by far the most interesting side of him. He lives at
17 Rue Méchain (near the rue de la Santé). You must handle
him tactfully, because his undeserved solitude has made him as
awkward, faddy, and mistrustful as any beginner.

I wish I had your turn of mind—so welcoming and (in the
English sense, I must add) so catholic—and could see the good in
everyone ! I have grown tough and callous in my solitude, and I
know that I am often unjust and intolerant. I really cannot
sincerely interest myself in pure literature. Of all the papers
that I am sent, I turn first to the *Écho de Fourvières*. I need to be
edified, if I am to be moved. All this has to do with poor Signoret's
poems, for which you wrote a fine preface, and which I've received
from the *Mercure*. (Why do you hit out at Jammes' Catholicism ?
You can't still believe, surely, that asceticism is the mark of a
pliable and enfeebled spirit. On the contrary, it is the discipline
for natures that are joyful, virile, martial, and heroic.) Try as I
can, I cannot really admire these vague and diffuse poems. I find
them ill-planned, ill-constructed, without either images or ideas—
nothing but a distracting babbling for which I can feel no indulgence. He belongs, with Lamartine, to that class of writers who
don't even manage to blacken the paper. I find his impudent
boastfulness profoundly shocking. It's like hearing poetry read
aloud in society. It might be all right in Italian or Provençal.
He thinks himself drunk with dew when really he's drunk nothing
but the nose-droppings of a monkey. *He likes Renan !!!*

I should like to make a fine edition of my *Five Odes followed by
a Processional*. I've found for the cover a marvellous white felt
from Korea. Do you think that it's still possible to print letters in
gold, and that the gold really stays on the paper and doesn't drop
off ? I'd also like to have some five initial letters engraved—
square, monumental letters without any figures. Perhaps one could
find them in some sixteenth-century folio.

I should have liked to do something else, but in spite of myself I
found that I had embarked on a series of liturgical hymns in which
I attempt to take up the tradition of Nottker, Adam de St.-Victor
and Prudentius (what a great poet ! Do you know his hymn on
fasting ?). The plays are put off till later. Besides, my ideas are
not yet ripe and I must revisit my country first.

I am happy to know that you are keeping company with Pascal.

When you are a Christian you will like him less. His light, now
blinding, now uncertain, and always spasmodic, is only for me at
night. Just so did the Hebrews, when they had crossed the Red Sea,
glimpse Mount Sinai by lightning-flashes. *Montes exultaverunt ut
arietes et colles sicut agni ovium.* An admirably observant line—
first the distinction between the great he-goats and the long frothing
line of the hills ; then it's perfectly exact that in a tropical storm
the background of almost uninterrupted lightning makes the
mountains seem to leap into the air. It's difficult to understand
the impression which Montaigne made on Pascal. His sceptism is
simply the talk of a man of letters who can't make up his mind.

I grasp your hand with affection. My wife is most anxious to
meet Madame Gide and sends her her greetings.

P. Claudel.

37.—*André Gide to Paul Claudel*

Cuverville, 17th October 1908.

Dear Friend,

I was waiting (and waiting very impatiently) to finish my
book before writing to you. It's done ; to-morrow I go back to
Paris ; the book, which was giving me trouble even yesterday, is
as near finished as it can be until I have revised it in proof—and I
don't expect to do more than a very little to it at that stage. I've
had it in mind for so many years (the first project goes back to
1891 ; it was then called *L'Essai de bien Mourir*), it was so profoundly
a part of me, and I had such difficulty in getting it away from
myself, that even now it seems to be still inside me and I can hardly
believe that I am rid of it. No doubt you will realize when you read
it that it's not a question of a purely literary subject (if any such
really exist !). And perhaps you will be able to distinguish the
secret, confidential element which will enlighten you in respect
of a childhood which you have thought was oppressed, but which
in fact was oppressed only by religion and morality—let's say, if
you prefer, by Protestantism—for you will certainly feel that the
book is furiously, deplorably Protestant. Anyway, I hope that the
Protestantism of the book will not make you think too irritably of
its author, because you will certainly sense that the very idea of the

book carries with it an implied criticism . . . and after all perhaps you will find the book Jansenist rather than Protestant, and perhaps you will understand that we think more or less alike when Pascal is concerned. I speak of the book as if I could send it to you at once. . . . Forgive my impatience.

My dear Claudel, I must know Suarès. It doesn't matter if some of his articles arouse in me the same exasperation that I always felt at the first things of his that I read. All the same, he knows how to give his scorn a quality of great loftiness—and that's what I call having his heart in the right place. But though I want to see him, I don't want to be importunate ; I want to know that he also would like to see me ; until I am sure of that, I shall wait.

My dear Claudel, I often think of you, and always with a special intensity. If I am not a better correspondent, it's because each of your letters sets up a great commotion inside me and it's a very serious matter for me to reply to you. I'm not replying to-day, but I'm writing none the less, for friendship's sake. What's become of you ? What are you writing ? Not being in Paris I couldn't find out about the publication of which you told me. I am most impatient to read it. I'll hear from you soon, won't I ? Do not imitate my long silence. Now that my book is finished perhaps I shall write to you more easily.

My wife remembers you and sends her regards. Our respects to Madame Paul Claudel, and a smile for your son.

Yours in friendship,

ANDRÉ GIDE.

38.—Paul Claudel to André Gide

Tientsin, 8th November 1908.
[Dedication of the Churches.]

I have just received your letter. I am alone in the house. My wife has just gone out with my little daughter, wrapped up like a big bear in order to profit by the good winter sunshine—as exhilarating and as cold as real champagne. So I shall reply to you at once, profiting by this dominical peace. I am still full of the Mass, at which I was present in my consul's chair which stands in the choir on the north side of the church. Facing a most ghastly painting which shows a pallid St. Louis burying bodies like children's gollywogs in front of a castle that looks like a petrol tin.

The moment after one finishes a book is both painful and agreeable. One is at once consoled and empty, unsatisfied with what one has done, and already nervous about what one will do next. I am most curious to read your new book. You say that it's very Protestant. All the better ! I know full well that in your case Protestantism is only a reagent. That its effects should be violent is no disaster. A poet like yourself is made to understand the mystery of liberty within Grace, which is the whole secret of both art and theology. A day will come when you hunger and thirst for bread and fermented wine.

You are kind to remember me. Shall I confess to you that you have always impressed me by that quality of " distinction " to which children are so sensitive, and which has a special effect on a nature as heavy and plebeian as mine ?

Nearly a year ago I finished a new book called *Five Grand Odes, followed by a Processional for the new century.* They are long lyrical monologues in which I resume, in poetry, certain themes from my philosophical book—for example : That which is at once bounded and inexhaustible, the circle which is the archetype of all forms, finite and yet infinite—the egg, the seed, the open mouth, the figure zero. If Columbus had gone off with the object of finding the new world he would have been simply an adventurer of genius. What made him a man of incomparable grandeur was his faith in the perfect circle. What my *Odes* portray is the joy of a man who no longer stands in fear of the eternal silence of infinite space, but who walks truthfully at ease in it, knowing that God who has made only what is perfect has but to make finite things, and that He who knows the number of His sparrows must also be able to count His stars. There are people it seems who are always possessed by the sensation that all is fugitive and momentary ; I on the contrary have the strongest notion, when I see that ever-pure sky, of permanence. It is impressive to see how the laws of astronomy (those of Lagrange, for example) are tending towards a permanence which it is an exquisite pleasure for one's intelligence to grasp.

I have spent this year in writing four hymns in the popular form of the old sequences on the festivals of Pentecost, St. Paul, St. Sacrement, and the Assumption. Also, I have been thinking of a great ensemble of plays which will keep me busy in the years to come. It's still too vague and too complicated to talk about. However, I have about completed the sketch of the first play and have even written the first scene.

I have just made the acquaintance of a great English poet whom I did not know—Robert Browning. He has all the defects of the authors of his race—prolixity, bad taste, and an unbelievable lack of order. But the imagination is of the first rank, and he excels all other English poets in this respect—that he finds poetry quite naturally everywhere, in the most ordinary walks of life. And his poetry is not vague and un-anchored like that of Shelley, for whom I don't much care, but curiously complex and highly-wrought, like that of the Latin satirical poets. Like myself, he has translated the *Agamemnon* and I was delighted to find that we agree on the great majority of points.

Have you read Blei's translation of *Partage de Midi* ? Chéring, the translator of Strindberg, has written from Berlin and wants to translate *l'Échange*.

What's new in France ? Since I left, several writers have appeared whom I really think very talented—Bonnard, Giraudoux, and perhaps above all someone called Romains, who wrote something very good in the paper published by that odious Marinetti.

What do you think of Jammes' *Ruchenfleur* ? I think it quite masterly, and find in it wholly new qualities of strength and an almost primitive severity.

I have a small service to ask of you. This country of sand, wind, and electric light has had a very bad effect on my eyesight. Could you find me a cheap edition of the *Imitation* printed *in fairly large type and including the Latin text* ? All the French versions are detestable. Berche and Tialin, rue de Rennes might have it.

Adieu, my dear Gide. My respects to Madame Gide.

P. CLAUDEL.

P.S.—I shall come back in July—it's quite certain now.

Speaking of Marinetti—he once asked what I thought of his heaven-sent genius. I replied at once that I thought him the equal of the greatest living French poets, *i.e.* of Verhaeren and Gustave Kahn. No doubt he scented the joke because he quoted me as having said he was the equal of the greatest French poets, and didn't mention the two cacographers.

39.—*André Gide to Paul Claudel*

9th January 1909.

My dear Friend,

I think you will have received the *Imitation* which I had them send to you ; I didn't much care for its looks, but I couldn't find anything better that gave you the translation and the Latin text in sufficiently large print. I hear that if I put " Via Siberia " on the envelope I can save two weeks ? I've started doing it.

I wanted to write to you when I was looking for the *Imitation* (which I am glad to give you), but I had too many worries to distract me ; I can't improvise letters to you. If I'm doing it to-day it's because I met Philippe Berthelot yesterday and he told me that you'd just sent your MS. to the *Occident*. What is this MS. ? Is it the collection of your new Odes ? Or just one of them ? Is it for the *Occident*-review or for the Occident publishing house ? This is why I am putting these indiscreet questions. . . . A Review [1] is being started here of which I am not officially the editor . . . but it's just as if I were, and in fact even better, because the Review will be directed, to all appearances, by three younger friends who are throwing themselves, heart and soul, into the job.

I know that there's *Vers et Prose* ; but it's more of a magazine, and publishes almost nothing that's new ; and I know what you think of it. *L'Occident* is the only paper which might overlap with ours, if it weren't that our rôle, parallel with theirs, is to give less room to theory and more to original work. We should like to print the most important work of the best writers. For instance I'm giving them the new novel of which I've often told you, although the *Revue de Paris* asked for it. (But if our Review becomes what I want it to be, the novel will fit in better there than among a lot of society gossip.) We think of following up with the new novel of Charles-Louis Philippe.

If this Review does not publish something important by you it will have fallen short of its destiny.

I think it necessary and urgent that the *real* writers should unite

[1] The *Nouvelle Revue Française*, of which you may have received the first number, was no sooner born than dead. The tiresome and incompetent director has gone, together with the clique of deplorable scribblers whom he brought with him. The Review which I've talked about to-day is arising from the ashes of the *N.R.F.*

against the great flood of journalistic rubbish which is being let
loose upon our country : there's no point in pursuing the metaphor
further, because I remember you telling me how much it distresses
you to see the waste of print and paper, and how you admired the
gesture of St. Francis when he lovingly picked up a handwritten
sheet which he saw lying on the ground. . . .

But, my dear Claudel, here is something that worries me : I
think that, whether from pure zeal or from friendship for myself,
you would not refuse to give our Review (which ought to publish
its first number in February) what you used to give to *Ermitage* . . .
but will not my request reach you too late ? That you should
have sent that MS. to *L'Occident* makes me very anxious ; I shall
be deeply distressed ; for, if you are not in it, our Review will, in
my eyes, have lost nearly all its point. But if, like *Les Muses*,
your MS. was not destined for the *Occident*-review—or if you have
another, and could give it, or part of it, to us—ah ! how deeply
happy I should be to hear from you at once, and if necessary by
telegram (if there are urgent amendments to be made in respect of
indications which you may already have given) ! Philippe Berthelot
knows all about it, so that two or three sent through him would be
enough to guide us—at any rate until we had your letter.

I often think of you, my dear Claudel, because the thought of
you is bound up with certain grave reflections towards which I am
drawn alike by the natural bent of my mind and the ghastly pressure
of external events. I am immensely impatient to read your newest
works.

Since you last wrote I have met a young man from the Sorbonne
who greatly admires you and, I am told, is in correspondence with
you—his name escapes me for the moment. I have also met
Suarès. He talked a lot ; he is a violent, fine-souled being, drunk
with solitude and pride. To speak the truth, I was appalled by
the atmosphere of mourning and gloom in which he lives. One
must attain to joy in the end ; by way of sadness, if you like, but
joy must be at the end. Whatever is sad is well within the truth
. . . that is really the subject of my book, for anyone who can read
it properly.

I have also met Jules Romains, whose poems you said you
liked ; I, too, found the book quite remarkable ; if he didn't send
it to you it's because he didn't know your address ; I've given it
to him.

To-day I've too much to do to write any more. Please give Madame Claudel my respects, and my wife's regards. Au revoir. Believe me, I am your friend,

ANDRÉ GIDE.

P.S.—Need I say that if I can render you any service (proof-correcting, etc.) I am wholly at your disposition. If it's a matter of proof-correcting I shall arrange it so that I am not the only person concerned—I am still embarrassed at the thought of two errors that I let pass in your *Art poétique*.

40.—*Paul Claudel to André Gide*

French Consulate, Tientsin,
28th January 1909.

Thank you, my dear Gide, for the *Imitation* which you say is on its way. I shall be so glad to have it from you.

The MS. I sent to *L'Occident* is that of the *Four Odes* and the *Processional* which, with *Les Muses*, will make up my new book. None of them are intended for separate publication. I want it all to appear as a whole, without the effect being diminished by any prior publication. Believe me that if I could depart from this design, it would certainly be in favour of a Review in which you took an interest.

But :

During 1908 I wrote four long hymns which will later make up part of a large four-volume collection which I shall call *Corona benignitatis Anni Dei*. It will not be at all an imitation of the breviary, but a cycle of songs inspired by the holy calendar. I am sending you one with this. You can publish it in your Review. I attach great importance to these hymns, which are the expression of all that is best in me and the flowering, after twenty years, of all those feelings and ideas which I accumulated during my long years at Notre-Dame. I should ask you that the printed text, unlike the MS., should always begin each verse on a fresh page. The print should be in large and very clear italics. At the fifth verse, after " *goûté* ", please leave a blank space of twice the usual size.

I have other hymns, but I am reserving *Pentecôte* and *Noel* for

L'Occident, where they had always behaved perfectly to me, and
which I like, as a Review, because I have never seen in it anything
impure or immoral. I am sure that the same will be true of the
one which you are founding. Our generation has a great mission
to fulfil and must repair the crimes of our predecessors, whose
horrible consequences are to be seen everywhere. The Flauberts,
Taines, Renans, Goncourts, Zolas, *e tutti quanti* are full of nothing
but darkness, nothingness, scepticism, despair, pessimism, and
mockery of everything in human nature that is sane, good, confident,
hopeful, and joyous. The conversations of those ghastly cold-
hearted men of letters in the Goncourts' Journal make me sick at
heart. Their stupidity, their vanity, and the feeling one has of
their poverty, of the secret hatred which each cherishes for the
others, and their sinister preoccupation with trifles—all these form
a truly infernal spectacle. Believe me—everybody is beginning
to feel the same, and to turn away from these poisoned cadavers.
Whatever our talents may be, the best men of our generation are
at least striving, within the limits of their vision, to repair and
rebuild. If man cannot live by bread alone, still less can he live
on the diet of sawdust which he gets from the famous writers whom
I have named (and named with disgust). Anatole France is the
last of their sad line.

I grasp your hand with affection,

P. C.

41.—*André Gide to Paul Claudel*

31st January 1909.

My dear Claudel,

A contingency has arisen (and some younger friends consider
it a very happy one) which may soon make it possible for them to
applaud the *Jeune Fille Violaine* on the stage. But none of us here
is entitled to give or to withhold consent to the project. Philippe
Berthelot, and after him Mithouard, declined to do so. I myself
wrote to Jammes ; Chapon wrote to Suarès ; but we don't dare
to decide collectively on your behalf, any more than we do indivi-
dually ; all the less so as we are none of us absolutely convinced,
not so much of the timeliness of the enterprise as of its potential

excellence. But it's for you to judge. I am charged to give you the facts, and I shall set them simply before you.

M. Bour, who wants to put the play on, is no beginner ; I'm told that he is a great admirer of yours ; not so much so, perhaps, as Mlle Marie Kalff who wants to play Violaine—and I don't think you need have any fears about her. They claim to have enough money to put on the play decently—they even want to spend much more on it than has been their wont with other plays. It would be put on at the *Athenée* perhaps—or in a theatre hired for the occasion. I enclose, moreover, a specimen of one of their most recent programmes—it won't mean much to you, but they asked me to send it. They asked me above all to put it to you that this combination of possibilities is unlikely to recur. If M. Bour cannot begin rehearsals at once (*i.e.* as soon as your answer arrives), he will have to undertake a long programme of other plays and Mlle Kalff, who is free at present, has to join the Théâtre Gémier next year on a long-term contract.

I should like to give you more information ; unhappily I've never seen any of Bour's productions—and I can only rely on the word of friends who represent him to me as a good producer. I haven't seen Mlle Kalff either ; but she came twice to see me last week and I must admit that I was touched by her enthusiasm. And look here : *they can't wait for a letter from you, if they are to begin rehearsals.* You must telegraph a simple *yes* or *no* to Gide, Villa Montmorency, Paris. You can send detailed instructions by letter.

Au revoir, my dear Claudel. I don't want to go into other matters to-day.

Your friend,

ANDRÉ GIDE.

———

42.—*Paul Claudel to André Gide*

Tientsin, 18th February 1908.

My dear Gide,

I have just had your letter about the Théâtre d'Art. I answered at once (by telegram, as you asked), "Regret Impossible".

I am really touched by the goodwill that reaches me from every side and I must ask you to express my sincere thanks to the Théâtre d'Art, to M. Lenormand, to Mlle Kalff, and to M. Bour. It was a real sorrow to me to renounce, yet once again, all idea of a public performance. But like all our friends, you will understand my reasons, which are irrefragable and leave me no ground for hesitation.

1. No play of mine can be performed in my absence. I have never written with the stage in mind. I never go to the theatre and I know nothing of its requirements. There would therefore have to be, not a performance, but a veritable transposition, which might perhaps be possible, but which would involve me in a whole category of study and reflexion for which I am not yet ready.

2. Of all my plays, *La Jeune Fille Violaine* is the one which I consider at once the most saturated with poetry and the least perfect. The story and the action are childish. Whole sections like the architectural digressions of Pierre de Craon (in fact his whole part, perhaps) must be cut out. And then again—how much of the compunction, the devotion, and the pity (which are the whole interest of this religious play) would get across on the stage ? It would be like a photographic negative, in which white would appear as black, and black as white—I mean that the story-telling, which is naive, ridiculous even, would be dragged violently into the foreground. The only play of mine which *might* be acted now is *Partage de Midi*. The one I'm writing now will be much more dramatic and stageable.

3. Finally, and much the most important : I am by no means sure that the performance would be welcome at the Ministry, where I am already out of favour for my religious views, and where Berthelot is my only supporter. I could not compromise my position for the sake of momentary fame. Understand my disjointed existence—to be a consul, a poet, and a man of God all at the same time is too much, and then I am a father into the bargain.

Once again, my thanks to everybody and especially to you, my dear friend. A better occasion will one day present itself, and I look forward eagerly to it, for I have a great many thoughts about action and declamation in the theatre which I want very much to verify. If the occasion never comes—what would you ? As the Chinese say, *maski*.

I grasp your hand with affection,

P. C.

43.—*André Gide to Paul Claudel*

24th February [1909].

My dear Friend,

I am deeply grateful to you for sending your admirable *Hymne*. We sent it at once to the printer and it will appear in our April number. By then you will have received our first two numbers, which include two-thirds of my novel—you will not need a preface to convince you that the first two sections are meant to explain Alissa's diary which, so I think, is the best thing I have done. May you find in it a quality of piety which is not too unworthy to stand beside the *Hymne du Saint-Sacrement*.

I am leaving for Rome in four days and cannot therefore correct the proofs of your poem ; but I shall leave your instructions with Jean Schlumberger who, with Ruyters, will correct and reread the whole text ; they have both a deeply respectful admiration for you and will bring a minutious zeal to their task.

Do you still think of coming back to France in June ? No doubt I shall be back from Italy by then. I already rejoice at our reunion.

I can't write any more to-day, being busy with preparations for my journey. Did I tell you that I have met young Jacques Rivière ? Most congenial—and we talked about you for a long time. He is very sad that you did not consent to the performance of *Violaine* ; for my part I think you were quite right. But I don't think that you should have to pay for the telegram—I'll discuss it with the actors who asked me to write to you, and with you yourself on your return.

Au revoir. My wife was pleased to be remembered. Believe me.

Most affectionately yours,

ANDRÉ GIDE.

44.—*Paul Claudel to André Gide*

Tientsin, 27th February 1909.

My dear Friend,

If my *Hymne du Saint-Sacrement* has not yet appeared in your Review, would you please either stop it from appearing or let it appear unsigned or with the initials P. C. ? It seems that I have

often been denounced at the Ministry for my religious opinions ;
and with a dossier like mine it's better for the moment that I'm not
too much talked about.

I send you a cordial handshake,

P. CLAUDEL.

45.—*André Gide to Paul Claudel*

Cuverville 19th April 1909.

My very dear Friend,

Your last letter reached me at Monte Cassino where I had
gone to make a short retreat. Alas ! it was too late for me to do
anything about it. The third number of the *N.R.F.*, bearing your
name in full, had already appeared, and contains the admirable
Hymne which you kindly confided to us. . . . I was distressed that
you might have to suffer for your kindness to us, but Ruyters,
whom I met in Paris the day before yesterday, has reassured me.
May you not have any new cause for alarm at the expression of your
point of view. . . . On returning I found the proofs of my new
book and have to correct them in a hurry . . . no time for more
than this note.

Yours ever,

ANDRÉ GIDE.

46.—*Paul Claudel to André Gide*

Tientsin, 10th May 1909.

I have just received the third number of the *N.R.F.*, in which
I find the last part of *La Porte Étroite*. I am still suffering from the
emotional shock (and the great perplexity) which its perusal
provoked in me. Having read it in serial form, I have carried your
book within me for a long time, but I shouldn't like to say that I've
understood it perfectly, despite the high quality of an admirable
style which insinuates itself into one's being like some warm and
intoxicating liquor. One seems to be enveloped on every side in
that solemn end-of-summer atmosphere, that " gilded ecstasy " of

which you speak in your concluding pages. The language is suave
and mature—a suavity full of anguish. A Dantesque sweetness,
but beneath it is something terribly bitter—I don't like to say
despairing.

Allow me to examine your book from two angles—first as a work
of art and then from my point of view as a Christian.

As a work of art there's nothing to be said—it's logical from
beginning to end. The coarse literature of the last hundred years
has put us off the scent, where the study of our deepest feelings is
concerned. NO, sexual satisfaction does not mean the satisfaction
of love and passion ; it is a diminution, sometimes a caricature of
them—more often that a deformation, and always a transformation.
It's not a question of Platonic niceties. The sentiment of " refusal "
lies deep in the heart of womankind and is even found among the
animals ! There is no richer or more complicated dramatic
subject, and none more filled with pathos for a masculine reader
—whence our interest in all those books (*Dominique* is the most
moving of them) in which we watch passion at grips with duty.
The strength of your book is that there is no question of external
duty, but only of an inner voice. That is also what many readers
will find exasperating.

Let us turn to the Christian problem, which leaves me very much
in doubt—what was your intention ? Is yours a Christian book ?
Have you simply represented God as an atrocious, unspeaking
tormentor ? Your noble Alissa, dying broken-hearted between
your clean bare walls, distressed me deeply.

For me, your book was an invaluable document on Protestantism,
and through it I now understand many things which were formerly
incomprehensible to me. Protestantism has no sacraments, there is
no longer any real substance in God's relations with mankind,
and no longer any religion in the true sense of the word, where
both parties loyally provide their share. Man has to rely on
himself for everything, and it is only rarely, and undefinedly, that
God intervenes. The noblest souls are left in anxiety if they seek
to draw near to him. God never speaks directly. Whence that
strained, quibbling, sorrowful morality which at first sight seems
so much at variance with the dogma of predestination. Hence
your use (so astonishing to a Catholic) of the word " self-improvement " (*perfectionnement*) which recurs often in your book. A
saint does not strive to improve himself—that's to say, in short, to

varnish and whiten himself, to become a bigger man—but to become smaller. If the love of God necessarily robbed him of the compunction and the humility of penitence, then he would do almost better to remain a sinner. The nearer we are to the mountain, the smaller we are : the nearer we are to eternal Sanctity, the more sinful we seem to ourselves to be, and the more sinful we truly are, in our own eyes. The protestations of the saints are not just hypocritical formulas. It is not by our virtues, but by our infirmities, that we have the right to God's attention.

Two other passages touched me to the quick—those in which you revive the old quietist blasphemy which was developed *ad nauseam* in the last century, and which says that piety needs no reward, that the noblest love is the most disinterested. How could God's love be more perfect if it were contrary to reason and had no rational origin ? For the whole of creation God is the supreme and unique Good ; how should he not be the same for us ? Shall we love him more purely when we have robbed him of his very essence ? What an insult it would be, when the gift of a poor man is so sacred ? We have nothing more to ask, no more prayers to offer, nothing to do but to admire him coldly as an *objet d'art*— though even an *object d'art* yields us profit and instruction. God's bounty cannot be separated from Himself. To deny the one is to reject the other. Love that is not nourished by interest would be a poor sort of love. . . . I hear that tender cry " Alissa ! Alissa ! " which fills the whole of your book. What a problem is that of the complete union of two souls !

I grasp your hand with great affection, my dear friend,

P. CLAUDEL.

47.—*André Gide to Paul Claudel*

Cuverville, 18th June 1909.

My dear Claudel,

Ruyters tells me that you are not now coming back till September ; you had talked of coming in June, so that I didn't dare to write. Your excellent letter of 10th May gave no sign, and I was already preparing to answer it by word of mouth !

Your letter was a great source of joy to me, for everything you say about my book—even your reservations, whether psychological or dogmatic—everything shows that the book is a success. You realize that it is animated by pure, religious feelings ; and also—what is equally important, you realize that the drama of the book resides entirely in its unorthodoxy. I can't imagine what can be *the* drama of Catholicism. It seems to me that there isn't one, that there couldn't and mustn't be one (unless one can say that it is all comprised in the Mass). Catholicism can and must bring peace and certitude, etc., to the soul ; it is admirably devised to this end ; it exists to *quieten* drama, not to *provoke* it—whereas Protestantism hazards the soul in adventures which may end in the way I described. Or in free-thinking. It is a school of heroism, the error of which emerges pretty clearly, I think, from my book. It lies precisely in that sort of superior self-infatuation, that exhilarating disregard of all reward (which you took offence at), that gratuitous reversion to the spirit of Corneille. But it can be accompanied by real nobility, and I shall have done enough if I persuade someone like you to pity and to love my Alissa—with a love that includes some small mingling of admiration.

What I wanted to draw, quite simply, was the portrait of this womanly soul ; a soul with which I fell in love for the same reasons that made you, also, pity and love her. A Protestant soul, in whom was enacted the essential drama of Protestantism—the drama which very few Protestants can glimpse, but which you descried perfectly.

This drama would not emerge in all its purity unless the element of external constraint were entirely removed. But I was afraid that, if all external motivation were discarded, it would seem paradoxical, if not monstrous and inhuman. So I invented the double intrigue, the fear of buying her happiness at the cost of the happiness of somebody else—and, above all, the mother's " crime ", and the resulting vague need of expiation and so forth. . . .

Forgive this hasty, awkward letter. I dislike explaining my book, and as soon as one is written I think of nothing but the next. But your opinion was of supreme importance to me and I could not leave your letter unanswered.

You will see in the next issue of the *Nouvelle Revue Française* a letter from Jammes to a certain " P. C., Consul ", in whom you will recognize yourself. You know how deeply happy we shall be on the

day when you entrust it with a new composition of yours. I think
it most important that we should band together to fight against the
infamous rubbish that pours out from most of our " literary
journals ".

Your friend,

ANDRÉ GIDE.

48.—*Paul Claudel to André Gide*

Tientsin, 1st July 1909.

My dear Gide,

I am sending you with this a letter addressed to the Editor
of the *N.R.F.*, and I should be very glad to see it published in that
journal. I haven't signed it—you know why. The state of French
printing is now so ignominious that the time has come, in my
opinion, to make a protest.

What do you think of my idea of a co-operative organization for
the publication (without any idea of profit) of five books—each as
near as possible to the *editio princeps* and the author's intentions, and
with no illustrations ? Might it not really be a lofty form of charity ?
And perhaps it might even make money ! The books we get now
are beneath contempt, and most injurious to one's sight.

I grasp your hand with great affection,

P. CLAUDEL.

49.—*Paul Claudel to André Gide*

Tientsin, 2nd July 1909.

My dear Gide,

On thinking it over, I shall ask you, if you publish in the
N.R.F. the letter I sent you yesterday, to cut out the passages
relating to Barrès and Madame de Noailles. My object is not to
attack writers, but to defend them—even against themselves.

I believe there really is something in that idea of a museum of
written thought, both ancient and modern. Many people are
sick of luxury editions and illustrations, and I think that a " Society

of Friends of Good Printing " would have no difficulty either in being founded, or in flourishing. Once a book was assured of preservation in some decent format, the publishers could always be asked for permission to print cheaper editions.

I grasp your hand,

P. CLAUDEL.

50.—*Paul Claudel to André Gide*

Tientsin, 8th July 1909.

My dear Friend,

This time I can give you definite news of my return. I have been given leave, and I mean to leave Tientsin on 6th September, arriving in Paris on about the 20th. But I only mean to stay in Paris from November onwards, and even then I shall certainly go to Rome during the winter for a fortnight or three weeks—this being absolutely necessary for the various books I have in hand. I am rather nervous of this long journey to France with two children, and a third on the way.

I am glad that I understood your book, which seems to me one of the most interesting and significant books I have read for a long time. Above all, I am happy that I was not mistaken about its sincere, religious character, although Alissa's end is a cruel one and is likely to disconcert many of your readers. For my part I like to think that so noble a soul was made rather for a convent cell than for a madhouse. Her Protestantism is worth more, after all, than the nihilism which would see only madness and unhealthy derangement in the employment (however injudicious) of the best and healthiest forces of human nature.

So as not to lose the habit, I am going to break a lance with you over what you say about Catholicism—that being in possession of the truth, it is therefore a position of rest. Nothing is farther from the truth. " I come not to bring peace, but the sword." The marriage contract which we call religion establishes a strict relationship between an infinitely perfect being and an infinitely imperfect being ; this relationship cannot be pacific. Even our salvation is not won once and for all, as the Calvinists believe. On the one side are infinite exigencies, on the other a weakness and an ignorance almost as infinite. What is more tragic than the struggle of what is invisible against all that is visible ? The Christian does not live in a state of equilibrium like the sages of old, but in a state of conflict. Every one of his acts has its consequences ; he feels himself in a continual state of re-adaptation.—And how enthralling is the drama in which not death nor marriage is in question, but life or death to all eternity, and where you yourself have a part, not in some fictitious intrigue, but in the perpetual drama of humanity ! No goad is as sharp as the truth ; the life of St. Paul after his conversion was not the life of a man who complacently takes his ease. Even Christ was tempted. And from the intellectual point of view, what a heroic stimulus for the mind is there for us in all those revelations which we have got to understand ! The Christian alone has this ambition. And the traveller who saw the vast supine civilizations of the Orient can judge how inestimable a ferment Christianity has been. Precisely because there is no part of human nature which it has suffered to remain in peace.

And then again, from the historical point of view, what drama there is in the evolution of dogma ! (I am only speaking, of course, of expressed dogma.) What a spectacle is that of century after century of great Councils, with kingdoms and empires groaning, like the timbers of an enormous wine-press, when their designs were thwarted—and all so that the *homoousios* or the *filioque* should flow into the chalice of the *Credo* like a few drops of a pure wine ! Read in Mgr. Batiffol's fine book the splendid story of the euchar- istic definitions, and with what effect the supreme formula has been wrung from the very heart of humanity. What tragedy can compare with that which has whole centuries for its scene and millions of men for its players !

A propos of the dramatic, almost vertiginous character of Ortho- doxy, I am sending you a fine passage from an inspired volume of G. K. Chesterton.

You do wrong to provoke me to write for your Review. I am on the point of invading it. I shall shortly send you a diptych on St. Peter and St. Paul with which I am quite pleased.

My respectful regards to Madame Gide. I clasp your hand with great affection.

P. Claudel.

APPENDIX TO LETTER 50 FROM CLAUDEL TO GIDE

From Chapter VI of *Orthodoxy* by G. K. Chesterton
(Dodd, Mead & Company, Copyright 1908)

This is what I have called guessing the hidden eccentricities of life. This is knowing that a man's heart is to the left and not in the middle. This is knowing not only that the earth is round, but knowing exactly where it is flat. Christian doctrine detected the oddities of life. It not only discovered the law, but it foresaw the exceptions. Those under-rate Christianity who say that it discovered mercy ; anyone might discover mercy. In fact everyone did. But to discover a plan for being merciful and also severe—*that* was to anticipate a strange need of human nature. For no one wants to be forgiven for a big sin as if it were a little one. Anyone might say that we should be neither quite miserable nor quite happy. But to find out how far one *may* be quite miserable without making it impossible to be quite happy—that was a discovery in psychology. Anyone might say " Neither swagger nor grovel " ; and it would have been a limit. But to say " Here you can swagger and there you can grovel "—that was an emancipation. . . .

This is the thrilling romance of Orthodoxy. People have fallen into a foolish habit of speaking of orthodoxy as something heavy, humdrum, and safe. There never was anything so perilous or so exciting as orthodoxy. It was sanity : and to be sane is more dramatic than to be mad. It was the equilibrium of a man behind madly rushing horses, seeming to stoop this way and to sway that, yet in every attitude having the grace of statuary and the accuracy of arithmetic. The Church in its early days went fierce and fast with any warhorse ; yet it is utterly unhistoric to say that she merely went mad along one idea, like a vulgar fanaticism. She swerved to left and right, so as exactly to avoid enormous obstacles. She left on one hand the huge bulk of Arianism, buttressed by all the worldy powers to make Christianity too worldly. The next instant she was swerving to avoid an orientalism, which would have made it too unworldly. The Orthodox Church never took the tame course or accepted the conventions ; the Orthodox Church was never respectable. It would have been easier to have accepted the earthly power of the Arians. It would have been easy, in the Calvinistic seventeenth century, to fall into the bottom-

less pit of predestination. It is easy to be a madman : it is easy
to be a heretic. It is always easy to let the age have its head ; the
difficult thing is to keep one's own. It is always easy to be a
modernist ; as it is always easy to be a snob. To have fallen into
any of those open traps of error and exaggeration which fashion
after fashion and sect after sect set along the historic path of
Christendom—that would indeed have been simple. It is always
simple to fall ; there are an infinity of angles at which one falls,
only one at which one stands. To have fallen into any one of the
falls from Gnosticism to Christian Science would indeed have been
obvious and tame. But to have avoided them all has been one
whirling adventure ; and in my vision the heavenly chariot flies
thundering through the ages, the dull heresies sprawling and
prostrate, the wild truth reeling but erect.

51.—*André Gide to Paul Claudel*

Cuverville, 19th July 1909.

My dear Claudel,

I read your letter with the liveliest interest, for I have this
question of printing, paper, etc., very much at heart, as you already
know, I think. And the *N.R.F.* would be most particularly ready
to wage a campaign in this sense, beginning with the publication
of your letter—and then (if you will grant *me* this licence) by making
certain comments on it ; for while I am passionately of your
opinion, I fear that by mingling with the two main questions—
(1) our wish to have fine and correct editions of Baudelaire, etc.,
etc., (2) our vehement reprobation of the ignoble editions of our
time—by mingling with these your attacks on the critics of yesterday
and to-day, and on the recent elections to the Academie (deserved
as these may be) you may prejudice the practical results which we
desire : a sort of revival of French typography, which was once so
admirable—a patriotic enterprise, attempted by a group of disinterested people (disinterested at the beginning : I can well
believe that such an enterprise, if well directed, would have every
hope of success). *Quorum pars.* . . .

But, my dear Claudel, I come now to the main point. Will you
let us publish this letter in the body of the number, and with your

signature ? Not at all because of the banal theory that everyone
should be ready to bear the responsibility of his attacks, but because
the public will judge the importance of the attack by the importance
of the person who signs it. Spoken by a voice as authoritative as
yours, these words will seem important and may bear fruit ; for
my part I shall help with all my strength towards this end—and so
will a few scattered friends (I should like the nationalizers to
espouse this question). Spoken by an unknown person, your letter
might seem merely an irritable outburst, and the noble passion
which you put into it (and which, coming from you, might have a
good effect), will seem, I am afraid, nothing but exaggeration.

As there is nothing particularly urgent in your letter, I shall
wait without impatience for your answer before giving it to the
Review—and I am returning you the typed copy in case, when
signing it, you care to make any amendments. (In particular, I
think that the word "crapulous" might be changed—though
more because it is inexact than because it is too violent.)

And then, finally, your collaboration is too precious for the
N.R.F. to consent willingly to publish anything of yours unsigned.

I am writing this very hasty letter in order to have your reply as
soon as possible.

Your friend,

André Gide.

52.—*Paul Claudel to André Gide*

[Tientsin], 10th August 1909.

My dear Friend,

Pedibus et manibus incido in sententiam tuam. I wrote to you under
stress of the violent emotions with which I reacted to that ignoble
edition of Banville. From time to time I have these fits of rage
which are like veritable apoplectic strokes. Hitherto I've been
preserved from my worst follies by the fact that I had no magazine
to welcome my invective. You are perfectly right to demand
corrections. Hack about in that rubbish as much as you like, if
you feel that something useful and presentable can be made out of
it. What I cannot do is to put my signature to it ; I've never yet
signed an article of merely accidental or temporary interest. I
don't trust myself, and I don't want to be led on into excuses to

which I am, unfortunately, only too much inclined by nature. . . .
Besides, I am a civil servant. If the letter isn't interesting
without my signature, just throw it into the wastepaper basket.
It'll be no great loss.

All this in the happy excitement of departure. I leave on the
16th by the Trans-Siberian railway. This letter will no doubt
reach Paris at the same time as myself. I shall only be there for
the beginning of September. In November I shall make a longer
stay.

I grasp your hand with great affection.
My respects to Madame Gide.

P. CLAUDEL.

_____

53.—*Paul Claudel to André Gide*

37 Quai d'Anjou, Paris,
29th October [1909].

Dear Friend,

You can give my lucubrations the general title of *Three
Hymns*.

I am in Paris till the end of November. I am looking, at present,
for somewhere to live.

Heaven knows when my Odes will appear ? Chapon is looking
after them, and he's in no hurry. It's now a year since I sent him
the manuscript.

My most friendly greetings,

P. CLAUDEL.

_____

54.—*Paul Claudel to André Gide*

[Paris], 3rd November 1909.

My dear Friend,

Come and see me when you like, at the hour that suits you
best. I shall be so happy to talk with you !

But let me have a word in advance, because at the moment I am
out of the house nearly every day.

After to-morrow my address will be : 7 rue de la Trémoille.

Of course I've forgotten your address. Put it on all your letters, for there are certain things that I can never get into my head. I grasp your hand. My respects to Madame Gide.

P. CLAUDEL.

Gide :   *Journal*

Sunday, 7 November 1909.

Ruyters, Philippe, Rivière, Copeau, Drouin, and Claudel came. Tuesday : dinner at Claudel's with Philippe and the Frizeaus (much to be said—but no time).

55.—*André Gide to Paul Claudel*

[Paris], Christmas 1909.

Dear Friend,

I am just back from Cérilly, where I went to bury poor Philippe. Ray told me that you knew about it. I wanted to tell you myself, and then I had neither the time nor the strength to do so. I loved Philippe tenderly and it's not easy for me to *realize* this bereavement. The cruel negligence of the four or five particular friends who looked after him (with great devotion, I must add) left us in complete ignorance of his illness until almost the last moment. In fact it was only by chance that I knew he was married, and when I saw him he was already unconscious—or unconscious of us at any rate.

I know, my dear Claudel, what a profound influence your works, and still more your strong and tranquil belief, had had upon Philippe. Did he express this in any letters to you ? (I have found one which is admirable in this respect—but perhaps you had others which were still more significant ?) Would you consent to let me have it (or them) for a day or two ? This is why :

We mean to publish in February a supplementary number of the *N.R.F.*, devoted to Ch. L. Philippe. Jammes is to send us a few pages ; if you care to send us a few more, they would be welcome ; next will come an article on his work, one on his life at Cérilly, by the peasant Guillaumin, who wrote *La Vie d'un Simple* ; another on his early years by Marcel Ray. Finally I shall describe his last days and give some recollections. We should like to include in this number some unpublished work by Philippe, and no doubt half a dozen of his letters, chosen among those which are most significant and have the widest general interest. If one of these letters were to throw light on the religious preoccupations of the time immediately preceding his illness, then no doubt those of his circle who do not care to admit that religion could *interest* Philippe would have to think again.

You will write to me about it before very long, won't you?

Shortly before he fell ill, Philippe brought us the *Charles Blanchard* which you will read in our January number. It is his cut-down version of the novel on which he laboured for a long time, and which he had abandoned, a short time earlier, in favour of another.

Au revoir, my dear Claudel. Our best remembrances to you all.

Yours,

ANDRÉ GIDE.

56.—*Paul Claudel to André Gide*

French Consulate, Prague,
27th December 1909.[1]

My dear Friend,

Returning from Mass on Christmas Day I found on my table a letter from an unknown schoolmaster in Montpellier, who told me of the death of Charles-Louis Philippe. I did not want to believe it, but the paper that I opened this morning confirms the dreadful news. May God have pity on that fine soul, that deep and ingenuous heart! Death did not come to him with the secret connivance of a life and a talent whose substance had already been consumed. Our friend was still growing and *Croquignole* foreshadowed the great work of his maturity.

Do you know how Philippe died? Tell me what you know of his end. I once had a long conversation with him which I now blame myself for not having resumed during my last visit. But it is a sad consequence of one's own moral inferiority that one no longer feels entitled to speak to others. Redoubtable dangers are in question, and people don't even suspect that they exist. Now Philippe, in his turn, has opened and silently shut behind him the

---

[1] Paul Claudel wrote this letter before receiving No. 55.

door through which I formerly saw Schwob disappear. I blame myself for not being enough of a fanatic, enough of a preacher. But well-being puts us to sleep, and art prevents us from feeling the sad reality of things and makes us see everything as an unimportant fiction. Poor soul !

I gave Philippe the manuscript of *Partage de Midi*. Could you discover what has become of it ? No doubt his heirs set no value upon it.

Write to me. You are the person whom I consider to be in a certain sense the executor and the representative of Philippe's thought.

I grasp your hand,

P. CLAUDEL.

57.—*Paul Claudel to André Gide*

French Consulate, Prague.
30th December 1909.

Dear Friend,

Alas, I never received so much as one word, one line, from Philippe—not, at any rate, on the subjects with which you are dealing. In 1905 I had a long talk with him, but he so much enjoyed life as it is that I had the impression he wanted nothing more. Besides, his mind was so encumbered with obvious and elementary objections to religion. I'm sure they didn't go very deep, but it would have taken time to pull them out. They had all but stifled the lovely little soul of *La Mére et L'Enfant*.

Could I be wrong ? Was his simple heart more sensitive to the idea of God than I imagined ? Tell me all you know on this subject, at the risk of making me more sorry. The sin of causing somebody to lose their faith is ranked as " homicide " in the hierarchy of self-examination. But those who have seen the light and do not strive, as if in desperation, to propagate it in all directions and in all circumstances—they also bear a heavy load of guilt.

I am sending you a poem I wrote last night.

I grasp your hand affectionately,

P. CLAUDEL.

58.—*André Gide to Paul Claudel*

[Paris, early in January 1910.]

Dear Friend,

I could not help weeping as I read the poem you sent me :
thank you.

I am copying for you a short letter which Philippe wrote to me
on 2nd July 1907. It will show you, better than anything I can say
to you, where Philippe stood. He had just received my *Retour de
l'Enfant prodigue.*

" Dear friend, I am very much disappointed in you. I said to myself
as I read the speech of the elder brother : Now Gide has understood it
—I am no longer alone in my understanding ! How we should have
encouraged one another !

But you had to show me that you were still a romantic. If I had written
that book, what should I not have said to the younger son ! I should
have shown him all the tenderness that can exist in a home, all the intelligence that goes to make a well-ordered life, and I should have told him
that our human dreams of the wild pomegranate are as nothing compared
with what one finds in one's own orchard.

And yet you have never written so purely or thought so clearly. Make
haste now : be a man : choose. I know in advance what you will choose.
We shall all make the same choice.

Love from

C. L. P."

I'm sure that this letter will make you more sorry that you did
not speak to him at greater length. For my part I cannot console
myself for his death, and since I saw him in the country in his last
agony, I can think of nothing else.

None of the most elementary measures to preserve his papers
had been taken by those around him ; surprise and distress had
made them quite lose their heads ; *I don't doubt that they are perfectly
honest*, but when, with the permission of his mother, I went with
some of them to visit the flat (the door had not been sealed) we
could not find any of the manuscripts (of published books) which
he had kept—or the manuscript of *Partage de Midi*, or *any* of his
letters (except, in two untidy drawers, the letters of the last two or
three months). All those things had undoubtedly been kept
together—but what can have become of them ? We are looking ;
we are making enquiries. . . . I will inform you of the discoveries,
if there are any. I consider it so unbecoming to go and argue

over somebody's grave that I keep myself to myself and curb
every movement of my heart—but as you can guess these movements
are sometimes rather violent. In haste (I have a million things to
do)—all our best wishes to you all from us both.

Yours,

ANDRÉ GIDE.

———

59.—*André Gide to Paul Claudel*

8th January 1910.

Dear Friend,

In a cupboard, which we had at first overlooked, we found
all Philippe's manuscripts and several boxes filled with letters ;
but not the manuscript of *Partage de Midi*. What can have become
of it ? There remains a lost hope—did Philippe send it to be
bound ? Francis Jourdain is going to enquire. . . .

I should like to have your *admirable* poem printed on an oblong
page (I know nothing, even among your works, which moves me
more than the last six lines), but I think that, printed in big capitals,
as we did with your *Hymns*—despite what was thrown out—they
would have just as majestic an appearance.

Don't you agree ?

Yours,

ANDRÉ GIDE.

———

60.—*Paul Claudel to André Gide*

French Consulate, Prague,
15th January 1910.

My dear Friend,

Do not wear yourself out by looking for the manuscript of
Partage de Midi. Fundamentally I don't much mind either way.

I have had a very amiable letter from Franz Blei about the
Odes. But when will they appear ? It's becoming more and more
desperate.

I have read with great interest your article on St. Bartholomew
and the political theories of Maurras and Balzac—neither of whom,
as you remark, is a Catholic. You may be sure that the Church,
when represented by reputable theologians, never in any instance

advocates either violence or assassination. But being what she is
—believing herself, that is to say, the only and the exclusive
possessor of absolute truth, and believing also that departures
from doctrine involve the soul in terrible risk of eternal damnation,
she cannot admit what people call liberty of thought (or rather
liberty to publish one's thought) or consider that expression as
unimportant or free from danger. She therefore seeks not to
exterminate the heretics—that is a question for the State, and a
question of one social outlook—but to prevent them from doing
harm. You will allow that her point of view is quite logical. That
is why, even to-day, morality forbids the reading of obscene books,
and the offenders are sought out and punished by the police and
by the law. In this latter case a rule of hygiene is in question—in
the former, eternal salvation. From the Catholic point of view,
as I told you the other day, a book which takes away a man's faith
constitutes a veritable homicide.

As for the religious zeal which animated the rulers of the sixteenth
century, it didn't exist. Every decision was taken for base reasons
of immediate interest—as is the case now with electoral interest.
It was the most Christian kings who, at a moment of supreme
crisis, allied themselves with the Turks against Christendom and
threw their whole weight on the side of Protestantism in Germany
(and had such great success in France !). St. Bartholomew's Eve
was the opposite of an abuse of force—it was an abuse of weakness,
the sudden madness of the weak.

All these lofty political theories remind me of our school orations
on Richelieu and Mazarin. In the practice of affairs such theories
are soon unlearnt. The whole art of the statesman can be reduced
to providing for whatever is most urgent, profiting by every opportunity (despite a great many stupidities, blunders, and misappre-
hensions), and doing just what one can every day. The story goes
that Bismarck, when speaking in the Reichstag at the very end of
his career, once said, " At the end of a life devoted wholly to public
affairs, and with all the experience that I now possess, I think I
can see *one year* ahead of me. The rest is outside my competence."
That is the language of the statesman.

All the same, St. Bartholomew's Eve was not so terrible. Catholics
have never committed crimes like Cromwell's extermination of the
Irish—he sold 40,000 of them to the West Indies as slaves. Not to
speak of the appalling ravages of the Reformation in Germany.

Christianity is not an element of social construction, like indifferent brick or stone ; it does not lend itself, like an indifferent
element of construction, to the fantasies of any architect who
happens to come by. It constructs, like life itself, by means of the
fermentation, the boiling-up, which is brought about in our lives
and in our earthly ideas by the germ of something that is foreign
to them. We ourselves try either to eliminate or to assimilate this
germ, but in neither case do we altogether succeed. It is the wine
which bursts the old bottles. " I come not to bring peace among
you, but the sword." All those people, and all those minds, who
do not know this ferment must live in torpor and die in putrefaction.

I grasp your hand with great affection,

P. CLAUDEL.

I am just back from Vienna, where I saw *Tannhauser* and was
deeply moved by it. I don't know that Wagner ever wrote anything
finer.

61.—*Paul Claudel to André Gide*

French Consulate, Prague,
Candlemas, 2nd February.

My dear Friend,

Poor Rivière has written me a letter which fills me with
terror and consternation. He wants to give up teaching and give
all his time to literature. I wrote to him to-day, rather severely,
—but if he knew what he was doing ! The haggard look of the
Verlaines, the Villiers de l'Isle Adams, and the other derelicts has
always been ineffaceably engraved on my mind.

You, who have so great an influence on this young man, must
try to knock a little sense into his head and make him see, in its
true aspect, the way of life which he wants to adopt, and which is
unworthy of an honest man. To be a journalist one must rally to
some flag, sword in hand—like Veuillot, for instance, who for me
is a real hero. But to sell one's " literary impressions ", to write
" like an escalator ", to dash off prefaces to books on art—and all
for a wretched pittance, in order to distract a hard-working public
which reads it all with contempt for a man ? Have we need of
another Mauclair ?

Rivière has the highest qualities, and his last Notes in your Review bespeak the highest intelligence, but he lacks what the English call " grip ", strength of will, driving power. He wants to see religion itself as a sort of morphia, and seemed quite taken aback when I told him that on the contrary the supreme form of health is that of the combatant, and that Christ had promised us no other end but the Cross. I am sure that the old feudal chiefs who had their castles on the other side of the Dead Sea, and who fought what was, in human terms, a hopeless fight against the surrounding pagans—I'm sure that they were completely happy and filled with joy. That is our Christian situation, and how honourable, how exciting it is !

I count on you to put that dear boy back on the right road, and with this hope I grasp your hand.

P. CLAUDEL.

There are things in *Charles Blanchard*, especially in the second half, which are of the loftiest beauty, and touched me sublimely.

62.—André Gide to Paul Claudel

15th February 1910.

Dear Friend,

Here is the little announcement. Our tenderest wishes for little Reine ! A word from you to say that it all went off well would complete our happiness.

I sent your letter on to Rivière—a line from him, yesterday, described his perplexity. (Add the fact that he is overworked and has influenza, and you will not be surprised if he doesn't reply at once.) My brother-in-law, though he finds his work terribly tiring, has spoken to Rivière in just the same sense. His young wife takes the opposite view ; for my part, not knowing what to say, I don't say anything ; I'm very much worried about him ; I'm afraid that his physical strength may not be as great as his moral integrity and his determination.

You will receive by this same post the number of the *N.R.F.* which is devoted to Philippe and contains the admirable text of another *Charles Blanchard*. It seems to me that the letters of Philippe which we quote throw a very good light on his character. Two numbers of the *Figaro* (the last, its literary supplement) and other more serious papers have published long articles on this number and are proof that it is a success.

You will also receive Péguy's *Jeanne d'Arc*—which I offer to you because he *did not dare* to send it to you, and because I think it admirable. Perhaps it is partly the reason (very indirectly and quite involuntarily) why I can't go on with Scantrel's book, as I could when his essays came out in the *Grande Revue*.

What's become of your work ? Your play ? I need not tell you, no doubt, what a great pleasure the *N.R.F.* would take in publishing it—and the especial pleasure it would give to me if you were good enough to entrust it to me—but I must add (and on behalf of the *N.R.F.*) that it has been decided that you should be properly paid for it. I say this in a whisper—for we cannot, for some time as yet, hope to pay all our contributors. But the delight (and the all too exceptional honour) of publishing a new work of yours will tempt us to make an exception, as we have already done with the posthumous work of Philippe.

Our magazine has made giant strides in the last three or four months and has expanded far beyond our expectations. None the less, any subscribers whom you could secure for us among your acquaintance, in Prague or elsewhere, would be very welcome.

For my part I am not working at all well, and my head is giving me trouble again. We took refuge at Cuverville, to get away from Paris ; and now we've just come back to Paris to get away from the dreadful weather. Many affectionate greetings from us to you.

Yours,

ANDRÉ GIDE.

Mithouard tells me he is getting on actively (?) with printing the *Odes*. Those you gave to us were widely read at Monte Cassino I learnt not long ago.

———

63.—*Paul Claudel to André Gide*

French Consulate, Prague,
17th February 1910.

My dear Friend,

First of all, my congratulations on the superb number which you've devoted to Philippe. As a monument it is admirably composed, and its many points of view provide a complete idea of the central figure : one can walk round it. It makes one want to be dead. Arnauld's article is excellent, the Comtesse de Noailles' rather mediocre, despite *one* very beautiful phrase. Who is Marguerite Audoux ? As you say, the *Charles Blanchard* series is extremely beautiful, even better than the one in the last number. There is in it a sweetness, a majesty, and a sort of pretaste of everlasting joy. The true form of the book would not have been a novel, but a *suite*, like those of Schumann or Moussorgsky.

I was deeply sorry not to see Jammes' name on the cover. I hear that you had had a disagreement in the matter. But you are too fond of one another to sacrifice the place which each occupies in the other's heart.

Your notes are very moving—but we give the name of *sacristain* to the person whom you speak of as the *diacre*.

I've all but finished my play. I shall only have to rewrite it, which is very pleasant work and will take six or seven months. But I am in a very awkward fix. To my profound consternation, the play assumed, as it grew, an unmistakably reactionary and antirepublican character and, further, it is appallingly obvious. I am like King Midas' barber, who after twenty years' of whispering into the earth that his master had the ears of an ass, noticed that the reeds were beginning to grow and pass on the tale. The play is full of movement and very dramatic and it will be annoying if I have to keep it to myself, as no doubt I must.

Lugné-Poe is still offering to put on *Partage de Midi*, but for many reasons (my conscience among them) I cannot let him do it.

The *Odes* are being printed with maddening slowness—about eight pages a month. And we haven't broached the question of the cover, over which we are likely to stick fast until the Last Judgement ! The manuscript was sent to Chapon in November 1908.

L'Enfant prodigue arrived this very morning. May I send you another long effusion on this subject ? I very much want to do so, after the beautiful letter of Philippe, which very much touched me.

I've written again to young Rivière who accepted with charming good humour the letter of abuse which I had sent him. But I haven't changed my mind, alas ! He is all too well suited to the profession which tempts him.

We have just had a very painful upheaval, with our child born

before its time and my wife carried out on a stretcher. Still, all
has ended fairly well.

Thank you very much indeed for your financial proposals. We
can talk about them later. I could perhaps give you one of the
Five Odes, but the format of your Review is not adapted to them.

My wife wishes to be remembered to you—and to Madame Gide,
as do I myself. I grasp your hand with affection.

P. CLAUDEL.

At Prague the bookshop called TOPIC FERDINANDOVA ULRIA
sells a lot of French books. I should advise you to send them the
N.R.F. on trust.

64.—*André Gide to Paul Claudel*

23rd February 1910.

Dear Friend,

I did not know that the birth of little Reine had caused you
such anxiety. No doubt the expression of our sympathy will
arrive very late, since you tell me that Madame Claudel has almost
completely recovered, but please give it to her none the less.

Yes, in spite of many blurred edges, the Philippe number seems
to me fairly satisfactory, and the approval of Philippe's friends is
some small reward for the trouble I took.

I, too, had wished with all my heart for the name of Jammes to
appear on the cover, and I had at once asked him to contribute,
not knowing (as I discovered later) that Jammes' relations with
Philippe had cooled, or become a little strained, after the appearance of *Triomphe de la Vie*, a book which Philippe had not sufficiently
admired. That explains the peculiar manuscript which I received
from Jammes. This is how it begins :

" I am asked to open this number of the *N.R.F.*, which is devoted
to Ch. L. Ph. It was simple for me to keep silence when nobody
asked me any questions, and silent I should have remained. But
now that the question has been asked, I am led to answer briefly
that . . . " (then follows the text of an *admirable* letter from
Philippe to Jammes, dated June 1898). Many of us, including
Arthur Fontaine, thought *unseemly* to open our number with these
reservations ; for my part I thought that not only would Philippe
be done scant honour by it, but his friends would take offence and

Jammes would do himself the greatest possible harm. So I asked
him, in friendly and timid style (for I know how intolerant of
criticism he is) to be good enough to let us publish Philippe's letter
without the mysterious and disobliging prefix which he had devised
for it. Alas ! I was all too right in my apprehensions. . . . And
yet I had hoped that his author's pride would give way at that
graveside. . . . The prancing self-satisfaction of his letter hurt me
to the bottom of my heart—and angered me, I must admit—for I
had been living for some time in Philippe's humble, loving and
suffering company, and I was thinking only of the homage which
the .*N.R.F.* wanted to offer him in a number which I wanted to be
as noble and as harmonious as possible.

What should I say now ? I've no *grievance* against Jammes (the
very word is ridiculous). He behaved too much in character for
me to begrudge this manifestation of his nature. Some days ago,
in sending him Péguy's book, I took care to send with it a warm
letter which will show him how far I am from taking up arms
against him ; but if he wishes to harbour resentment, what can I
do ? It prevents me *even from seeking* a reconciliation. . . . Forgive
me for talking so long about something that is no doubt as painful
to you as it is to me.

I am most impatient to see your new play, and all that you tell
me about it heightens my curiosity. But seven months is a long
time to wait, and we have taught our readers to be as hungry for
your works as we are ourselves. I am very distressed by this
question of format which prevents you from giving us one of the
Odes ; I was discussing the day before yesterday, with Ruyters and
Schlumberger, the possibility of " folding in " to the magazine
some sheets printed the other way—as we did with Philippe's
autograph . . . ? Of course, we want so much to have you that
we would do the impossible for it, and if you envisage any solution
which seems to you satisfactory. . . . But, even in the big edition
of the *Muses*, not every line will go on to one line of print. I must
own that your poem on Philippe, which I already so much admired
in manuscript—and which I wanted at one moment to be printed
in a special, transversal way—seemed to me to gain, and to take
on a more natural solemnity, on the two pages of the Review. (On
the other hand we did not like the XXX which were put on the
cover in place of a title ; we had asked for three asterisks, but *one*
such request is not enough, and when we were passing the final

proofs we left it to our secretary to correct the cover.   One should
supervise and re-supervise everything oneself.

I have had the great pleasure of meeting a number of readers
who profess to admire your funerary poem even more than I do—
among them Jacques Blanche and Madame de Noailles !—which
leaves you, I hope, perfectly indifferent.

Au revoir.   My wife and I send you and Madame Claudel our
best remembrances.

Yours,

ANDRÉ GIDE.

I reopen my letter, having just received yours about Péguy's
book.[1] How glad I am that you like this book. . . . But you are
mistaken on one point : nothing could be less *literary*, nothing more
authentic, more sincere, more submissive.   Péguy-Paul of
Tarsus and those like him may have been—or seemed to be—your
enemies when it was dangerous to be so ;   but they are generous
enough, and devoted enough, to turn away in disgust from the
material advantages of such a position, and the hideous rush for
the spoils.   And to-day they are the most valiant and significant of
your allies.

Yes, I know what you pick out as " Protestant " in the character
of Jeanette, and I foresee what strands of Protestantism you will
find in my way of speaking about Péguy ; but . . . no ; it's
better talked about than written.   You will allow me, won't you, to
show your letter to Péguy, who, I know, values your opinion above
any other ?   No doubt he will understand what you meant to say.
But at any rate you must believe me that the " Protestantism " of that
book is quite involuntary and that in intention it is wholly orthodox.

Yours,

A. G.

────────

65.—*Paul Claudel to André Gide*

French Consulate, Prague,
26th February 1910.

My dear Friend,

Show my letter to Péguy if you think that it will not give
pain to a sensitive and generous-hearted man whom I should be

[1] This letter about Péguy's *Jeanne d'Arc* has been lost.

sorry to distress. What you tell me about him gives me great
pleasure and I should be very happy to count him as one of my
friends.

I am very much perplexed about the *Odes*. It's not so much a
question of how much will go on to one line as of how much will
go on to one page without the reader having to turn over too
often and so distracting his attention and creating a rhythm which
is not that of the poem. There is a certain unity of the page, just
as there is a unity of the stanzas. Perhaps the best would be for
you to ask Chapon to show you the *Magnificat*, or rather the *Fifth
Ode*, which is shorter, and that you yourself should give me a
perfectly objective opinion (provided, though, that the printing,
already so slow, should not be delayed still further).—And then
the parcel of Chesterton which I sent you must satisfy your appetite.
You can quote to Péguy, a propos of the denial of St. Peter, a
saying of that same Chesterton which I greatly admire : " A
chain is never stronger than its weakest link ". Later, I can also
send you some translations from an admirable and unknown
English poet, Coventry Patmore, who only wrote about a thousand
lines, all of the highest interest. He, too, foreshadowed that
doctrine which, in my view, will be the doctrine of the twentieth
century—that of the " closed system ", the inexhaustible definitive
content of the thing fixed from the very beginning. You see that,
so far from being a grudging contributor, I shall, on the contrary,
overwhelm you. I think I can find you some subscribers here. I
can give you the names of some people who would take out a trial
subscription for several months.

As for my play, it's far from being ready. Only very recently
have I seen clearly what I want to do, and it will mean long months
of hard work.

As for Jammes—alas, literary *amour-propre* is one of the strongest
of human sentiments. St. Jerome in the desert subdued his flesh,
but when he learnt that Rufinus was making fun of him at Rome
he came out of his solitude like a lion.

Household troubles as usual. My small daughter has an abcess,
my small boy whooping-cough, my wife exhausts herself among our
clumsy servants, who don't understand her. She thanks you and
Madame Gide for your affectionate greetings.

I grasp your hand,

P. CLAUDEL.

66.—*Paul Claudel to André Gide*

French Consulate, Prague,
3rd March 1910.

Dear Friend,

I am delighted that the Chesterton interests you.

Could you find for me Napoléon Landais' diatribe against modern books ? I should like to write something on it—at Chapon's request.

I see that the jubilee of Henri Fabre is being celebrated at Avignon. Do you know this admirable naturalist ? If he were English, he would be more famous than Darwin—and very rightly so. If you don't know the ten volumes of the *Souvenirs Entomologiques* (published by Delagrave), go and buy them at once. It's one of the most astonishing and the most stimulating books, alike for the intelligence and for the imagination, that I know.

I have just received the *N.R.F.* and I turned at once to the pages on Péguy. Why do you think I should object to them ? On the contrary, I like them very much.

I grasp your hand with great affection. My respects to Madame Gide.

P. CLAUDEL.

67.—*Paul Claudel to André Gide*

French Consulate, Prague,
11th March 1910.

My dear Friend,

C. sent me a letter and a telegram about the manuscripts which you had to ask him to make over. Don't torment him further. He is already so embroiled in this question of the printing that I'm afraid he may go quite off his head. I can myself send you the proofs of the *Magnificat*, if you are not appalled by the quarto edition which you know—the lines are as long as those of the *Muses*. The poem cannot be split up, and must appear in one piece. I have not found any way of isolating any one section of it. It remains true that the use of big letters is not essential ; the question is not the same as it was with the *Hymns*.

Moreover, I should like it to appear without too much delay.

If I decided to do it, it would be mainly because I want to make a little publicity for the edition, of which the enormous expense (more than 2000 francs) is bearing very heavily upon me.

I grasp your hand.

Answer me quite frankly,

P. CLAUDEL.

68.—*André Gide to Paul Claudel*

Cuvervlle, 12th March 1910.

Dear Friend,

I left Paris abruptly, worn out and exasperated at never having time for any of the things that are dearest to me ; and having almost forgotten what it is to sleep. A few days in Normandy will suffice, I hope, to get the machinery in good order again.

Remember that we were left in anxiety by what you said, in the last but one of your letters, about your children ; a word from you to reassure us about you all would be very welcome.

After some hesitation we have decided not to print one of the *Odes* in the *N.R.F.*—as much because of the very reasonable typographical points which you submitted to my judgment, as because of the size of the poem ; and also because we were very short of time (if we were not to delay its publication in book form we should have had to put it in our April number) and ran the risk of not being able to print it to our complete satisfaction—something which would have left me inconsolable.

All the same, I asked Chapon (as you had suggested in your letter) to send me the *Ode IV* and the *Magnificat*. After promising me the proofs for the 10th, he said that he had scruples about it and had written or telegraphed to you in order to secure a more direct authority. I am so sorry about this complication, which he could have avoided, and could have spared you, if he had let me know of it in advance for the *N.R.F.* had already given up the idea of publication. Nevertheless I wrote again at once to Chapon, because I don't want Mithouard to be surprised or offended by what I did. It will at any rate have the good result of egging on the *Occident* who have suddenly become full of zeal and are getting on fast with your book.

As for the Chesterton, we mean to put it at the top of our May number, in view of its magisterial grandeur. And in view of the sad ignorance of the public we should like to preface it with a few lines of information about the work and the personality of Chesterton ;—where the chapter in question is placed in the book, and the place of the book in Chesterton's *Oeuvre*. Valery Larbaud, a great admirer both of yourself and of *Orthodoxy*, has agreed to write these lines (he is very well informed about the whole of English literature and delighted to hear that you mean to translate Coventry Patmore). They would appear in smaller type, signed by his initials—but of course they would first be submitted to you so that you can alter them, or add or cut out, as you wish—(Valery Larbaud already agrees to this)—because I am anxious, and the *N.R.F.* is anxious—to do nothing in this matter without your approval. But it's to the good, don't you think, that the reader should realize the *importance* of this chapter.

Where Chesterton is concerned, have we nothing to worry about ? Have you, have we, a sufficient authority to print ? What about the author's rights ? A word in answer, please, to reassure us on all these points.

I read the *Nigger of the Narcissus* and thought of you. But H's translation gives me goose-flesh.

Read in our next issue the prose-pieces of Saint-Léger, a friend of Rivière whom Frizeau sent to us ; at first I disliked them but now I find them delectable—and violently influenced by you, I must add.

Au revoir, my execrable pen ruins my pleasure in writing to you.

My respects, and my wife's best regards, to Madame Claudel.

Yours,

ANDRÉ GIDE.

———

69.—*Paul Claudel to André Gide*

French Consulate, Prague,
16th March 1910.

My dear Friend,

I am replying at once to your letter of the 13th. I quite agree with you. It is better that none of my *Odes* should appear before the complete edition. I agreed to it out of friendship for you, and also, I admit, out of the wish for a little publicity, for the edition is a sort of insanity on my part and I should like to be comforted by a few subscriptions to it. So if you could publish in your review an announcement or even a little note at the end of one of your next numbers, I should be very pleased. Having failed to get what I wanted by typography, I am going to have the title engraved here : I think it will be magnificent. But if you know the trouble I've had with C. . . . ; only by violence of some sort can one get anything out of him. It's a pity, because he's conscientious and has good taste.

As for Chesterton, I know nothing of him as a man ; I believe he's an Anglican ; with the illogicality of the English, anything is possible. I wrote to him once, when I was first under the spell of *Orthodoxy*. He could perhaps be reached either through his publisher, or through the *Illustrated London News*, where he writes every week, as brilliantly as our Lavedan (do you read his weekly articles in *L'Illustration* ? I find them dazzling. How can a man who has written so much rubbish reveal his full stature all of a sudden ?) I am delighted that M. Larbaud should undertake the introduction which, as you say, it needs. I have taken a few small liberties with the text, which can well bear them. One could have quoted other and much more striking examples of the paradoxes of Christianity : the man-God crucified, the Virgin-Mother, the Pope, and St. Francis, etc.

I have finished *L'Otage* and am beginning the period of " immersion " and development. I am very glad to have reached the end of this play, which seemed to me horribly difficult.

The little children are well and I am very happy to have them. My wife wishes to be remembered to yours. I salute her with respect and grasp your hand.

P. CLAUDEL.

70.—André Gide to Paul Claudel

Cuverville, Monday [March 1910].

Dear Friend,

My wife has forwarded from Paris (whither I return to-morrow) your letter of the 11th. For a moment I thought of telegraphing to you to send the proofs of the *Magnificat* to the *N.R.F.* offices. But, even with the help of the telegraph, they would reach us too late for the April number, which is already made up, and of which we shall have the proofs the day after to-morrow. Besides, they would entail an entire re-arrangement of our number, because the article (on Rémy de Gourmont) which opens it—and which I had been preparing for months—would seem to be part of a conspiracy, and your poem to have been put after it as an example and support.

But your authority, your advice, to publish it in small Roman characters has revived all my ambitions. No doubt it could be arranged so that the text was laid out and divided exactly as in the big edition, the proportions of page and characters remaining almost exactly the same.

We would put off the Chesterton till a little later and you would appear on 1st May ; we should only ask Chapon for a formal assurance that your volume would not come out before the 15th of the same month.[1] And as we should take care to announce the book in a note after the *Magnificat*, it would be given an honest and natural advertisement and would in fact be given a sort of send-off.

I know that the *N.R.F.* (whose projects in respect of your play I have, I think, described to you) already intended to offer you 200 francs for the *Magnificat*—with their regrets that it should not be more. But our great concern is to stay in existence, and we don't at all want to founder through an over-hasty generosity.

So I shall wait for the proofs, if you still stand by what seems to me an excellent decision.

I finished last night the prodigious *Nigger of the Narcissus*. Au revoir. I am impatient for you to read my *Gourmont*. I am afraid it may provoke a fearful storm at the *Mercure* . . . I am afraid . . . and I hope ! For it's time.

You will have had my letter of yesterday.

Yours most affectionately,

ANDRÉ GIDE.

P.S.—I am taking this letter with me and will send it off from Paris.

---

[1] I don't think that this will hold it up for long.

71.—*André Gide to Paul Claudel*

Sunday evening [17th April 1910].
Dear Friend,

A word in haste : You *do* mean " especial ", don't you ?
We intend to put on the cover of this number a special notice,
as we did with the Philippe number, to announce that " this
number contains Paul Claudel's *Magnificat* ". (You don't, I take
it, see any objection ?) We can print the word *Magnificat* in red ;
but I don't think that that would be possible in the magazine itself.

Despite our indications, the printer has felt bound to print, or
has allowed others to print, the title in capitals. We are now
insisting once again that it should be in italics. You know how
difficult it is to get what one wants out of them.

Yes, we here vote unanimously for the special notice. The
importance of your admirable poem must be asserted, in spite of
those who would not recognize it. I see, too, that the note which
calls attention to your forthcoming volume has not been included,
although we had asked for it ; one can't tell whose negligence is
responsible—you will see if it would be better to add it at the foot
of the first page or (as I think preferable) at the foot of the last
page. " This *Magnificat* is the fourth poem of a volume of *Odes*, to
be published by the *Occident* ", etc. As for the subscription, you can
see if you have room to indicate that subscriptions can also be
received at the *N.R.F.* . . . but I should like to be assured that
neither Chapon nor Mithouard will take umbrage. Perhaps it
will be better simply to say that subscriptions will be received at
the *Occident* offices. But your decision shall be final.

In haste—am quite submerged by proofs.
Yours ever,

ANDRÉ GIDE.

———

72.—*Paul Claudel to André Gide*

French Consulate, Prague,
20th April 1910.
My dear Gide,

I've just received your letter of the 17th, and by the same
post the proofs which I am returning to M. de Lanux by this

courier.—Yes, it must be *espéciale*. I prefer this very French variant to *spéciale*, which is dry, and scholastic, and insufficiently emphatic. The initial *e* must jab like a thumb. I am very flattered by the idea of that special announcement. As for the red, it can't be helped. It was a preference, not a stipulation. Could you put the " Magnificat " a little to the right instead of in the middle ? And a question of fact : the *Magnificat* is the third, not the fourth, of my *Five Odes*. I think it would be better to give the *Occident* as the only place where people can send their subscriptions. Thank you none the less for your kind offer.

I am happy that you should like this " Ode ". I think it represents something quite new in literature. It's built up like a symphony on different themes : the theme of the forest, the theme of the cold, the theme of the child which recurs in every possible form and in the end is metamorphosed in the canticle of the Eucharist, etc.

I grasp your hand with affection,

P. CLAUDEL.

L'Otage is finished, and I have even completed the definitive version of the first Act.

I'd like it best if the note were put at the bottom of the first page.

———

73.—*Paul Claudel to André Gide*

French Consulate, Prague,
25th April [1910].

My dear Gide,

The title can stand—after all, it hasn't any great importance. In revising the poem for the *N.R.F.* I noticed that, despite all the trouble I took, I passed over several errors in the large-paper edition. It's heart-breaking.

Have you read *Un Etre en Marche* ? Romains has sent it to me. He is an interesting poet, and there are two or three points in the book at which he achieves greatness. He's very hard on that side of us which cares for the plastic, sensual side of literature, and his appalling blank verses are a continual torment to one's ear. But he is right in thinking that the man who walks is a different being from the one who remains seated. The movement of our ideas, and the movement of everything that passes across our field of vision—both assume a quite different aspect. And then his idea of *unanimity* has something in common with Plato's : at the beginning of the *Republic*, Socrates explains the psychology of an isolated individual is too difficult and that it's easier to analyse a whole city, which is in reality no more than an enlarged individual.

Are you coming to Prague this summer, as you promised ? I am famous here now and a hatter in the Wentzel's Platz has even launched a new hat, named after me !

I grasp your hand with affection,

P. CLAUDEL.

74.—Paul Claudel to André Gide

French Consulate, Prague,
20th April 1910.

Dear Friend,

Yes, I am very pleased with the form which my *Magnificat* has assumed in your Review. The different types have the effect of glasses which allow me to look at my thoughts now from one distance, now from another. It seems to me the least bad thing I have yet written, and I hope that the three other *Odes* and the *Processional* will not seem to you unworthy of it. But when will they be ready ? No news from Chapon, and I am still feeling my way towards the cover and the title-page, which I have decided to have engraved here. At Pilsen, which not only manufactures 150 million litres of beer every year, but possesses a pretty museum which I have just visited ; I saw some enormous pages of antiphonaries which sent me into a dream. They are wonderfully beautiful. There, one can follow the history of the decadence of the letter from the remotest times down to our own.

I wrote to Chesterton, but have had no reply, and am not really surprised. I see him as one of those great English schoolboys—you know the type. I think that my two letters are enough to show him what's going on. I shall need to see the proofs again—not for the material corrections, of which I should be quite incompetent, but for certain details of the translation. Your friend Larbaud (who is publishing a most interesting novel in the *N.R.F.*) has saved me from two gross mis-readings.

While on the subject of the *N.R.F.*—you should speak seriously to the distributors. The three subscribers whom I secured for you in Prague have not yet received the May number. Nothing is more important for a Review than an astronomical exactitude.

I haven't yet congratulated you on your courageous article on Rémy de Gourmont. You said what needed saying, though I thought you too indulgent towards this repulsive polygrapher who, at bottom, like all those who have neither heart nor conscience, is incapable of understanding anything about anything. You have started a regular campaign—soon after your article I read another in *La Phalange*.—Yes, I no longer read the *Mercure*, and very glad I am.

A propos of Gourmont : why are the philologers and bookworms always, without exception, cowards ?

As for my play, it's not getting on so fast. I was held up by my second act, which gives me the greatest difficulty, or at any rate takes up a lot of my time. For my method of " work " when I am not inspired is to do nothing and wait for inspiration to come. But I shall have nothing to change in the third act.

What you say about Rivière's health very much distresses me. Tell him to write to me and give me his news.

My respectful regards to Madame Gide. I grasp your hand.

P. CLAUDEL.

75.—*Paul Claudel to André Gide*

Prague, 21st May [1910].

My dear Friend,

I saw Blei yesterday when he passed through Prague and very much enjoyed meeting him. He has a very interesting face —finer than is usual in a German. He told me that Chesterton, whom he has translated, is a very difficult customer. He had trouble with his publisher about an article he had translated—he had asked permission, but had had no answer. That is how we stand. Would the *N.R.F.* not do better to take up the translation rights of the whole of *Orthodoxy* ? It would only cost 300 or 400 francs and this very important book would certainly sell enough copies to cover this little sum. It seems to me that M. Valery Larbaud would translate it very well.

I am going to try and get *The Cross and the Ball* which has just come out.

Blei tells me that you are preparing for the autumn a book which will " make a scandal " ?

I grasp your hand most affectionately,

P. CLAUDEL.

────────

76.—*Paul Claudel to André Gide*

Prague, 2nd June 1910.

My dear Friend,

I am very interested in your projected publishing house and hope that something will come of it. The whole question is to find out if a commercial enterprise can live by publishing nothing but books which are excellent both in form and in substance. Even for a Society, like that which I momentarily envisaged, it seems to me very doubtful.

What you simply must organize, I think, is not so much the publishing part as the publicity. The book trade seems to me to be to-day in a barbarous, un-organic state. This is what I mean :

The book is to-day the only form of merchandise which people buy blindly, without knowing if it corresponds to their needs. When one is not guided—and very insufficiently—by the author's name, there is absolutely no way of keeping abreast of the output of books which interest you. Literary criticism is useless from the practical point of view. What ought to be done is to enlarge and perfect the rôle played in France by the arcades of the Odéon and the book-racks of obliging booksellers—that is to say, to put books within the reach of every scattered and isolated reader. To bring this about, two main schemes (which could be combined) seem to me possible :

I

To put samples in the hands of the public :

1. By means of a very full prospectus, accompanied by extracts, which would be sent to all the possible clients (of whom one would gradually establish a directory).

2. By means of a magazine containing an analysis, without any critical appreciation, of all the new publications, together with well-chosen quotations. This would be an intelligently executed extension of the *Bulletin de la Bibliographie Française*.

II

To put the books themselves within easy reach of the public. And, with this end, to develop in an intelligent and up-to-date way the institution of " circulating libraries ".

I maintain that most books need only be read once. Every avid reader ends up by being encumbered with a heap of costly waste-matter which is as useless as its digestive equivalent. Few books need to be kept.

Yet circulating libraries have little success in France :

1. Because their books are disgustingly dirty.

2. Because they have not enough copies of the new books, and because their resources in general are insufficient.

3. Because their catalogues are badly made up and include only names and titles—and to look on their shelves is a dirty and pointless procedure.

4. Because the subscriber has to clutter himself with awkward parcels and later endure the bother of re-packing.

The circulating library I have in mind would be based on the following principles :

(*a*) It would only provide the new books summarized in I, paragraph 2.

(*b*) It would send them packed in such a way that they could be returned in the same package—for instance, a box divided into compartments and closed with a buckle or a lever. The address of the circulating library would be printed on the box and would come into view as soon as the label bearing the customer's address had been removed.

(*c*) Wherever possible, a representative should pick up the boxes on regular days, as is done with household refuse.

Put the average price of a book at 5 francs, binding included. Put the subscription at 10 francs a month (an average of 12 books borrowed each month, 6 to be issued every 15 days). A book would only have to be taken out fifteen times to recoup its purchase price and a good part of the general expenses ; the rest is sheer profit.

A " consumer's co-operative " among this sort of French reader could end by having all the publications at its mercy.

One of the advantages of circulating libraries is that publishers have to make their books solid and easy to read—printed in good type, therefore, on good paper. Illustrations lose their point when it is no longer a question of egging the customer on to buy.

All books should be carefully inspected when they are returned, and any damage should be punished by a fine or expulsion.

One must absolutely realize that for most people a book is not one of the most necessary of pleasures. It must be put under the hand of the indolent reader. We must realize that a book should be above all a thing which can be picked up, taken about, and sent on its travels ; it is above all a thing made to be lent—and never to be returned, because it will have been passed on to somebody else.

I am reading Chesterton's *The Cross and the Ball*—full of interest, though not equal to *Orthodoxy*.

I have almost finished *L'Otage* ; another fortnight's work will do it. I am very embarrassed about publishing it. Most readers are hasty and superficial and will take it for (in the most current and contemporary sense) a reactionary book. In point of fact I've tried to portray many conflicting forces, none of whom, not even the Pope who has the principal rôle, not even God himself, has the field completely to himself.

And the printing of the *Odes* is still despairingly slow. I am having the cover engraved here, in gold, vermilion, and ultramarine. It's rather loud, but I think that the contents justify these trumpetings.

I grasp your hand with affection,

P. CLAUDEL.

77.—*André Gide to Paul Claudel*

Cuverville, 14th June 1910.

Dear Friend,

Here I am, back in the country, where nothing remains to disturb me in my work. Blei has sent me some rather fine specimen proofs of what they would like to do at Leipzig ; but I've already

written to say that : this enterprise loses all interest for me if all
the technical side is in German hands (of the three specimen pages,
a title-page of the *Comédie* (sic) *humaine* confirms me in my decision)
and I don't now doubt that we can do more and better in France
(not, however, from the commercial point of view, where the
Germans are undoubtedly stronger ; but no matter). Your last
letter very much interested me ; perhaps, in view of the impersonal
character of your advice, I may ask you, at some opportune time,
to turn them into an article ? I think that hardly anything would
have to be changed. I should ask for it when we launch the
publishing firm of which I told you briefly in my last letter—in
October or November of this year, I hope. We envisage two under-
takings—one, entirely non-commercial in its intentions, would be
concerned only with very fine limited editions of books that are
specially worthy of . . . respect. Possibly we shall set that in hand
this summer. The other side of the firm would have as its contrast-
ing object the widest possible diffusion of the work of writers who
are being suffocated at the *Mercure* (if you take Mithouard, Griffin,
Valery Larbaud, and add the names of Jammes, yourself, and
myself, you have already a pretty promising list).

That's what is being enquired into.

An obituary article on Jules Renard has had to be substituted
for the Chesterton in our July number ; but the Chesterton will
still seem urgently *topical*. What plans have you for your play ?
May I hope that you will be good enough to confide it to the *N.R.F.* ?
I've already told you, haven't I, of our fatuous intentions in that
respect ? If it could appear towards the end of the year—or
straddled across the turn of the year—that would be perfect. I
think I also asked you (forgive me if I am indiscreet) if I might
have it typed and keep the manuscript. Please answer me quite
frankly on this point.

I saw that you have offered some copies of *Partage de Midi* for
sale at 10 francs each at the *Occident* bookshop. (Ruyters points
out to me that second-hand copies of it have always been priced
at 20 francs.) I didn't know that it was on sale at the moment
when (persuaded by his enormous wish to have the book and his
understanding of your whole *œuvre*) I advised my friend Dominique
Dupouey to write and ask you for a copy. The letter he wrote to
me a few days ago shows that you were kind enough to send him
a copy Here, anyway, is what he says about it :

" No sooner had I decided to keep silent and given up the idea of possessing *Partage de Midi* than I was seized by the need to possess and reread that book. So I wrote to Claudel. My friends " (he is a Naval officer : A. G.) " hurled themselves on it, as I need hardly say, and I can only glimpse it as it passes distantly from hand to hand."

I hope that one day I can introduce Dupouey to you, for he deserves your esteem and your affection. Thank you for sending him your play.

Au revoir, my dear Claudel. We greet you both and smile upon your children.

ANDRÉ GIDE.

78.—Paul Claudel to André Gide

French Consulate, Prague,
17th June 1910.

My dear Friend,

I have got your letter of the 14th and envy you the country and your solitude. As for me, who am shut up at the end of a smoky valley, I could only momentarily enjoy the marvellous spectacle (which I had almost forgotten) of a European spring—a spectacle put on and carried out with such superior art.

My plan for a " circulating library " has, I think, a practical, commercial value and I fancy that it would be premature to publish and put it in the hands of people who would spoil it, without being certain that there would be some, among our own friends, who could bring it off. Literary man-power is cheap and of good quality in Paris—how is it that better use is not made of it ?

I put " The End ", last week, to the third act of *L'Otage*. Nothing remains but some unimportant formal corrections. I thought for a long time about your proposals, and here is my answer to them :

1. First of all, my wife, who leaves for France towards the 1st of July (she will spend the four summer months there, for the children's health) will bring the manuscript with her. If you can arrange a rendezvous in Paris, she will give it into your hand. I cannot bring myself to entrust it to the post. It's the only copy and I've no complete duplicate of it.

2. I gratefully accept your suggestion about having it typed and am very happy to present the manuscript to a bibliophile such as yourself.

3. When you have read the manuscript, please give me your advice about its publication. Don't forget that I am already suspect at the Ministry and that it's only through the generous and energetic support of Berthelot that I have kept my position. Last year the amiable Berteaux (who is spoken of as a coming Prime Minister) asked for my head. I had been so imprudent as to deal harshly with one of his rascally friends, who is a valiant supporter of the régime.

Couldn't we publish the play in my name, with just the initials P. C., which would leave no doubt of my identity and yet spare me the trouble which could be made for me on account of the regulation (nothing can be published without authorization) ? I admit that I should not at all care for serial publication. It should be read straight through—not with these month-long interruptions. Could you not make a special number, as you did for Philippe ? A sort of supplement ? I should not release the play in any other way, and probably wouldn't publish it for a long time. Give me your advice when you've read the book.

Charles Morice asked me to contribute to a collection of tributes to Verlaine, which will serve to pay for the hideous simulacrum which they want to erect to the poor man's memory. At first I refused, and said what I thought of monuments—hypocritical and derisory tributes to people who have been allowed to die of hunger. He insisted, though, and invoked the authority of Mallarmé— knowing that this would be decisive in my case—who is apparently the initiator of the enterprise. I therefore sent my poem, but I don't know if it will please everybody.

I forgot to tell you that *L'Otage* comprises 125 large quarto pages of fairly small handwriting. You could save space by putting the characters' names in the margin.

I have had the last proofs of *Cinq Grandes Odes*. I'm now only waiting for those of the cover and the title-page, which are to be printed from the zinc-engravings I had made here. Would it be indiscreet to ask you to announce it in the next two numbers of the *N.R.F.* ? Could you perhaps reproduce the prospectus ? You could reach an agreement with Alfred Chapon on this point.

I am very annoyed to hear from you that people have lowered

themselves to the point of selling copies of a book which I had given them, and which I gave to nobody (except my intimate friends) unless I was asked for it.

Will you follow up your *Rémy de Gourmont*, which I read with delectation? I am very anxious that the *N.R.F.* should become more pugnacious, like the old *Revue Indépendante*. There has been a change of attitude in the literary press since we were young. To-day the reviews, and the big newspapers too, are full of nothing but flavourless eulogies and whiffs of incense. It's all miscalculated. There's nothing in all human nature so deep, so widespread, and so dependable as cowardice. These iniquities allow scoundrels to hold their heads high. Scandals, like the election to the *Académie* of such literary " hodmen " as the Aicards, the Brieux, and the Prévosts—such things go on with nobody to protest against them. Ah, if I weren't a civil servant and the father of a family . . . but then everyone has his reasons for not belling the cat. That's why I admire your *Gourmont*.

And I see that I've said nothing of your publishing projects. That will be for another time. What type-face will you choose? There are lovely ones in Prague.

The *N.R.F.* is now prominently displayed in the main bookshop of Prague.

Won't you come and console me in my solitude this summer?

I grasp your hand with affection. My respects to Madame Gide.

P. CLAUDEL.

79.—Paul Claudel to André Gide

French Consulate, Prague,
20th June 1910.

My dear Friend,

If I had a small service to ask of you, it would be to get me the last two books of Péguy : *Notre Jeunesse* (if it's out) and another which, I think, is called *Histoire d'une Famille sous le Second Empire* or something of the sort. I should like to get a clearer idea of this copious writer. For, though I spoke of his " last books ", are they really his last? I see him rather as Goethe's *Sorcerer's Apprentice*, with papers overflowing on every side of his work-table, cascading from the windows and blacking up the ventilator. I have always hitherto forgotten to tell you something which will please you : I gave my wife *La Porte étroite* to read and she enjoyed it enormously. She has a very delicate natural taste, and hers is the most valuable sort of approval. She read the book at a sitting and could not put it down.

I suppose it is to you that I owe the volume of stories by Ch. L. Philippe that has been sent to me ? It led him into bad paths, parallel with those of Maupassant and Renard, writers of the objective, " picturesque " type. All those stories about peasants whom we are supposed to see as special, picturesque beings— they lack depth, truth, and, I should say, charity. It is always man in general who is most interesting : the picturesque should be kept for details. It's like those people who go all out for exoticism, local colour, etc.

I grasp your hand,

P. Claudel.

80.—André Gide to Paul Claudel

[June 1910].

We are agreed on this, dear friend ; we shall not speak of the possible advantages of your scheme till the project is far enough advanced for us to be able to announce the programme, and to put it into effect, at one and the same time.

How delighted I am that I shall be able to read *L'Otage* ! If Madame Claudel comes to Paris at the beginning of July, it is better, as you say, to entrust the manuscript to her, and she can give it, if not to me—for I have to go to Paris the day after to-morrow and I don't know that I can go back again so soon afterwards— then to Jacques Rivière who is to come with his young wife for the month of July—or, if the Rivières have already left Paris, to our secretary Pierre de Lanux. To arrange all this properly I must know when Madame Claudel will be in Paris.

Not till I have read *L'Otage* shall I re-discuss the question of publication and examine, with you and Jean Schlumberger, what can best be done. Fortunately, we have time before us. It seems to me better that we should not give the new play until the publication of the *Odes* has more or less made its first effect (forgive this vulgar phrase) ; so we here shall act in concert with you, after having envisaged the problem from every angle, but with, as our prime object, the wish to please you.

I'm sorry that you didn't warn us sooner about the *Odes* ; we could have begun with the July number. But we won't fail you in August. (If there is a prospectus, would you ask Chapon to send it to us ?) Have no fear in any case ; you'll have quite a large number of subscribers. How many do you need to cover your expenses ?

As for the tribute to Verlaine, I've done as you first thought of doing. The book will appear without my name.

Are you certain that no copies of *Partage de Midi* have been stolen ? That would explain their being on sale . . . without your having to suspect any of those to whom you gave it, or caused it to be given. Or perhaps one was sold after the owner's death ? I don't remember that Philippe's copy, for one, was ever found. Has Lucien Jean got it ? I will ask Ruyters again if he has the catalogue in which the book was announced.

I am glad you liked my *Rémy de Gourmont* and understood that it needed a certain courage to write it—for I had no illusions as to what would happen to me in consequence of it. Have you read Monfort's attack in the last-but-one number of *Marges* ? I should very much like you to see it ; you would appreciate the perfidy of it. As his object is to do me harm, he doesn't worry at all about the truth ; but plausibility is on his side, and that's enough for him—as it is also enough for the public. So now I have to defend myself and reveal my own position rather faster than I wanted to. (I'm doing it in our July number.) I hate the ways of journalists, politicians, and torpedo-men in general. It doesn't matter to them if they're in the right or wrong. What they want is to torpedo the other man and *discredit* his word.

I'm in all the great need of a few people's esteem.

Au revoir, my dear Claudel. My respects to Madame Claudel.

Yours,

ANDRÉ GIDE.

Serial publication, which I, too, very much disliked in the case of *La Porte étroite*, is not without its advantages. One's more sure that the book will get about. People *don't stop* talking about it, and the stir of interest which is created by publication comes back again and again, and *insists* on being noticed.

P.S.—A letter this instant from Rivière tells me that he can't leave Paris before *the third of July.* So if Madame Claudel could meet him before then, all would be for the best. (2 rue Cassini.)

———

81.—*Paul Claudel to André Gide*

French Consulate, Prague,
24th June 1910.

Dear Friend,

Yes, I read Montfort's article, but without attaching much importance to it. Your article against Gourmont is a positive act, the other is just an outburst of useless words and doesn't even manage to be insulting—for I don't consider it as an insult when he reproaches you for the religion in which you were brought up. You haven't to excuse yourself for anything there. Believe me— the Gourmont article is more than a fine page : it's a fine action. Those things had to be said, and they could not have been said better than by you. You have relieved all our consciences. In this country I can see all the harm that that poisoner has done to the poor people whom he has misled. Your article made a great impression here, and they even want to translate it in a local Review. It's not a polemical article, it's a definitive execution. Despise all those little annoyances. You have said out loud what everybody thinks in private—for, at bottom, there's nobody who doesn't regard the object and idiotic epiloguist of the *Mercure* with the contempt which he deserves. You have your responsibilities, as one of the guides of the young people of to-day, and you've done well not to back away from them. Your authority, already great, will be greater still after this courageous pronouncement. After all, you've only been scratched, whereas your adversary has been wounded " in his black liver ", as Homer says.

My wife leaves for France on the 7th. Her address from the 8th onwards will be : Madame Claudel, Villeneuve-sur-Fère, par Fère-en-Tardenois, Aisne.

Must I give up all hope of seeing you in Prague this summer ?

I grasp your hand with great affection. My respects to Madame Gide.

P. CLAUDEL.

82.—*André Gide to Paul Claudel*

Cuverville, 27th June [1910].

Dear Friend,

That brief conversation the other day left me more anxious to resume it than if we had not seen one another at all ; decidedly it is only in Prague that I shall see enough of you, and no doubt I shall soon be going there to pay you a few days' visit.

Before leaving Paris—that's to say on the evening of the same day that we lunched together—I managed to see Marcel Ray from Montpellier, who was himself passing through Paris. He was, as you know, Philippe's oldest and most intimate friend. He would very much like to know if you have any evidence that Philippe ever *received* the manuscript of *Partage de Midi*. It seems to him implausible that Philippe, who knew that he admires you, should never have mentioned the manuscript to him—unless you asked him to keep the gift a secret ; but even then you would have had a letter of thanks from Philippe. Otherwise what are we to think ? That the manuscript got lost *before* it reached Philippe ? It seems to me more and more unlikely that some unscrupulous person could have sneaked it after Philippe died.

If you saw Vallette again before leaving, please let me know what you decided. Do not think it indiscreet that I should wish not to see your name disappear in four years' time from our catalogue—but no ; you know very well, don't you, that I am animated by admiration, friendship, and esteem ; and, for all my zeal, I can't do a thing without help.

An urgent and admirable letter from Jammes has quite bowled me over. . . . Au revoir.

Yours ever,

ANDRÉ GIDE.

83.—*Paul Claudel to André Gide*

Friday [end of June 1910].

Dear Friend,

I also was very sorry that we had not been able to talk m ore seriously than is possible in the general commotion of a meal. I am delighted with your idea of an early visit to Paris. Unhappily, I couldn't entertain you then, as I should be able to do later. My wife has taken away all the servants and I am living a bachelor life. But come all the same. You will be fulfilling a charitable duty— I am terrified of the two months I am to pass by myself. You will see in Prague the completest ensemble of that interesting " rococo " art which is now so little known. Then Dresden is quite near, there are interesting castles, and then Slovakia with its fantastic costumes is not far away. In short, there's more than enough to fill an enjoyable fortnight. I hope that Madame Gide would come with you ?

As for my plans for future publications, I told you exactly how I was placed. Apart from my links with the *Mercure*, it all depends on whether I shall republish *Partage de Midi*. I am still far from being sure about this, and in any case I'm waiting for the *Mercure* to finish printing the first volume of my plays. But, as I told you, the first volume of my *Corona* is available, or soon will be. If you want it ? . . . It's also probable that one of these days I shall make a volume of the different articles I have written, or shall write, such as *La Justice, Les Charges, Contre Pascal, Contre l'idée d'infini, Sur la Décadence des Raisonnements résultant de l'emploi des méthodes dites scientifiques*, etc. It could be called—except for the irreverence of such a title—*Contragentes*. We will go into all this in Prague.

I grasp your hand with great affection,

P. CLAUDEL.

What you say about the manuscript of *Partage de Midi* is quite possible. I had asked X to send it on, after it had been set up in type. In any case Philippe never acknowledged its arrival.

84.—*Paul Claudel to André Gide*

Prague, 15th July 1910.

My dear Friend,

My wife left eight days ago for France with the children. She is to be in Paris to-day and will give Ruyters the manuscript of *L'Otage*. Could you possibly make fifteen roneographed copies of it ? This would be as far as I should go towards publishing it.

Besides, I'm sick of publishing. I no longer have the illusion, cherished hitherto, of being able to do good. All literature is sterile except for evil. One gives a stray impulse to a few more or less frivolous minds—and there it ends. It's perfectly right. The fruit is worth just what the tree is worth. In *L'Otage*, for lack of the necessary books, I haven't been able to complete the Coûfontaine coat of arms. Would it be an abuse of friendship to ask you to put it into heraldic language ? The escutcheon is divided horizontally. I learn that a sword with its point in the air is called " *Space* ". Instead of putting " with the cry ' Coûfontaine, Adsum ' ", I ought to say " with the cry and device ' Coûfontaine, Adsum ! ' " (The heraldic device is not enough.)

I have received several prospectuses of the *Cinq Odes*. Chapon tells me it will be out in a week, but I don't believe it.

I grasp your hand with affection. My respects to Madame Gide and my best regards to Rivière, who must be near you at this moment.

P. Claudel.

85.—André Gide to Paul Claudel

Toulouse, 6th August 1910.

Dear Friend,

This hideous paper does not inspire me and I have only a moment to tell you that when passing through Paris I received your admirable play from Ruyters, read it at once, and gave it to be typed. I was only on my way through Paris (between Cuverville and Toulouse) and had just enough time to serve as a link between Ruyters and the typist. But when I had *L'Otage* in my hands I went at once to the post-office and telegraphed to Eugène Rouart that I should arrive twenty-four hours late. My yesterday was given over entirely to you. I travelled all night, with hardly a moment's sleep and this morning I can only tell you that I was deeply moved. The *urgency* of your play was beyond all my expectations—though you know that they were lively enough. The placing of your various characters is admirably effective ; you give a new scale, a new dimension to yourself. And Turelure is *not* less than Sygne, Coûfontaine, or the Pope.

I am having three copies made : one for me—one for the *N.R.F.*
I can't help believing that the reverberation of this play will be as
deep as it will be long ; far from wishing (I am here speaking
from your point of view—not that of the *N.R.F.*, for which I have
no authority to speak) that it should appear in one single number,
so that those who don't want it can easily ignore it, I think it an
excellent idea that it should return to the charge.   Besides, each
act has its own persuasive power ; and perhaps it's better to have
digested the first two before taking the strain of the last act, which
will antagonize more than one reader.   Less so, however, if the
first two acts have already imposed themselves on the public.

Au revoir, I thought I had still a lot to tell you—but my head
is splitting.

Yours ever,

ANDRÉ GIDE.

Ruyters is definitely appointed the government's representative
(or something of the sort), for the time being, with the Ethiopian
Railways at Addis Ababa.   I am delighted, because it shows that
his superiors at last appreciate his worth.   No doubt he will start
in four or five weeks and will be away eight months.

He will be writing to you and will ask for the names of people
who could usefully be sent the issue in which the Chesterton
appeared.

———

86.—*Paul Claudel to André Gide*

Prague, 1st September 1910.

My dear Friend,

Have you any news of the typed copies of *L'Otage* ?   I admit
to being in torment until it comes, because I have no second copy
of the manuscript.

The *Odes* have been printed in the end, after two years of effort.
I hope you will think the book beautiful, even though I could not
prevent Chapon from printing the title in three vertical lines on
the spine.

Rivière has written a marvellous article about me in a little
review called *L'Art libre*.   He is a very discriminating boy and very
gifted as a critic—we haven't so far been allowed to appraise him

in any other capacity. He does at least say something and isn't content with threading adjectives together. He has even revealed to me certain things about myself—why, for example, I returned, in the *Hymnes*, to regular rhyme and stanza : he is quite right and most ingenious. Some of his *N.R.F.* articles also pleased me, though I knew little of the people he discussed.

I shall no doubt be in Paris towards the end of September. Will you be there then ? Don't forget that you and Madame Gide have promised to come and see me this winter. You have many admirers here (no doubt you know that *La Porte étroite* has just been translated into Czech by one of the best of the local writers). If you would consent to lecture here you would do infinite honour to the town, and you would give great pleasure to the French Consul.

Would you believe that I've never read *Les Mémoires d'Outre-Tombe* ? I am reading them now. I began with mistrust, read on with admiration, and know that I shall finish as an enthusiast. Something that does not inspire me with similar feelings is Pascal's *Pensées*, which I hadn't reread since my twentieth year and which I mistakenly had ordered in the Brunschvicg edition. This Jewish professor has had the idea of arranging all these scattered *pensées* in categories—thoughts on style, on Man, on God, and so on. The effect is disastrous. It's the same mistake which was made at the Louvre when they put all the Rembrandts together, and all the Ruysdaels : you leave those rooms with an impression of disgust and indigestion. Professors have ideas which are not those of an artist. A man's thoughts must be contrasted, and have air between them. I should not have believed that I could regret the Navet edition. What I resent above all in Pascal is that he so maltreated and calumniated human nature—not only that which has been sullied by sin, but that which has been created by God and glorified by grace. It's not Christianity—it's an invalid's bad temper. And what pitiable arguments he uses. It's astonishing to see the fascination with which this great man regarded such mediocre and superficial spirits as Montaigne. He watches this Gascon with the wonder of a man from the Auvergne. For instance : Montaigne and Pascal say that if it's ridiculous to esteem a rich man for his clothes, it's equally absurd to love a woman for her beauty or a man for his talents, since these are things which may easily be taken away. As if clothes, and innate physical qualities, and an acquired spiritual superiority, were each equivalent to the other, and could disappear and leave the fundamental human being intact ! That is a confusion of the *habit* with the *habitus*—the outer envelope with the qualities which spring from the being itself and are joined to it by intimate and quintessential ties. Pascal would no doubt like us to love a being, or to love God himself, after the fashion of the Quietists, independently of the good which they do us and the quality which makes us love them. To love for no reason would be, in his eyes, the only reasonable excuse. Everything he says is on the same level. It's not enough to be a geometrician to know how to argue. If Pascal had spent more time with the scholastics whom he so much despised, he would have spared himself many errors. And yet his book is very beautiful.

I don't know if all this interests you very much. When I have a pen in my hand I let myself be carried away to I don't know where. I was even going to talk to you of the Papal decree about first communion. On this subject I have had a very fine letter from my friend Louis Massignon, the orientalist, of whom I believe I've spoken to you.

A charming friend in Prague has given me a translation she has made of Slovak stories. Many of them are charming. Would they interest the *N.R.F.* ? I could bring them to you when I pass through Paris.

I grasp your hand with affection,

P. Claudel.

You've no doubt read that Junius in the *Echo de Paris* spoke of my translation of G. K. C. I suppose that René Bazin wrote the article.

87.—Paul Claudel to André Gide

Prague, 12th September 1910.

My dear Friend,

As regards the publication of *L'Otage* (if it is to appear in the *N.R.F.*), I would ask you not to let it come out before 1st January. It's probable that I shall accept your generous offers, but I still need to think it over a little. I have other practical reasons, and I want also to have a lapse of time in order that the

play can decant itself before I re-read it. Tell me if this isn't a
nuisance for you.

You are lucky never to have read *Les Mémoires d'Outre-Tombe*.
You have a great treat in store. You must read them in the
excellent Biré edition (hideous from the typographical point of
view) which is the only edition that preserves the admirable scheme
of the work, which is conceived in *books*, like an epic poem. Your
resistance, like my own, will not last for long. Never has anybody
written such admirable French. One soon gets used to the note of
grandeur and dignity and there is much more truth, fundamentally,
if one makes the necessary adjustments, in a book of this sort than
in little memoirs encumbered with little facts. An instantaneous
photograph is false, and contrary to nature in that it fixes something which nature never meant to be fixed.

Friendly greetings,

P. CLAUDEL.

88.—*Paul Claudel to André Gide*

French Consulate, Prague,
14th September 1910.

My dear Friend,

I have just received the typescript of *L'Otage*. Thanks.
As for its publication, I gave you my views in my last letter, three
or four days ago. I still prefer January. I don't in the least want
to get myself talked about—on the contrary. I hope that this will
not anger the *N.R.F.*

I leave to-morrow and shall be at Hostel on the 16th. There a
short motor-tour in Burgundy with the Berthelots. Then a short
stay at my house at Villeneuve. Then a few days in Paris where I
hope to meet you ?

I had heard talk of that recantation of Pascal, which people
have tried to suppress as much as they can. (There is on this
subject, in Brunschvicg, a very amusing conversation between the
Archbishop of Paris and the publisher of the *Pensées*.) I am curious
to read Brémond's article. I should like to think that the great man
had broken with the hideous individuals of Port-Royal, whom
Joseph de Maistre has disposed of so ably. At bottom there's not
an immense amount of Jansenism in the *Pensées*. The capital

heresy which is the kernel of this Apologetic is rather that of "fideism", condemned during the last hundred years with increasing vigour by Gregory XVI, by the Vatican Council, and finally by the admirable "Pascendi" Encyclical. The error of this consists in saying that we can only reach the truth, even where nature is concerned, with the help of faith, and that human nature of itself and without grace, is incapable of knowing what is good. That is contrary to *Genesis* which says that God made man in his own image and saw it was "very good", that is to say, perfectly proportioned to his object. Evil, which according to St. Thomas is a non-essential thing, is well able to sully human nature, but not to destroy it. Pascal mistakes the essential condition of human nature for its defects ; for instance, he describes as *divertissement* the power to fix one's attention on objects in succession. "All evils come from not being able to stay quietly in one room." Well, of course—or rather from the fact of being alive and not dead. The sanctity of the hermit derives not from his cell, but from the will of God. Man, of himself and by his reason alone, is perfectly capable of reaching the loftiest forms of knowledge : God, the immortality of the soul, etc. (Vatican Council). He is even capable of natural virtue. But it's all finite—he can only of himself deserve the finite, never the *infinite*. For this also to be accorded him, there must be some purely gratuitous action. A roadmender can earn two francs a day by breaking stones, but he can't earn for himself the throne of France, or eternal life. These are, after all, quite simple truths.

I grasp your hand with great affection,

P. Claudel.

––––––

89.—*Paul Claudel to André Gide*

Prague, 16th September 1910.

My dear Friend,

I received your telegram, but I didn't see any need to telegraph back, since my letter has already brought you my answer. It is materially impossible for the proofs to be ready by 1st October. I have only just got, and reread, the typescript. The play is decidedly too—and too markedly—royalist, feudal, and reactionary.

No government official could sign it. I should lay myself open to denunciation and I could always be confronted with the Order which forbids all officials of the Ministry to publish anything without authorization. I should therefore like to sign it simply " Paul C. ", which would make my identity plain to all and yet cover me against attack. That may affect the amount of money which the *N.R.F.* can give me, but, of course, that is a secondary consideration.

I have a lot of small corrections to make—one of them rather delicate ; and then the heraldic problem is still unsettled.

I thought of leaving yesterday morning, but then it didn't work out as I'd hoped. When can I go ? One can't tell—given the amiable indecisiveness of the Slav countries.

I grasp your hand with great affection. Don't bear me any grudge.

PAUL CLAUDEL.

90.—Paul Claudel to André Gide

Villeneuve-sur-Fère (Aisne),
20th October 1910.

My dear Friend,

I am sending by bag the typescript of *L'Otage*, most carefully corrected. It only remains to modify the device of the Coûfontaines (if need be, it could stay as it is). As soon as you consent to the signature " Paul C. " you can print it as soon as you like. Thank you for your kindness.

I am here till the 5th and thereforward at Paris till the 10th at least : 15 avenue du Trocadéro, c/o Dr. Millon.

I grasp your hand with affection. My respects to Madame Gide.

P. CLAUDEL.

91.—Paul Claudel to André Gide

Prague, 12th November 1910.

My dear Friend,

I note what you say about *L'Otage*, but have you set in hand the heraldic indications ?

For the money, send it whenever you like to my bankers, Dossan and Co., 5 rue de Lille, less 20 francs for the Philippe memorial.

The good Chesterton wrote to me through his secretary to say that he was " extremely pleased " by what was said about him in the *N.R.F.* (please tell Mr. Larbaud) and that he found my translation " particularly good ". I thought for a moment of translating the whole book, but the publisher's conditions are too exorbitant.

My compliments on your excellent article relating to Baudelaire ! There are above all a dozen lines that go right to the heart of the matter.

Paris-Journal mentions that in your lecture you say that Philippe escaped the " redoubtable " influence of Claudel's Catholicism. Alas, alas ; how small that influence really is !

I grasp your hand,

P. CLAUDEL.

———

92.—*Paul Claudel to André Gide*

Prague, 18th November 1910.

My dear Friend,

I have your letter of the 15th and am replying at once to your request—as best I can, for you cannot imagine how few contacts I have with the Catholic world and how completely unknown I am in that world. Here, however, are a few names :

René Bazin (the Academician) ;
Mgr Baudrillart (Rector of the Catholic Institute) ;
Théodore de la Rive, Présinge, near Geneva (Switzerland) ;
Élie Baussart, Couillet (Belgium) ;
M. Sainte-Marie-Perrin, 13 rue du Plat, Lyons ;
Émile Baumann, 14 rue Jacques Raveau, Sens (Yonne) ;
Louis Massignon, 91 rue de l'Université, Paris ;
R. P. Dom Besse, Abbaye de Chivetognes, near Namur ;
Ch. Henrion, 45 rue Isabey, Nancy ;
G. Dumesnil, Professor of Philosophy, University of Grenoble.

I am returning you the extract from your fine lecture. I didn't know before that poor Philippe had certain leanings towards Catholicism. I once talked to him and he seemed to me still too immature for certain ideas, full of a naive appetite for life and still encumbered with evolutionist mythology. Poor boy ! It is, even so, a consolation for me to think that I was able to introduce into his heart a particle of faith, no larger than a grain of mustard seed. Death is a marvellous gardener. My friend Massignon, the orientalist, whose conversion has been really miraculous, was telling me that, when he was left for dead at Bagdad and had apparently lost consciousness, he kept on repeating to himself the Arabic word " hak " (which also means " debt ") and that, though at that moment he was completely without faith, he had the impression that there was some formidable debt that he had to pay.

The news of Tolstoy is very moving. Unhappy sower of the wind, who reaped nothing but the whirlwind and dies at the age of eighty on the public highway in a waiting-room ! " He who is not with me is against me."

I grasp your hand with great affection,

P. CLAUDEL.

93.—Paul Claudel to André Gide

Prague, 22nd November 1910.

My dear Friend,

As you realize, I am extremely vexed by the contretemps which prevents the name of *Coûfontaine* from being printed with the correct orthography. For various reasons I attached the greatest importance to it. Do at least put the note you speak of on the first page. For the other acts, could you not adopt for the designation of the characters another type-fount in which the exact orthography would be respected ?

Shall I see the proofs ? I must point out one gross error which I have corrected on the first page.

Thank you for whatever you can do and
Believe me,
Always your devoted,

P. CL.

94.—*Paul Claudel to André Gide*

Prague, 22nd December 1910.

My dear Friend,

Your letter, and one that I received a few days ago from my relation René Bazin, are of the sort that made it quite excusable for me to get something of a swollen head. I own that I was very pleased myself on reading my second Act, which comes off very well in print. *L'Otage*, for me, is a victory from two points of view : for the first time I've managed to hold in check the over-riding lyricism which is my great enemy : for the first time I've succeeded in creating objective and external characters, which means to say that the faculties of vision are beginning to develop to the same extent as the faculties of expression. But what trouble it takes one to reach that point ! How often have I despaired and been on the point of dropping everything ! And what a job the writer has ! Past experience is no help ; each new work sets new problems, in the face of which one feels as anguished and uncertain as any beginner, with the additional handicap of a certain treacherous facility which one must brutally suppress. . . . Anyway, our motto is that of the sardine firm Amieux (" One better each time "). I am working now on a new version of *La Jeune Fille Violaine* (retaining hardly more than a few lines of the original) which will be, I think, more piercing, more affecting than *L'Otage* ; without any philosophical palavers. After that I've nothing at all in mind, except a very vague plan for a series of plays continuing the story of the fortunes of the Coûfontaines throughout the nineteenth century.

What you say about the *Cinq Odes* distresses me. Yet a writer has enough to do to learn his own trade, and cannot teach their own to the workmen he employs. Perhaps I shall have the first part of the *Corona* printed here ; they have a fount which I like very much.

And now Christmas and sunshine have arrived at the same moment.

I am going to Communion to-morrow. Ah, my dear friend, what enormous joys you renounce—joys beside which all others are nothing ! There is the source of all my inspiration. When I think of the blessings which God has heaped upon me, my eyes fill with tears. No man has been more favoured than I. I thought of that when my wife and I were making the *Crèche* for those three lovely children who are now with us and are so sweet and affectionate. If only I can pass on to others a little of the joy with which I am overflowing.

Adieu, my dear friend. I grasp your hand with affection. Remember us kindly to Madame Gide and give her my respectful regards.

P. CLAUDEL.

———

95.—*Paul Claudel to André Gide*

Prague, 26th December 1910.

My dear Friend,

My sister-in-law, Elisabeth Sainte-Marie-Perrin, tells me that she has sent to the *N.R.F.*, for which she has the greatest respect, a little essay called *Les Beaux Cœurs*. I think she would be very flattered if you were to put it in. She isn't without talent, though she's a little too much influenced by the American essayists. Perhaps you've already seen her signature in the *Revue des Deux Mondes*, *Correspondant*, and in *Débats*. She is the daughter of René Bazin, and through her your Review might penetrate quite an influential world—and one which might be useful to you if—as I hope you soon will—you ever put up as a candidate for the Academy !

Would it be too much to ask you to send the numbers in which *L'Otage* appears to my dear Élémir Bourges (51 rue de Ranelagh) and to Barrès, if he doesn't already get it from the *N.R.F.*

Being out of sorts these last few days, I amused myself by translating some little poems of Coventry Patmore. If they interest you, you can have them (for nothing, of course !). In order not to seem to intrude myself too much in your Review, I have signed them with pseudonymous initials.

I am sickened by the fuss which is being made about that perfectly insipid book of Mademoiselle Audoux, whereas our dear and great Philippe never became known in his lifetime. It is just a year since I received the news of his death. I was going to pick on you about Chateaubriand ! But I know that one is only fair to the people one loves.

I grasp your hand,

P. C.

96.—*André Gide to Paul Claudel*

7th January 1911.

Dear Friend,

You cannot imagine the pleasure I got from your last letter but one ! [1] I don't remember ever having such intense happiness from your letters—except once when you wrote to me of your " passionate love of souls ". Admirable as are the great *Odes*, they could have made me fear that thenceforward you would trust to your own momentum and be content to free-wheel. That is why the character of Turelure, and the phrase in your letter about " the over-riding lyricism which is my great enemy ", have made my friendly heart leap up with new hope. It is good to have worthy enemies.

Yes, I duly received, with a very amiable letter from Madame E. S. M. P., an essay which was very prettily written, and showed great purity of emotion, but which seemed to us to be so very much better in intention than in execution that we did not think it would fit very well into our Review.

I should be very interested to read your translations of Coventry Patmore, and you would give me great pleasure if you sent them. I've no idea what they may be like, but it would very much surprise me if the *N.R.F.* was not delighted to welcome them.

Barrès and Bourges have been sent the Review from the beginning —whom would we send it to, after all, if not to them ?

What am I to say about the end of your letter ? It touches all that is deepest in me ; but I can remember enough of the burning piety of my adolescence to understand the felicity which you describe to me to-day. . . .

Au revoir, dear friend ; I take leave of you with an unfinished phrase. Here are my wife's best remembrances ; accept with them my respects to Madame Claudel and believe me,

Yours in friendship,

ANDRÉ GIDE.

[1] Paul Claudel's letter of 22nd December 1910.

97.—*Paul Claudel to André Gide*

French Consulate, Prague,
31st January 1911.

Dear Friend,

Yes, of course—print the C. P. when you like, and with a note by Valery Larbaud, if you think fit. Nor have I any objection to my initials.

Thanks for the 500 francs. I will let my banker know.

As for *L'Otage*, in principle I am ready to talk it over with your publishing house. But I'd like to reserve the right to reprint it later (after an interval which we could decide upon) with the rest of my plays.

Thank you for Chateaubriand ! I shall repay you in kind if ever Stendhal falls into my hands—like the barons of the Middle Ages who exchanged their prisoners !

Have you read a book which the Germans are making so much of—written in the eighteenth century and just re-issued : *Der arme Man von Tokenburg* ?

I grasp your hand with affection,

P. CLAUDEL.

98.—*Paul Claudel to André Gide*

French Consulate, Prague,
18th February [1911].

My dear Friend,

I am sending you (please let me have it back) a letter I have just received from the firm of Plon-Nourrit. Of course, you have my word, and your firm shall have first refusal ; but I should be glad if you could give me a few details about the exact date of publication.

Barrès writes that he is about to publish a long essay about me.

I am working with great excitement on my new play, *L'Annonce faite à Marie*, and am completely possessed by it. There won't be much left of the poor *Jeune Fille Violaine*. Even the fourth act, which I wanted to leave more or less intact, will no doubt be

demolished.   The whole thing should be ready in four or five
months' time.

My respects to Madame Gide.

I grasp your hand with affection,

P. CLAUDEL.

I am hearing Wagner's *Ring* for the first time.   What superhuman
genius—in the midst of so many errors and so great a chaos !

———

99.—*André Gide to Paul Claudel*

22nd February 1911.
My dear Friend,

You would have had some time ago a letter from Jean
Schlumberger if he had not been suddenly recalled to the South of
France on account of the illness of one of his children—but now
he is back again and all ready to discuss with you the publication
of *L'Otage*, which will appear, if you are agreeable, as soon as
possible.   As, with the *N.R.F.*, we are Verbeke's main clients, we
have no doubt of the diligence, the zeal, and the care which he
will bring to the printing of any book with which we entrust him.
As regards the quality of his work, I don't think we could do better,
and I know (for example) my opinion is shared by Jammes and
Suarès, who gave him their last books, thereby breaking with the
traditions of the *Grande Revue* and the *Mercure*.

In the collection which we hope to inaugurate with your *Otage*,
a book of Philippe's, and my *Isabelle*, we don't intend to have either
a uniform price or a uniform format.   I want *Isabelle* to have the
same appearance as my *Porte étroite* (a small blue edition) ; but
as this old-fashioned format is no longer in regular commercial
use, we have to order the paper specially (from Perrigot-Mazure,
I think.   I find it shameful to go abroad for one's paper and abandon
those admirable *vergés d'Arches* which Chapon also regards as
superior to the *Hollandes*).   I find that the sheet which served for
the octavo of my little volume makes up with a very beautiful
quarto format—preferable even, I think, to the format of *Partage
de Midi*.   Take a look at this specimen sheet (as it's rather flimsy
for the printer I shall order it thicker—another kilo for every ream).
I shall order a greater or smaller quantity according to whether or
not you would like it for *L'Otage*.   The cost price would compel us

to ask 6 frs. for your book, but as we should be sorry if some of your readers were discouraged by a rather high price, we should be quite ready, if you have no objection, to sell it at 3.50 frs. on more ordinary paper as soon as the first impression had been taken up ; I shall do the same for *Isabelle*.

Don't you think that the lay-out already adopted by the *N.R.F.* would be well suited to the quarto format—bearing in mind the felicitous change of appearance which will follow the suppression of the running title ? But of course we shall carry out all the indications and modifications which you may like to send us ; I suggest this simply as a basis for discussion—and in order to save time. The question of the capital U for Coûfontaine is going to come up again. You must decide specially if there is a case for having the letter manufactured—it doesn't exist, as we told you, in stock.

A few words more, not especially about *L'Otage*, but more generally about our projects. While we are anxious to profit by Rivière's youth, enterprise, and well-developed business organization, we don't want to leave our budding collection entirely in his hands, for fear that he should make of it just what we want to avoid—a commercial undertaking. We mean to retain complete control—just as we have retained complete control of the *N.R.F.*— so that we never publish anything unworthy of it ; and for this reason we have declined his offer to take over all the expenses. After the deduction of :

1. The percentage given to Rivière and to the booksellers—who must be persuaded (we must study how) to take a real interest in us.

2. The percentage given to the author, which (precisely because we don't want to make a huge profit ourselves) we can promise will be at least as large as that offered by any commercial publisher. (If you like we can take as a standard of judgment the percentage which Vallette offers you, or Plon would offer.) The profits, if there are any, after we've paid off our overheads and the *faux frais* and balanced our losses, would be put into a reserve account, which would allow us later on to publish some fine book which would have only an uncertain commercial appeal—the second part of Bourges' *La Nef*, for instance.

This publishing venture is to remain, financially speaking, quite independent of the *N.R.F.* (I mean that it wouldn't contribute towards the expenses of the Review), so perhaps we could invite one or two people (I have in mind Arthur Fontaine, Valery

Larbaud, Philippe Berthelot, for instance) to help and advise us. But we don't need to wait for all this to be settled, because we are quite ready to bear, if necessary, all the cost of the enterprise.

What else can I tell you ? That I should instantly advise you to accept Plon's offer if I thought it genuinely advantageous for you ; but I can't persuade myself that it is. . . .

On his side, Fasquelle is tempted by my *Isabelle* ; but I hold fast to our project, in the conviction that we can at last put into force (in respect both of the texts themselves and of their typographical presentation) some of the reforms which you, as much as I myself, have at heart. Naturally, I cannot found this collection all by myself ; I am only embarking on the adventure because you are with us ; since we are beginning with your *Otage* and the two other books I mentioned, I have *every confidence* in the enterprise ; and I even hope for an extraordinary return to health in Literature (and in typography). The results obtained by the *N.R.F.* are most encouraging.

And then Marcel Rivière is anxious to try the honourable system of advertisement which is so widespread in Germany and which, in your letter about (and against) French printing, you wanted to introduce here—the despatch, in an envelope, of a prospectus with a specimen page of the book in question, so that the reader can see at once the quality of the text, the paper, the print, and so on. . . . The Philippe Barrès, in company with whom I dined the other evening, had already told me of Maurice Barrès' project, which absolutely delighted me. Had I told you that he wrote to me about my article on Baudelaire ? He was just recently very good to Jean Schlumberger and has more than once shown his sympathy for us all. I very much hope that one day he will contribute to the *N.R.F.* and I am happy to think that the fact of being in your company would do much to attract him. If my letter were not already so long I should write about quite different matters—Jacques Rivière, Saint-Léger—and even of the *Ring*, but I have written enough for to-day.

Forgive this hideous writing ; I don't want to keep you waiting and I write in a great hurry. As soon as we receive your precise instructions about format, lay-out, and number of copies, we shall tell Verbeke to begin setting the type, and we shall order the paper.

All friendly greetings,

ANDRÉ GIDE.

100.—*Paul Claudel to André Gide*

Prague, 25th February 1911.

My dear Friend,

I am replying to the different points which you touch on in your letter about the publication of *L'Otage*.

1. The type-face of the *N.R.F.* printer suits me perfectly. Nor have I any amendment to suggest for the lay-out of the page—except for certain details in the list of characters, etc. So we shall have a little volume of 150 to 200 pages.

2. The same with the format—we can keep to the standard *N.R.F.* model.

3. I don't insist on a first edition at 6 frs. The play, unlike the *Odes*, doesn't need to be shown off or introduced with trumpets, so I don't see why it shouldn't come out straightaway at 3.50 frs.

4. As for the paper, I don't want anything extraordinary—simply something very white and very strong. The *N.R.F.* paper is perfect for a review but too light for a book. Besides, I like the paper to have some fibre in it.

5. In my last contract the *Mercure* gave me 40 centimes for each copy sold (a book of about 350 pages). We can stick to this arrangement for *L'Otage*.

6. We ought to decide for how long *L'Otage* will be at your disposition, and also to stipulate that subsequently I have the right to publish it elsewhere in my *Collected Plays*.

7. I suggest you print at once an edition of 1500 copies.

8. I insist absolutely on a capital U with a circumflex accent. If there isn't one, you must have it made—at my expense if necessary.

If you are agreeable, and no further points need to be settled, you can send me as soon as possible the contract for signature, and we can get on at once.

Please compliment M. Schlumberger on the *Epigrammes Romaines* which he kindly sent me. They are very fine. My wife and I are waiting impatiently for the rest of *Isabelle*.

Please give my respects to Madame Gide.

I grasp your hand with affection,

P. CLAUDEL.

101.—*André Gide to Paul Claudel*

[February 1911.]

My dear Friend,

I left Bruges at noon on Wednesday, after spending the morning in re-reading your proofs. I was considerably moved when, at 11 o'clock, I gave them over once and for all to the printer. The big capitals make a much better impression ; we had to have the U's made specially, but by telegraphing to the foundry in London we got them in the morning of the following day and the work was not held up for a moment. I hope it won't be held up by any doubts about the exact number of copies to be printed. Verbeke will already have had your telegram in reply to my letter ; and in any case if you insist on an alteration the delay would only, I hope, be a matter of three or four days. It was agreed with Verbeke that they would print all the rest of the book, leaving only the title-page to be altered if you wish (with or without inset) even at the last moment.

When I re-read it yet again, your *Otage* seemed to me greater than ever. Couldn't you get someone like Barrès or Junius to speak of it in the *Echo* ? Surely you could easily do it.

How I want you to be satisfied with this edition of *L'Otage* ! From every point of view. Au revoir. My respects and our affectionate remembrances to Madame Claudel.

Yours,

ANDRÉ GIDE.

102.—*Paul Claudel to André Gide*

French Consulate, Prague,
27th February 1911.

My dear Gide,

About the printing of *L'Otage* in book form, could you please, for the time being, consider our negotiations as suspended ? The news from Paris makes me fear that my personal enemy Berteaux will come to power, and in that case I shall have to look out for myself.

I grasp your hand,

P. CLAUDEL.

I shall consult with Berthelot and write to you again.

103.—*Paul Claudel to André Gide*

Prague, 4th March 1911.
My dear Friend,

I should be most grateful if you could have them send me a copy of the numbers of the *N.R.F.* which contains Acts II and III of *L'Otage*. The people to whom I asked you to send the Review —among others René Bazin—have not received those issues, so that I am now sending them myself. Perhaps it would be a good idea if you spoke to the people whose job it is to despatch the Review regularly and to the right addresses. Several subscribers in Prague have complained to me of its irregular arrival.

I grasp your hand,

P. CLAUDEL.

Are you sure that Barrès gets the Review ? I very much want him to read *L'Otage* and I wonder if I shouldn't myself send him the three numbers which contain it.

104.—*Paul Claudel to André Gide*

French Consulate, Prague,
6th March 1911.
Dear Friend,

We can go ahead. My friend Berthelot's answer disposes of all my anxieties.

Do you know where I could find a good translation of Calderon or Lope de Vega (the latter especially) ? I've recently read extracts from them which interested me. I think I should find in them some interesting pointers for the art which at the moment most interests me—that of dialogue.

What J. Schlumberger says about translations is quite right. Nothing is more difficult or less appreciated than a good translation. It was in that school that all our great writers of the past perfected themselves. Do you know the admirable preamble to Tacitus' *Histories*, translated by d'Ablancourt ? The other day I thought of copying it out for you. Besides, it's a very topical passage, in view of the reign of Combes which is about to begin.

All the last part of *Isabelle* is very moving. It's a typical story of the fall of a great house. I watched a drama of the same sort not far from my own home. And what a beautiful violin that is, on which you play !

I grasp your hand,

P. CLAUDEL.

———

105.—*André Gide to Paul Claudel*

9th March 1911.

Dear Friend,

Why yes, of course, you must send us that passage of d'Ablancourt—if it's not a nuisance for you to copy it out. I don't know it, but I think, from what you say, that it would fit in very well either in our section " Texts of the Month " or in the section " Translations ", which we mean to continue. If you send it at once it could, I think, go into the April number, and that would be ideal.

I am delighted to see that Calderon and Lope de Vega attract you. Some years ago I read a great many of their plays (Calderon's especially). The most extensive (I don't say the best) translation was published by Charpentier, in an *ignoble* format which will fill you once again with justified indignation (three volumes of each author, if I'm not mistaken). But there appeared recently a translation of some religious plays of Calderon—much more carefully done and much better presented. I shan't give you the title because I want to reserve for myself the pleasure of giving you the book. I should be very surprised if disappointed.

Very glad to see your anxieties disappear ; I am letting Jean Schlumberger know at once. The U's have been ordered, and so has the paper. Need I tell you with what real happiness the *N.R.F* would welcome *L'Annonce faite à Marie* on the same terms as *L'Otage* ? (Of course, I'm speaking of publication in the Review ; we can speak of the book publication later.) In the autumn we're going to begin a collection of *good* translations—all our dispositions are ready for it. Our section of " Translations " in the Review is meant to lead up to it. When I think of all that I seem to be twenty again—and to have grown wings !

Yours,

ANDRÉ GIDE.

106.—*Paul Claudel to André Gide*

French Consulate, Prague,
17th March 1911.

Dear Friend,

Here is the transcript of d'Ablancourt. I enjoyed copying
out such magnificent French. You will see how mercifully free
from accents they were then.

Nouveaux Prétextes arrived yesterday and I went through all the
first part of the book, which was new to me. It is very interesting
for those who want to appreciate the working of your mind. I shall
speak of it again later on. Of course, I have good reasons for
believing in the existence of a Christian drama. The heart of a
Christian is one long school of tragedy. And do you remember
that profound passage in which Mallarmé speaks of " the Passion ",
and says he would like to substitute it for " the Passions " ?

Do you care for Sainte-Beuve ? I recently took a volume of his
with me on a little journey to Vienna. What a style !

Although there is a crisis in the French language, even Faguet
writes better than that to-day. Most of his little articles are
collections of quotations and offer no interest at all. *Madame
d'Épinay*, *Voltaire à Cirey*, Arvède Barine or Wyzewa or anybody else
could do as much.

Sorel has asked me to write for his *Indépendance*. I was astonished
by his letter—who is he ? I thought he was a revolutionary
anarchist.

I grasp your hand with great affection,

P. CLAUDEL.

107.—*Paul Claudel to André Gide*

Prague, 27th March 1911.

My dear Friend,

You are very kind about the Calderon. But I am really not
at all a bibliophile and I rarely re-read a book. So when I have
read the one which you are so kindly sending me, I need not
deprive you of it any longer, and I will send it back to you.

The Guêpes had asked me to contribute to their *Hommage à
Boileau*, an author whom I like above all because of my hatred for

the Romantics.   But as the number which contains my letter contains also some disgusting jibes at Jammes, I wrote to them and said that, as I shared Jammes' convictions, I should like to share his enemies too.   The schoolmasterly tone of these little youngsters infuriates me.

Do what you like about *L'Otage*, but let me know roughly when you think it is likely to appear.

As for d'Ablancourt's translation I don't really see the point of saying that it was I who sent it to you.   I don't want to clutter up your Review with my initials.

Do you know a young orientalist called Louis Massignon ?   He is a most remarkable fellow and I have been in correspondence with him for several years.   He says he has met you.

I grasp your hand in friendship.

My regards to Madame Gide.

P. CLAUDEL.

108.—*André Gide to Paul Claudel*

1st April 1911.

My dear Friend,

Here's the specimen lay-out—not quite the same as the Review, you will notice, but we ourselves prefer it, in view of the format.   We estimate that the book may be ready in the second week of May—or sooner, perhaps.

I know that the *Mercure*, on its side, means to republish successively all the branches of *L'Arbre*, and will shortly give us *Tête d'Or*, once again.

Do you think we should aim to publish before, at the same time as, or after ?   We'd try to carry out your wishes.

I think that it would be better to publish *after*—perhaps three weeks later.

We should aim to publish almost simultaneously *L'Otage*, *Isabelle*, and Philippe's *Lettres de Jeunesse*, spacing them with a week's interval between each in order to secure the attention of all the booksellers who subscribe to our books.   I thought of putting *Isabelle* first, in order to prepare the ground and generally " warm the house " ; what you said about this little book gave me pleasure, but I admit that I'm almost ashamed to bring it before the public in the company of your formidable *Otage*.

I applaud what you wrote to those young *Guêpes*. Those young people have got to realize, after all, that one can detest their insolence without being a socialist or a revolutionary or an anti-patriot, etc. Your letter on Boileau is excellent too.

Did I tell you that the disharmony between Jammes and myself no longer exists ? I am very very happy about it.

Au revoir. Yours in friendship,

ANDRÉ GIDE.

———

109.—*Paul Claudel to André Gide*

Prague, 3rd April 1911.

My dear Friend,

First let me congratulate you on your reconciliation with Jammes. I am deeply happy to hear it.

I have only one objection to make to the specimen lay-out for *L'Otage* which you sent me. I should like you to cut out the running title, which is all the more conspicuous as the page is rather short. That continual repetition of one word really makes no sense.

The second week in May seems to me a very good moment for publication. The publication dates of the *Mercure* are of no import-ance—and anyway I couldn't possibly say what they are. Vallette just told me that he would send page-proofs of *Tête d'Or* this week, and *La Ville*, of which I am just correcting the first proofs, will soon follow. I had them reprint the first versions without reading them, and the proof-correcting sent me into a cold sweat. God, how stupid one can be at twenty ! How could I have written such extravagances without a shudder ?

A last word about business—could you tell me if our contract is ready ? Think over what you want in respect of the number of copies and the length of time during which you will retain exclusive rights in the play.

I am going to send Sorel some pages he wanted for his magazine, *La Justice* (inspired by Proudhon's book).

I grasp your hand with great affection. My respects to Madame Gide.

P. CLAUDEL.

110.—*André Gide to Paul Claudel*

[Spring 1911]
[The beginning and end of this letter are lost.]

After going thoroughly into the question, we've decided to establish ourselves as a Company—in a way which seems to me solid and satisfactory—with Gaston Gallimard (the son of the collector and bibliophile), who is absolutely devoted to us, as manager.

Your extract from d'Ablancourt gave me some awkward moments. I'd thought, from your letter, that, being part of a preface, it was actually concerned with translations and ways of translating, so that the passage would fit very well into our section of " Translations ". Could I give it as a " prose passage " ? On what pretext ? However noble the language, there's nothing in it which would especially justify the choice of this Huguenot ; and certain sectarians would certainly think that we'd put it in for denominational reasons. (That was why I wanted to say that it had been sent to us by P. C.) Could I give it as a specimen of translation ? I admit that I don't admire it to that extent ! Have you compared it with Tacitus' own text ? D'Ablancourt's text seems loose and feeble beside it. The *atrox proeliis, discors seditionibus, ips'etiam pace saevum* becomes " *full* of wars, internal strife and cruelty even in time of peace ". The " *nobilitatus* " *cladibus mutuis Dacus* becomes no more than " The Danube, blood-red with our defeats and our victories ", and so on. So that, in the end, I decided not to make use of it, and filed the page among the pages of my Tacitus—which, thanks to you, I had had occasion to reopen.

———

111.—*Paul Claudel to André Gide*

Prague, 14th May 1911.

My dear Friend,

I don't altogether agree with you about the page from d'Ablancourt. It's of value in itself, and (to my ear at least) it sings with some of the fullest and most perfect music that language

ever gave forth. It also realizes my conception of a good translation
—one that is exact without being servile, and in fact takes note of
an infinite subtlety of values : in a word, it achieves a veritable
transubstantiation. Take, as a very obvious example, the English
word " fly " and the French word " *voler* " ; each expresses a quite
different aspect of flight—the one standing for flight towards a goal,
the other for the wing which hovers in the air. In some cases I
should think it a real mistranslation if the one were rendered by the
other. Let's apply it to the two examples you give from d'Ablancourt. I hold that in the contrary our compatriot has done his job
with most fastidious taste. Of course he could never rival Tacitus
in concision on his own ground. He had to transpose in accordance
with the special genius of the French language, and he did it so
perfectly that I think his version sometimes better than the original.
Atrox proeliis discors seditionibus deserves Pascal's rebuke, " Two
strong words are one too many ". He should have cut away the
support and let the light shine on the essential words—of which one,
" *guerre* " was rough and sonorous, while the other, " *divisions* ",
dragged on like a political manœuvre. The other example is
even better ; " *nobilitatus* " is rather an odious word—he could
have used " decorated " instead. D'Ablancourt rightly preferred
the word " *ensanglante* ", which is as majestic as a river roaring in
flood. Moreover, it gives something of the funereal timbre of
" *cladibus* " ; " *mutuis* " was not quite right and was more appropriate to a civil war. D'Ablancourt rightly amplified the diction,
replacing the dry Dacus with the magnificent Danube, and he
finishes with the blazing oriflamme of " *victoire* ". How fine an
art is translation, and what a pity it is to see it abandoned to-day !
But since we don't seem to feel quite alike on this subject I shall not
send you, as I had intended to, the translation of a passage from
Wells' new book, which seems to me to be full of good sense. Have
you read the *New Machiavelli* ? It's a book full of ideas, or the
appearances of ideas (I don't accept any of them, by the way), and
deserves to be discussed. As a picture of all that is most contemporary in English life it has some excellent things. Wells has far
surpassed the idiotic fantasies of his early days. Already in *Tono-
Bungay* there were very remarkable passages.

As I told you, I give you an absolutely free hand as regards the
format of *L'Otage*. I should only like the book to appear as soon
as possible—for several reasons, some of them quite serious.

I leave for France on about 8th June and shall be at Hostel until 10th July more or less.

My respects to Madame Gide. I grasp your hand with great affection.

P. CLAUDEL.

P.S.—Have you read Pierre Lasserre's article on me ? I confess that it is one of the things that has given me the greatest pleasure and tickled my vanity.

————

112.—*Paul Claudel to André Gide*

Prague, 19th May 1911.

My dear Friend,

I've just received your two letters and the title-page of *L'Otage*. I've nothing to say of the type and its setting—both most pleasing. But I don't much care for the three full stops under my name. Perhaps a simple line like this ——— would look better. I also think that the words A PLAY IN THREE ACTS would look better if they were spaced out more on the page, and especially if they were put on one line :

L'OTAGE

A PLAY IN THREE ACTS

There's no literary reason for going on to a new line after PLAY —and that should always be our guiding criterion, even in material questions. My most serious criticism is of the mixture of types in *EDITIONS DE LA Nouvelle Revue Française. Marcel Rivière ET CIE.* I feel that a title-page should be entirely in capitals. Nor do I like the two commas in 31, *rue Jacob, Paris.* Remember what Mallarmé said about pronunciation.

I've had some amusing letters from friends about Lasserre's article. One would think that I had lost a member of my family. But I can't hope to please everybody and I don't see why Lasserre should hesitate to say openly what he thinks about a book which is public property. It's interesting and instructive for me. I'm not blind, myself, to the defects of what I write, but L., like all schoolmasters, goes wrong when he fails to see that in any conscientious writer defects and virtues form a whole in which it is very difficult to separate. I know that I did what I could ; whether the result is bad or good is no concern of mine. My only complaint against L. is that he wrote in haste, and, anyhow, we are embarrassed by an altogether odious style—almost as bad as that of his master Sainte-Beuve (there's an article to be written in the " style Louis-Philippe ", the style of Renan, Lamartine, etc., which is the worst that ever existed and yet is often so absurdly confused with the " style classique ").

Why, of course, my dear Gide, do print my observations if they have any interest for your readers. I shall only ask you to let me correct the proofs, in case any errors may have slipped in. The extract of Wells can be translated by anybody, but the whole book deserves special attention (it's published by Tauchnitz). So does Chesterton's *What's Wrong with the World*. I grasp your hand and thank you for the trouble you are taking.

P. CLAUDEL.

113.—*Paul Claudel to André Gide*

Paris, 27th May 1911.

My dear Gide,

Forgive me for not having telegraphed. I was away from Prague for several days and the friend (Bourges' sister-in-law) who is designing my " trade mark " is Czech—which means that it's out of the question to count on her in respect of any date. Anyway the little seal is now ready. I'm sending it to-day to Verbeke, with a telegram to give him warning. If it gets there too late, it can't be helped. I am sending with this a list of the persons and journals to whom I should like *L'Otage* to be sent. Of course I know that the vignette in question serves no purpose, and it would be quite out of place for me to imagine that it could serve any purpose. It's just, for me, a sort of *sigle* which marks the date of publication and the circumstances in which I was at that moment. It could appear next the *justification du tirage* ; or next the printer's name and date.

I am also sending for your amusement a monogram which Mlle B. designed for me—the *N.R.F.* in the Wheel of St. Catherine. With the red band and the black lettering it would look rather pretty, I think.

Of the two pieces which Valery Larbaud told you about, the one doesn't seem to me very striking ; the other is very remarkable, but too long and blemished by that preciosity which is Coventry Patmore's great failing. That's why I didn't give you the two main pieces from the book, though I had translated them for my private enjoyment.

I grasp your hand in grateful affection,

PAUL CLAUDEL.

114.—*Paul Claudel to André Gide*

Prague, 7th June 1911.

My dear Friend,

Here is my little piece, slightly revised about d'Ablancourt. Call it whatever you like, but I feel that it shouldn't appear in the same issue as my translations from Patmore. I should seem to be crying my own wares too much. Better to keep it till the next number. At Valery Larbaud's request I have decided, not without very serious misgivings, to send him the translation of Patmore's great poem *Eros and Psyche*. I have often been on the verge of asking for it back. I fear that the mingling of sacred and profane love will be misunderstood. People will see in it the equivalent of certain poetico-feminine effusions which I detest, and yet it's the exact opposite ; the one drags the spirit down to the level of the flesh, and the other merely uses the flesh as an image and half-ironical symbol of a reality whose great strength lies quite elsewhere.

I grasp your hand with great affection,

P. CLAUDEL.

I leave for France on Friday and shall no doubt be in Paris between the 15th and the 24th. Don't spread it about too much. I shouldn't care to see it announced in *The Paris-Journal*.

My address : Château d'Hostel, par Virieu-le-Grand, Ain.

115.—*André Gide to Paul Claudel*

Cuverville, 16th June 1911.

Dear Friend,

I am so very sorry that I had to leave Paris without seeing you again. I stayed on as long as I could, hoping until the last moment for news of your arrival ; but certain duties, too long neglected, recalled me to Cuverville ; as soon as I was sure that *L'Otage* and *La Mère et L'Enfant* had been properly distributed, I left. Yes, we thought it wise to send out a rather large number of Review copies of these books to papers both in France and abroad. Could you not easily secure an article by Junius in *L'Écho*, and perhaps an article in the *Correspondant*?

I haven't yet re-opened the book. I'm terrified of finding some misprints. A friend has already pointed one out to me (a plural without its " s "). I'm telling you at once in the hope that you'll resent it less—if you don't have to discover it for yourself! I'm impatient to see your Patmore translation in the *N.R.F.*, but Larbaud has not yet quite finished his introduction. And as you say it would have been a mistake for that translation to appear in the same number as your remarks on d'Ablancourt, of which you will soon receive the proofs.

Have you no news of the new *Violaine* on which you said you were at work ?

In three weeks I expect to go to London to rejoin Valery Larbaud and put a new gloss upon my English.

Au revoir. Perhaps you will see Rivière in your way through. I envy him a little, but rejoice to think of his great pleasure at your visit.

Yours as ever,

ANDRÉ GIDE.

116.—*Paul Claudel to André Gide*

Hostel, par Virieu-le-Grand (Ain),
18th June 1911.

My dear Friend,

I leave to-morrow for Paris and shall be there till the 27th. Shall I have any opportunity of seeing you ? Address : c/o Madame de Massary, 37 Quai d'Anjou.

I shall bring with me the manuscript of *L'Annonce faite à Marie*. If you still have the same intentions, I am ready to give this play to the *N.R.F.* for publication next winter. It is much longer than *L'Otage* and would take up at least four issues, even if printed in smaller type.

My respects to Madame Gide.

I grasp your hand with great affection,

P. CLAUDEL.

———

117.—*André Gide to Paul Claudel*

Cuverville, 20th June [1911].

My dear Friend,

Our letters crossed. Deeply embroiled as I am, I shall try to come to Paris before you leave, for I am very anxious indeed to see you again, but I can't promise.

Yes, my intentions for *L'Annonce faite à Marie* are as faithful as my affection and admiration for you—and I am happy to learn that the *N.R.F.* can count on the new play (on the same conditions —as I told you, didn't I ?—as *L'Otage*). I am impatient to read it. May I have it typed out, like *L'Otage*, and would you let me keep the manuscript ? Speaking of typing, I know through Rivière that Frizeau would very much like a typescript of *L'Otage* (though I don't really see what importance he can attach to this anonymous relic) ; I should have liked to satisfy his wish, but I can't put my hand on any of the three (or four ?) copies that I had made, and which I probably threw away when the proofs of the magazine had rendered them superfluous ; but haven't you got a copy ? I seem to remember sending you one. If you don't want it (and I imagine you don't) couldn't you send it to him ? Anyway, it's possible that I shall one day turn them up at the bottom of a drawer, because I don't at all remember having thrown them away. . . . Yet I had a thorough search, before leaving Paris.

Yours ever,

ANDRÉ GIDE.

My wife sends her remembrances to Madame de Massary. Please offer her my respects.

118.—*Paul Claudel to André Gide*

37 Quai d'Anjou, Paris,
21st June 1911.

Dear Friend,

I am in Paris since yesterday and shall be at Villeneuve till Saturday ; then I shall come back, and no doubt be in Paris till Tuesday. Then I leave again for Hostel.

I am returning you the proofs of d'Ablancourt. I glanced at the text of Tacitus, which seemed to me to need very careful collation. I haven't the *History* at hand.

I was asked to sit on the Committee for the Rimbaud monument. I refused. I'm sorry enough that I played a part, however small, in the erection of that imbecility which has just been dedicated to the memory of Verlaine. I don't want to be an accomplice to a further profanation of the writer whom I hold in the highest regard, and whom I consider as a spiritual ancestor. I'm told that you have given your assent, but I imagine that you did it without enthusiasm and that you don't like monuments any better than I do.

I have in my suitcase the manuscript of *L'Annonce faite à Marie*, a fairly substantial bundle of 144 pages. I shall give it to you personally if, as I hope, I have the great pleasure of seeing you again in Paris. Otherwise I shall give it to Jacques Rivière to whom I am writing to-day.

I have had a very fine and very intelligent letter from Sorel about *L'Otage*. He understands just what I meant to do, not of set purpose but instinctively, in this book, which is not a historical but a symbolical, or rather synthetic drama.

My programme for next year is completely blank. That hasn't happened to me for ten years. Of course, I have some ideas, but nothing that really imposes itself. Only one idea tempts me—that of composing a series, or a canvas, of sermons.

I grasp your hand with great affection. My respectful regards to Madame Gide.

P. CLAUDEL.

I am lunching on Saturday at 12 at the Berthelots'. Bourges will be there. I think that if by chance you are in Paris on that day they would be delighted to see you. Forgive my handwriting, I am using one of those ghastly French steel nibs !

119.—*Paul Claudel to André Gide*

Hostel, 11th July [1911].

Dear Friend,

Alas, this is my last day in France. I leave this evening for the Jura, where I shall see René Bazin, and then to Geneva and on to Prague. Thank you for the little edition of *Isabelle*. The book is simply exquisite—perfect from every point of view. I shall read it during the long days of exile which are in store for me. But I have already read your article on Philippe. It is a curious and interesting idea to examine a writer in forms of the influences and reactions which have moulded him. " A spirit *rich in appetite* and impatient for joy." There is a deep-going definitive phrase ! It's why I, unlike you, should incline to see *Croquignole* as his best book, although I don't care for the end of it.

Remember that I consider your promise as definite and that I shall expect you at Prague between 20th July and 15th September.

I grasp your hand with affection.

My respects to Madame Gide.

P. CLAUDEL.

I gave the manuscript of *L'Annonce faite à Marie* to Jacques Rivière who was going to have it typed. Did he speak to you about it ?

———

120.—*André Gide to Paul Claudel*

Cuverville, 14th August 1911.

My dear Friend,

You will find in the back of this a letter from Blei. I don't want to answer it without first having your intentions. If you don't mind letting him translate *L'Otage* we could settle how much we should ask him for (200 or 300 marks I suppose), which will be shared, as usual—50 per cent. for you and 50 per cent. for the *N.R.F.*

Jean Schlumberger must have written to you recently about the books which you spoke of letting us have, and also to tell you that we have at last received V. Larbaud's essay on Coventry Patmore. It should begin to appear (it is enormous and highly interesting) in our September number with a first selection from your translations —which we have read aloud here and find *quite admirable.* *Eros and Psyche* would only appear in October, with the second part of the essay, which is well fitted to show it in the right light.

I received yesterday your *Chemin de la Croix*, for which I thank you very much.

Au revoir. You will tell me, won't you, if Prague is kindly in November ?

Yours ever,

• ANDRÉ GIDE.

121.—Paul Claudel to André Gide

Prague, 18th August 1911.

My dear Friend,

Settle with Blei as you will. From what I hear I am not overjoyed to have him as my translator, and the mere fact that he doesn't respect the arrangement of my lines proves that the criticisms I have heard are not unjustified. Obviously we can't ask him for very much, but I don't want to give him the *Otage* as I gave *Partage de Midi*—for nothing. I have another translator, who pays the *Mercure.*

Dark and dirty November is not a good month in which to visit Prague. I should rather advise January, which is always clear-skied and sunny. Perhaps we could take the opportunity to make a trip up into the mountains and the snow.

I am delighted to read Valery Larbaud on Coventry Patmore, about whom I know nothing. Is he still alive in England ? I'd like to write to him.

I grasp your hand affectionately.

My respects to Madame Gide.

P. CLAUDEL.

I shall be in France from 15th September to 15th October.

122.—*Paul Claudel to André Gide*

Villeneuve-sur-Fère (Aisne),
22nd September 1911.

My dear Friend,

Could you insert in the next issue of the *N.R.F.* a small
erratum about my Patmore translation ? I let pass, in the last
phrase of *Vesica Piscis*, " *On* ne parle que de. . . ." It was *Ou*,
with a *u*, that I wanted. As I never know if these translations may
not be reprinted elsewhere, it's important to have it put right.

You would do me a kindness if you thanked Jacques Copeau
from me for having bravely defended me against Reboux. I should
have done it myself directly if I knew your contributor's address,
and sooner if I had not been constantly on the move for several
weeks. I learnt about it from a sheaf of press cuttings which came
on from Prague.

Things are going as usual for me—silence, and then savage attacks.

The initial " I " in my translation has caused more talk than the
appearance of *L'Arbre*. Yet they need only call to mind the lawyers'
" *I* the undersigned " and the " I who formerly sang " of the
Virgile travesti. What idiots people are !

I grasp your hand with affection,

P. Claudel.

123.—*Paul Claudel to André Gide*

Frankfurt, 7th December 1911.

Dear Friend,

I am going to reply to M. Gallimard who has written to me
about that translation of *L'Otage*.

Insignificant as Davray may be, you know too much about a
writer's feelings to suppose that any criticism, whatever it may be
and from wherever it may come, can be indifferent to him. But
what can I answer ? This Davray seems to have no idea at all of
how very difficult it is to translate a poet like C. P. He thinks it
enough to render one word by another word. I can't make him
understand either French, or poetry, or Coventry Patmore—
presuming that he understands him in English which his letter
makes me doubt. Words mean nothing to him. The word *cime*,
for instance, gives him more of that sense of power and display,

that structural fullness which make it so strong a word in French.
French and English are not weighted in the same way. The one
relies on nouns, the other on verbs. The English *noun* is nearly
always saturated with action and—much more than ours—demands
an adjective to qualify it. How can one explain that to a Davray ?
Fundamentally, it's not myself that this wretched hack is aiming at,
but religion (which he hates) and the *N.R.F.* " *Le noir cimier* " is
merely picturesque, whereas the " *cime* " is eternal and carries
another sense within it. I am very much moved by your news of a
conversion in your family. When shall I hear of your own conversion, dear friend ? I'm much less shy—if ever I was really shy—
of talking about these questions. Religion seems to me such an
enormous, monumental affair, like the works of Nature ! Not to
acknowledge this great truth of Nature can only be a mutilation
and an artificiality. I thought of that the other day when I saw
the cathedral of Mainz—an edifice which is truly impregnated
with the imperial purple, seated foursquare with its vast caissons
on ground that for ever owes allegiance—the Church of the Councils,
the formidable Theotokos ! Pascal, so great a proselyte, has had
in other respects an extremely sinister influence. Ever since the
Pensées people have supposed that religion is an affair of sects and
fanaticism and requires one to stop using one's eyes, to make
oneself ill, to stay in one's small space, and to foreswear several of
the noblest of one's faculties. In point of fact it's something as
vast as the starry vault, where the Ocean itself has room to move,
and one can breathe to the limit of one's lungs. It is, on the
contrary, the unbeliever who lives in a shrivelled and diminished
world (" I believe in God, the creator of all things visible and
invisible ") and who has nothing above him but the smoke-
blackened ceiling of his study.

I grasp your hand,

P. CLAUDEL.

124.—*André Gide to Paul Claudel*

Sunday, 10th December 1911.

My dear Friend,

Just after your letter came I had a visit from Gallimard,
who tells me that the printing of the Coventry Patmore has not yet

begun. Don't you think it would be interesting to add, since there's still time, a *defence* of your translation on the subject? What you say in your letter makes me want to have it. And some reflections on " translating " from English into French? Gallimard was delighted with the idea. If necessary, and if you sent them in time, we could print it all in the Review beforehand ; V. L.'s answer, and the congratulations of Patmore's son, seemed to us too fulsome for publication.

I'm almost afraid to tell you how much I was moved by the other part of your letter. I still feel that I haven't the right to tell you of this until I make up my mind to go with you all the way. But just imagine what it is like to have been surrounded in childhood with admirable and saintly people whom I love, in death as in life, whom I revere, and who *watch over me*, as you were saying. Jammes talks of my heredity ; I let him have his say ; but I can very well tell *you* that the secret of my incapacity to believe does not lie there (my brain is made up of almost as many Catholic as Protestant cells, after all) ; it lies rather in the fidelity which I owe to those people, my relations and my seniors, who lived in such constant, noble, and radiant communion with God, and gave me my noblest images of abnegation.

If I have the happiness of seeing you in Frankfurt (but I can't promise to come, and in fact don't see when I could fit it in) I shall tell you of the conversion of my sister-in-law—who, like my wife's other sister, Mme Marcel Drouin (Michel Arnauld) had married a Catholic—and of the long conversations which I had previously had with her on the subject of Catholicism (which I defended— eloquently, it would seem—in the face of her contempt) and on the subject of Jammes, whom she knows (she used to live at Pau), and yourself.

Paterne Berrichon unluckily let himself be caught in the trap ; after Gourmont's ignoble article on Rimbaud he could easily have left the *Mercure* ; but he went on too long with his complaints to Vallette, and Vallette promised that Gourmont's article should be cut out of the next edition of the *Livre des Masques*, that Gourmont should take back his words (imagine what that cost him !), and finally that Gourmont should champion Rimbaud in the columns of the *Temps*, and in this way he put Berrichon under an obligation to him and got him stuck fast in the honey-pot. I am very sorry indeed that we shan't have Rimbaud, in *our* collection, next to you

(I was so delighted when Berrichon came to us and suggested it)—
and I am sorry too that Gourmont's article should be suppressed.
That ignoble article was what Gourmont *deserved* to write and I
am disgusted that he should now be preparing a hypocritical
recantation.

Au revoir, dear friend. My wife and I send you for the New
Year—for Madame Claudel, for yourself, and for your children—
our most affectionate greetings.

Yours ever,

ANDRÉ GIDE.

125.—*Paul Claudel to André Gide*

Frankfurt, 12th December 1911

Dear Gide,

Your letter and Gallimard's have arrived by the same post.
Despite your kind invitation I don't think I can preface my translation by a declaration of principles—something I've never done for
any of my books. Besides, I should seem to attach too much
importance to this Davray and to the other critics whose bad faith
is apparent to everyone even from the extracts which Davray
himself gives. The low pot-house jokes with which he replies to
V. L.'s courteous letter show pretty well what sort of person he is.
I don't want to involve myself in a discussion which would degenerate
into a tavern brawl, such as is represented by the general tone of
the *Mercure*. And then it's rather absurd to try to prove oneself
right to other people. If my translations from Patmore can appeal
for a moment to the heart and mind of some delicate reader, if I
can see in his eyes that I have been able to make him understand
what a foreign writer is saying in my borrowed voice—then I
need no other justification.

I very greatly enjoyed what you said in the *N.R.F.* about Gautier.
It was time that this bungling mediocrity, this twopenny-halfpenny
" stylist ", was put in his place. I could never stick his coarse
middle-class style, his insipid prolixity, his glibness. The *Voyage
en Italie* includes phrases of this sort—" the locomotive shortened
its stride ". Of all possible forms of bad writing none is more
atrocious than that which consists of saying commonplace things

in a pretentious way. How could Baudelaire, who was so intelligent
and had such exquisite taste, have dedicated the *Fleurs du Mal*—
and in what terms—to that demagogue ?

For several months now I've been in correspondence with
Berrichon on the subject of Rimbaud. I entirely approve his ideas
of letting the *N.R.F.* publish an edition of the *Illuminations : La
Saison en Enfer* ought to be put with it. I am always moved when
Rimbaud's name is mentioned—I've lived with him for so long
and feel myself so bound to him by the most secret of fibres.

I've just received from Mgr Baudrillart, the Rector of the
Catholic University, the beginning-of-term address which he
delivered to his students, and I was very much pleased and surprised
to find that he had taken my *Magnificat* for his text. It's no small
honour for me to know that my verses have resounded in church
from the full height of the principal doctrinal pulpit of France.
Mgr B. speaks kindly of the *N.R.F.*

One of these days we must talk together like those characters in
Dostoevsky who tell each other things so confidential that on the
morrow they no longer dare to look at one another and are seized
by a mortal and mutual hatred. It's a rôle that I'm getting quite
used to. How moved you must have been by that conversion,
by the intervention of Somebody so close to yourself and in such
astonishing circumstances ! But why do you suppose that you
would be unfaithful to those lovely and noble beings who surrounded
you in your childhood if you were to go further along the road
which was pointed out to you ? Religion consists essentially in the
love of God and of one's neighbour ; that closer union with both
one and the other which allows of the Real Presence and of obedi-
ence to a visible Father is entirely compatible with the examples
which you were given in childhood. Every theologian will tell
you that those souls (no matter to what doctrine they belong) who
have always acted according to the best of their lights do veritably
belong to the Church. Consequently they are saved—nor be it
surprising, in view of the principle that all the parts of Creation
are bound by a common solidarity and homogeneity, that they,
as souls, influence the souls of each of us. And not only can they
do good to us, but we in our turn can do good to them. They are
all round us—begging in hunger for the light which we can give
them.

Something which makes a great many people turn away from

the Church is that they see so many noble and lofty spirits who remain outside the Church and yet fulfil all their human duties— whereas, among ourselves, among most religious people, there is something disagreeable which gets in the way, a sort of crust which prevents all human contact. The fact is that we all share a common secret. The love of God (like that other love of which it is simply, and at last, the authentic version) does not address itself to the noblest faculties of the soul, but to that dead centre of our person- alities where body and mind are united. It is a need, rather than a virtue, and as such it is infinitely pitiable and pathetic. It does not destroy our external defects. On the contrary, one might say that it makes them all the more conspicuous by contrast with the extraordinary profession of faith which we have made. But it cuts off these defects at the roots : it ensures that they (like many other pagan things) no longer belong to us. They hang about us like an ill-fitted garment which no longer suits us and is no longer a part of ourselves. The convert is often like a man whom no woman finds attractive, but who has a wife who is blind.

Thank you for your New Year wishes, my dear Gide ! I send the same to you with all my heart, and also to Madame Gide. One more year ! But, as Rimbaud says, " of what importance is an external springtime to us who are concerned with the search for heavenly truth and have nothing in common with those who die at a given season ? " As we grow older, and the day of this world becomes darker and more clouded, so does the mysterious golden light shine ever more and more upon the inward sanctuary of our souls !

I grasp your hand with affection,

P. CLAUDEL.

126.—*André Gide to Paul Claudel*

7th January 1912.

Dear Friend,

How could I leave your letter so long unanswered ? Was I afraid of being led on to answer you in too confidential a tone ? No ; but a thousand anxieties withdrew my attention from you,

and from myself. Now that it's no longer a question of the
magazine or the publishing house, I am waiting for the greatest
possible state of calm in which to write to you. . . . Yet, after
having gone through with Rivière, the first act of *L'Annonce faite
à Marie*, I all but wrote to you even had it been only one word to
tell you again how much I admired it ; the departure of Anne
Vercors is one of the loveliest things I know ; tears came to my
eyes when I read that scene aloud. It must be put on the stage—
and soon ; I am counting on that (with impatience) as a certainty.

Have you seen some of the attacks on the *N.R.F.* ? Certain people
are beginning to be inconvenienced by its success. The attacks
are directed not so much against ourselves as against those who are
known to be our friends, in the hope that we shall take up their
defence. That defence could then be interpreted as a compromising
profession of faith. We shall look like a republican democrat if
we protest against the insults to Philippe ; we're already biting
our fingers for having answered back when Paul Desjardins was
attacked. Copeau, who answered in the *N.R.F.*, is simply a friend
of Fontaine's ; I'm in the same situation, and I don't at all share
Desjardins' ideas ; but it's so advantageous, strategically, to
portray us as the defenders of " lay principles " ! They don't
forgive me for being your friend, and this campaign is also intended
to destroy that friendship. I doubt very much if Sorel would have
attacked Philippe (and in such terms) if he'd known that you were
fond of him. I feel myself full of courage and zeal for the defence
of ideas which are dear to me, but not for the defence of ideas
which are not my own. The atmosphere of the *Union pour L'Action
Morale* is absolutely insupportable to me—quite as much as that of
present-day Protestantism. Outside of Catholicism only isolation
makes sense to me. I am isolated, my dear friend. I'm not at all
proud of it, for friendship is as necessary to me as bread—and
servitude—but what can I do ? For of all those who write
and play at politics, there isn't one whose Catholicism doesn't
manifest itself to me by the iniquity of its effects. (And it's because
you aren't like those others that I have listened to you with such
attention.) They use the crucifix as if it were a bludgeon ; and as
soon as they or their writings are called in question they hide
behind the holy sacrament. To draw near to Christ for me is to
draw away from them.

I should have liked to speak to you of Joseph Conrad, of Saint-

Léger, of Jacques Rivière . . . I haven't time to-day.   But let it
be soon.

All my best wishes to you.

Yours,

ANDRÉ GIDE.

127.—Paul Claudel to André Gide

Frankfurt, 9th January 1912.

Dear Friend,

Your letter has arrived and gives me real comfort.   I am
delighted to see that you don't side with Paul D.   Of course they
couldn't do more harm to the *N.R.F.* than by making you defend
that man, whom we can only consider as an enemy (that is to say,
animated by evil intentions towards us).   I think it would be best
if you remain silent and don't reply to Sorel's loutish and unbecoming attacks, which I deplore.   How can a man of his age
and education adopt such a tone ?

Alas, if you mean to delay your conversion till every Catholic or
soi-disant Catholic behaves like one of the saints, you will wait a
long time.   Even to-day the true visage of the Saviour is everywhere spat on and most hideously deformed.   And you must note,
too, that all these apostles of violence, the men of *L'Action Française*
and the rest, are Catholics only in name.   They don't obey the
commandments.   The true children of God suffer and pray in
silence ; they are more numerous than you think, but you have to
be inside to know them ; outwardly they may seem repellent, as
I know from what I felt myself at the moment of my conversion.
But what can be done ?   Note, too, that we've been persecuted
for over a century and that one can't always master certain defensive
instincts.   People who are hounded down, subject to daily insults
and misunderstood in their sincerest feelings, people who find
themselves constantly in the situation of a son who sees somebody
spit on his mother's face—such people are not always amiable,
although violence may be a culpable wastage of their strength.
Endure patiently, and in silence, the cruel mortification which God
is sending you ; it will put a certain distance between you and the
world, and it will make it easier for you to pray.   And, after all,

you've done quite enough to show your friendship for Paul D.
You've only yourself to think about now.

I am quite delighted with the sample sheet of *L'Annonce* which
Rivière sent me yesterday. The text is more compact than that of
L'Otage, and it's magnificently black and square. I am going to
send it back with a few amendments.

Adieu, dear friend, I grasp your hand in all affection.

P. CLAUDEL.

P.S.—I read in the *Phalange* an excellent article by Valery
Larbaud on Saint-Léger-Léger. Conrad's last novel is remarkable
—a Russian would have done a great deal with such a subject, but
one feels that Conrad wasn't moved for a second. It's just a story
that he writes down industriously, and seasons with the observations
of a true man of letters. I refer to *Under Western Eyes*. Of course
you don't read Bazin, but all the same there are pretty things in
Davidie Birot and a feminine sensibility that could easily pass
unnoticed, for instance : " the child who went on sighing long
after her tears had ceased to flow ". And then that most delicate
form of metaphor in which the material half of the image is set
down, and the rest left in silence. Another neglected writer is
Henri Lavedan whose weekly column in *Illustration* is full of good
things. No doubt you'll laugh at me for all this—to discover
genius in an Academician is a very dangerous symptom. In his
last, Péguy has excellent things to say about that unfortunate
fellow from the École Normale who declared that Lanson was a
genius !

———

128.—*Paul Claudel to André Gide*

Frankfurt, 15th January 1912.

My dear Friend,

I don't understand what you say in your letter about
Péguy. Have you quarrelled with him. What for ? I thought he
wasn't on speaking terms with Variot. It's all too confusing.

What vexes me a little is that you seem to take all these people,
these amateur Christians and recent converts like Sorel, Variot,
Péguy, etc., for the authentic representations of Catholicism. I

don't see how you can call them that ; and in any case a man ceases to be the representative of the Good from the moment he first does evil. If the priests themselves are not free from infirmities, and especially from that spirit of personal hatred which it is so easy to mistake for zealous devotion to good works—what are we to think of the others ? You know that the use of insulting language is severely condemned by our religion and ranked under the heading of " intentional homicide ".

I am not a friend of Desjardins. But neither am I a friend of those who see religion wholly in terms of authority and discipline and whose aim is Christianity with one's lips, if the heart does not move with them. As I once wrote to Ruyters, a Catholic has no allies—he can only have brothers.

All that is vanity and evil. It is not with the motes from one's neighbour's eye that the house of God can be built, but with the beams that one takes out of one's own.

But there is one very consoling truth : that the injustices of which we are the victims are never more than apparent. They act like those serums which disclose unexpected lesions in the working of our economy. *L'Indépendance* misunderstands the part which it should play in the recovery of our nation. But has not the *N.R.F.* ambitions of the same sort where art is concerned ? But it's beyond question that the decadence of Art is due to its separation from what people so stupidly call Morality, and which I call the Life, the Way and the Truth. That is the urgent question of the hour, on which we must absolutely take sides. Where does the *N.R.F.* stand on this question ? What is its doctrine ? Except for your admirable article on Gourmont, which hasn't been followed up, I can't see anything at all. We've absolutely got to save France from this literature of libertinage, scepticism and despair, which is exhausting the country and is itself falling into ruin. It's had its century and that's quite enough.

Whether we like it or not, everything that makes itself heard is accountable and must bear its own responsibility. " What went ye out for to see ? " said Our Lord, " A reed shaken with the wind ? " —something that bends before every breeze that blows, something that bears no fruit and makes no progress ?

I grasp your hand with affection, my dear Gide. Forgive this homily.

P. CLAUDEL.

Gide :   *Journal*

Zurich, Wednesday [January 1912].

I should like never to have known Claudel.   His friendship weighs on my thought, and obligates it, and embarrasses it. . . . I can still not get myself to hurt him, but as my thought affirms itself it gives offence to his.   How can I explain myself to him ?   I should willingly leave the whole field to him, I should give up everything. . . . But I cannot say something different from what I have to say, which cannot be said by anyone else.

———

129.—*Paul Claudel to André Gide*

Frankfurt, 13th February 1912.

My dear Friend,

First of all, let me say how delighted I was to learn that you may be coming to Frankfurt with Madame Gide, at the end of this month.   It is by no means as interesting as Prague, but there are fine things in the museums and outside the city.

The Comtesse de Noailles wrote me a very kind letter to say that she is not well enough, at the moment, to travel.   And what about you, dear friend ?   Would you feel like lecturing to our " Alliance " ?   I think that it could be arranged either this season or later.

I grasp your hand.   My respects to Madame Gide.   Let me know exactly when you are coming.

P. CLAUDEL.

Rivière's essay on you astonishes me—it's so penetrating and so well written.

———

130.—*Paul Claudel to André Gide*

Frankfurt, 20th February 1912.

Dear Friend,

I gave your name to the *Alliance Française* and they want to know if you would consent to give a lecture in Frankfurt some time

in March.   I should be very glad if you can accept.   They generally
pay 300 or 400 francs for a lecture.   Will you let me know if that
is enough ?

I hope to have a favourable reply, and I send, both to you and
to Madame Gide, my best greetings.

P. Claudel.

131.—*Paul Claudel to André Gide*

Frankfurt, 29th February 1912.

My dear Friend,

Returning from a four-days' visit to Paris, I find your
enigmatic letter which perplexes and disquietens me.   It's plain
that you are suffering, and have been suffering for a long time,
and I don't really see what you gain by slipping away any further.
You now know perfectly well where the truth lies.   I think that
your intelligence and your heart are both flooded with light, but
that you are a prisoner ; and your deliverance, far from being an
act of cowardice, is a difficult matter and calls for high courage and
the help of grace.   Perhaps I shall surprise you if I say that, like
all those who are feeling their way towards conversion, you have
long been under the influence of the devil, who is furious at seeing
you escape from his grasp.   Like all those who are nervous and
sensitive in an extreme degree, you are perhaps more open than
are most others to that sinister influence.   This idea came to me in
a lightning-flash after reading *Saül* and *The Immoralist,* and last
night it came back to me.   And I'm not talking wildly.   When one
knows what temptation means—that's to say, *when one has resisted it,*
once or twice only—one knows just where one stands.

In any case, do abandon the idea that anything you could say
or do or write would ever discourage or disconcert or scandalise
me.   The most disordered imaginings do not embarrass me ; they
have so often invaded my own heart !   For the moment you must,
at any cost, set your heart at rest and put an end to the dialogue
with yourself—and no worldly distraction will succeed in doing it.
So the best would be for you to come and see me, and for us to
talk it all over squarely and quietly, for there is nothing that frightens
our common Enemy so much as ordinary good sense.

Forgive me if I am indiscreet, but fundamentally I know you so little, and no one can say that you are easy to know. It's rather by guesswork that I proceed.

I grasp your hand very firmly,

P. CLAUDEL.

All these external circumstances which prevent us from meeting are really very strange. And then, with the Devil, one can go very low, but never very far.

————

132.—*Paul Claudel to André Gide*

Frankfurt, 19th March 1912.

My dear Friend,

Your news about Valery Larbaud fills me with joy. I don't know him personally, but his letters and what I have read of his work have given me a very good opinion of him.

I am happy to see that my last letter has not offended you. I was rather worried by the tone of your letter to me, and by the rumours that the book which you are writing will be " terrible " (?). Be that as it may, you know that I shall not fail you in my friendship, and in the help which I can give you to the limits of my strength. Everything will come in its own time. It's already a great deal that you should know and acknowledge Jesus Christ. But when one loves another person, is it enough to hear his voice, to read what has been written about him, to follow his teaching, or even to look into his heart ? No, all that is not enough. Only one thing can satisfy love : possession ; and it's because the Church has never wavered in its affirmation of the *real presence* that we recognize it as truly divine. The only way to prove anything against the Church is to prove that there is something, in its teaching and its practices, that is contrary to the love of Christ. But the exact opposite is the case—the Church is formed up like the pattern made when a magnetic needle is placed among a heap of iron filings . . . the simultaneous attraction which it exerts upon the souls of all who belong to it. Provided that I can go to communion, what do I care for all the rest ? To incorporate Christ in us is to become incorporated in Christ.   To communicate with Christ is to communicate with every other Christian.   But you feel yourself that one cannot be one of a body of people and yet retain complete liberty to act and believe as one pleases.   Religion is essentially a contract. One must give in order to receive, and if we are to give there must be someone who has a mandate, an external authority to receive our faith.   The proof of this is that, although you believe in Christ, you are anxious and in torment, like a debtor who can't pay up, because you on your side have given nothing.   Justice has not been satisfied.   God has given us the Word, and it is for us to give *our* word in return.

As for the fidelity of the Church to its own teachings, the proudest Protestants are no longer so sure of themselves as they used to be, and they have to make some very strange avowals (look at Harnack). And look at people like Soloviev and Newman, the one a schismatic, the other (while still an Anglican) writing one of the noblest works of Catholic apologetics that I know—*An Essay on the Development of Christian Doctrine.*   Do you know it ?   Anyway, I would debate with you more easily if you would consent to give a formal account of your objections.   I think that this would do you good.

I realize that your struggle is a terrible one and that you have many sacrifices to make.   But I think I know you quite well, and I know that you are magnanimous enough and inventive enough to set off on an entirely new road, Gide !   or rather *the only road* which *really* satisfies our need of open spaces, and leads to something other than marshlands and broken bridges, to horizons which are for ever renewed. . . .   It's quite useless to try to get there across country.

Write to me, won't you ?   I grasp your hand with great affection.

P. CLAUDEL.

133.—*Paul Claudel to André Gide*

Frankfurt, 2nd April 1912.

Dear Friend,

Your letter arrived here on Palm Sunday, just when we have finished the first of those terrible accounts of the Passion, and

moved me deeply.   What pathos there is in the spectacle of a soul
which searches for light !   No play can compare with it.

It seems to me that your mind is taken up with a lot of things
which don't for the moment concern you, and which will gradually
be illuminated for you from within.   *Unum est necessarium.*   Only
one thing is vital and necessary for you—that you should draw
near to Christ, to break bread after your long fast, even if you don't
much care for the baker's face or the decoration of his shop.   To
Christ you must go, and you can only get there through prayer—
but your prayers must be *long* as well as assiduous, and that isn't
easy for a beginner.   You have two subjects for meditation : the
first to review in detail all the events of your life, to make a thorough
examination of your conscience (I know only the Catholic methods),
and to see how wretched and impoverished is your condition ; the
second is to lift up, or rather to bow down, your heart towards
Christ, to read, for instance, the *Seven Penitential Psalms*, the resurrection of Lazarus, the four narratives of the Passion ; to shut yourself
up in your room, to take a crucifix and to kiss its feet.   Speak to it.
Then, in that immense solitude where there will be nobody but
Christ and yourself, you will be sure of hearing his voice.   And he
will tell you to come unto him and cast aside the prejudices of
nature, and to eat with him that passover which he desired with so
great a desire.   Believe that he will summon you, that for you alone
he would be ready to cut himself off for a second time from his
father, that it is *you* whom he needs, and that souls are not inter-
changeable.   How Christ loved us !   How sensitive and delicate—
as we can see from the story of Lazarus, and that of the Agony !
Infremnit spiritu et fremuit iterum . . . coepit pavere et taedere.

I am sending you two portraits of Rimbaud which I've had
reproduced from Berrichon's originals.   I've also read with great
joy, a certain surprise, d'Indy's book on Beethoven, where he stresses
the Christian and Catholic character (which earlier biographers
had carefully dissimulated) of this great man, and tells the edifying
story of his death.   *Lord Jim* is the last of Conrad's really good
books.   Since then he's become a manufactory, though an interesting
one.   But *factum non genitum.*

Courage, Gide !   my heart and my prayers are with you at this
holy time.

P. CLAUDEL.

134.—*Paul Claudel to André Gide*

Frankfurt, 25th April 1912.

Dear Friend,

I have an offer from a German publisher, the *Anstalt für Aufführungs* (which, I believe, handled your books?) They ask on what conditions I would allow some, or even all, of my plays to be put on the stage. I've no idea, but I suppose I should envisage a set sum and a percentage? Could you give me advice or some information on this subject, and in respect of the figures I should stipulate? Thank you in anticipation.

I've been thumbing through some Greek authors recently and I've thought once again of how little we know in France, of that immense and marvellous literature. Our professors (despite their handsome salaries) have done literally *nothing*. We have nothing but a few translations made in ridiculous style by persons of no account (those of Leconte de Lisle being by far the worst). What is needed is simply the text and a line-by-line translation, which would put even the most ignorant reader into direct contact with these holy sources. Some notes and a few words of introduction. Big print, cheap editions delivered direct. Who knows if such an undertaking, well launched, would not have a great success? The Greek authors have a double attraction for the public—their names are known, and their works are not.

The basic reason for the growing inferiority of our literature is : ignorance. We think of talent as scientists of the pre-Pasteur generation thought of spontaneous generation. In reality nothing comes of nothing. Talent, or genius, is something that does not replace itself when it is exhausted. It is transmitted by a sort of inoculation. We must regain contact with our Greek patrimony, which is as magnificent in the realm of thought as in that of art. (It is my reading of Aristotle that inspires my present letter.) I believe that one incontestable reason for the superiority of English poetry in the nineteenth century was our neighbours' traditionally superior knowledge of Greek.

I grasp your hand,

P. CLAUDEL.

I've lost your address in Italy !

Gide : *Journal*

8th May 1912.

Voluminous correspondence with Claudel.

———

135.—*Paul Claudel to André Gide*

Frankfurt, 10th June 1912.

Dear Friend,

I've always wanted to write on Rimbaud, but my attempts have never satisfied me ; it's difficult to express oneself, otherwise than in pagan parlance ! And then Paterne Berrichon seems to me to have said all that's essential ! (though in a style that I can't always approve). What are the unpublished works you mention ? The idea greatly excited me. The least phrase of Rimbaud has a tremendous effect upon me—like that of Wagner's orchestration upon the nerves of our generation. How poignant (to me, at least) were those three prose poems that appeared recently !

I've worked for nearly a year on a long poem which is made up, like a breviary, of dialogues and canticles, and is devoted to the night of the summer solstice (three women's voices). It's become a great deal longer than I had imagined and I am hardly beginning to understand what I wanted to say. I am now at that delectable stage in the work at which one is master of one's subject and ideas flow in in abundance. How moving are those letters of Keats which appeared in the last number of the *N.R.F.* ! Ah, Keats was *all* poetry ! Beside him all our French cerebrations, our *disciplines*, our theories, seem, ah ! how vain and cold ! Keats really was the man-butterfly, born for a single hour of ecstasy and filled with " a twice-distilled fire ". (The translation doesn't seem good to me. And the orthography ! " *Que nous ayions ! !   Que nous soyions ! ! !* " Is it the influence of the Belgian printer ? And of the *sodden* climate of Bruges ?)

A conversion is something so grave and so marvellous that I cannot admit that any living man can have any part in it—that of an instrument save in itself perfectly negligible. You deceive yourself if you think that your friendship for me has any bearing upon your thoughts at this moment. There is another factor—

and one which, thanks be to God, can never be discounted. I am sorry for you, and I pray for you, but I am a little impatient at your many delays. How sad and cold the world must seem, when the world of faith is not there to superimpose it! How much unsuspected wealth is going to waste within you! How much time is being lost! Don't take any notice of those who tell you that conversion is only a passing fashion. It won't pass, any more than the fashion of eating and drinking. The world of love which offers itself to you is as immense, in its variety, as the act of physical union. It is the world of the unbeliever that is poor and limited. May the Blessed Sacrament, whose Feast we are at present celebrating—may this covetable bread complete its work and summon you once and for all! When I went to communion the other day I felt that the whole economy of the Church was there : we are allowed to communicate, all the rest is put aside.

I am reading at this moment Plato's *Timaeus*—it's incomparably exciting and exalting. What naivety, what depth, what poetry— in the midst of a litter of extravagancies and absurdities!

An affectionate handshake,

P. C.

I am very curious about your book, and a little nervous!

———

136.—*Paul Claudel to André Gide*

Frankfurt, 15th June 1912.

My dear Friend,

Since you and Copeau asked me to write a few lines on Rimbaud and I said " No ", a sort of remorse has preyed on me. I feel I can't refuse to do public homage to a man to whom I owe everything. Anyway I wrote the following few pages this morning. Do with them what seems to you best.

I grasp your hand,

P. CLAUDEL.

But speak to Paterne Berrichon about it and show him the article.

137.—*Paul Claudel to André Gide*

Frankfurt, 22nd June 1912.

Dear Friend,

Now that Suarès has written on Rimbaud I am most anxious and in fact *I must positively insist* that my essay on R. must not appear in the *N.R.F.*

You know S., you know how crotchety he is, and I don't want to do anything which might offend his invalid sensibilities. (Besides, his earlier articles persuade me that we are very probably in agreement.)   My four pages can appear, if you agree, with the new unpublished texts of Berrichon's, and can very well serve as a sort of footstool to them.   Besides, I am going to Paris in a few days and shall try to satisfy my long-cherished wish to visit Berrichon at Roche.   After which I shall no doubt wish to alter what I have written.

I grasp your hand with affection,

P. CLAUDEL.

———

138.—*André Gide to Paul Claudel*

[These rough notes were found in André Gide's archives.]

25th July [1912].

On my return from Florence, I told Desjardins that he should no longer count on me as one of the guests at Pontigny ; but after these further treacheries in the *Indépendance* I haven't the heart to abandon him, although my point of view draws further and further away from his own.   I don't want, either, to seem to yield to their intimidation.

You will no doubt know that the reading of *L'Échange* attracted a public even more numerous than that which attended Copeau's earlier lectures.   I was very sorry that I could not leave Cuverville at that moment, either to go to the lecture or even, perhaps, to meet you.   At any rate I had news of you from Gallimard, who was very happy to make your acquaintance . . . [. . .].

139.—*Paul Claudel to André Gide*

Frankfurt, 3rd August [1912].

Dear Friend,

I found your letter on returning from a little journey to Bohemia. Marie Kalff had already told me of Lugné-Poe's projects for the *Partage*. I said No—not without regret, I must admit, for I had already heard this actress and she seemed to me to be a woman of feeling. But I don't want that play to be put on the stage.

I've had, from Blei and from a whole group of German translators and impresarii, a series of letters which mean nothing to me. It's a hopeless muddle.

I was very much impressed by my journey to the Rimbaud country, and I've added a few lines to my article. Berrichon and I still want the *N.R.F.* to have it, if your agreement with Suarès allows of this ? I wrote to him yesterday. I doubt if the unpublished R. material would make a book. Only two of the letters have real literary interest.

My dear Gide, if you start to worry, before you do anything, as to the effect which your actions may have upon this person or that, you will never have a moment's peace. It's quite difficult enough to please oneself, without wanting others to be pleased with us as well.

I met Variot in Paris and I'm bound to say that he spoke of you, of Copeau and of the *N.R.F.* in a very decent way. I didn't notice the insinuation you spoke of. But what a " Palace of Illusions " is Parisian life—where one's every gesture is at once reflected in a thousand distorting mirrors ! I spoke rather freely about Barrès with a soldier, and on the following day my conversation was published in the *Paris-Midi*. Let's away from such places ! I grasp your hand,

P. CLAUDEL.

I am ashamed of myself for not having thanked M. Copeau for his lecture. My small nephew, who was there, told me that it was " marvellous ". I have to spend the whole summer at Frankfurt. Did I tell you that my wife expects a baby about the middle of this month ? I shall try to be in Paris towards the middle of October.

You never tell me about your literary plans.

140.—*Paul Claudel to André Gide*

Frankfurt, 5th September 1912.

Dear Friend,

It's a very long time since I had your news. Your name no longer appears in any of the Reviews. You seem to have gone into retreat, like any ordinary Papist. But these periods of isolation are good, and bear fruit.

May I break into your solitude to announce the birth of a son, who arrived, a few days ago, to swell the numbers of my little tribe? It's always an affecting event, and the delivery itself is one of the loveliest and most tragic things that I know of.

The *N.R.F.* is being good enough to publish in October my essay on Rimbaud, and it will be followed by several unpublished letters. I forget if I told you of my journey to Roche and Charleville. It was profoundly interesting.

I've also sent Gallimard my *Cantate*, which will come out in the autumn. For the present I'm busy drawing up certain schoolboy précis—of the state of the body of Our Lord in the Eucharist, his Ascension, the state of resurrected bodies, of the Angels, etc.—certain theological questions which very much interest me. Those are the extreme frontiers of theology as it is to-day.

In the end I decided to let Lugné-Poe try to give *L'Annonce faite à Marie*. I have confidence in Marie Kalff, who has the supreme quality (the only one I can demand)—enthusiasm and faith in my work. Whatever its success may be, I shall learn something. So I shall have to go to Paris quite often this autumn and winter, because the play has to be given before 15th January. You see that this letter is all about myself. You should imitate me and send me an answer full of details about yourself and your plans. You know how much I am interested.

There is here a rather interesting exhibition of pictures of which the centre-piece is a portrait of Madame Manet—unknown in France—and an admirable *chef-d'œuvre*. It's worth coming here for that alone. There are also many other interesting things.

I grasp your hand with great affection. My respects to Madame Gide.

P. CLAUDEL.

141.—*Paul Claudel to André Gide*

Frankfurt, 28th September 1912.

My dear Friend,

I'm glad to have your news at last, and I envy you the joy of being at work on a big book, above all at that happy moment when, after a long period of inertia, the book begins to vibrate with a life of its own. My printed works belong to the public. You can therefore single out any passage you like, provided that you attribute it to the character in question and not to me myself. Even at the time of the Schism of the West, there was only one Pope, though it wasn't easy for everyone to recognize him. *The problem* you speak of has only one solution, as you well know. Why do you delay ? Why go on living in a condition of such dreadful hazard ? I'm impatient, after this long evolution, to see at last the complete and definitive Gide ; having suffered that change which eternity brings, and not that which he has wrought himself (not the result, *i.e.* of his own self-absorbed contemplation).

We need you : there are things that you alone, and not myself or any other person, can give.

I was already feverishly busy with the problem of how to put *L'Annonce faite à Marie* on the stage, how to manœuvre the actors, what décor and costumes to choose, and so on, when crash ! there came a letter from Madame Kalff to say that she is ill and must take a cure high up in the snows.

Adieu veau (it comes all too aptly), *vaches, cochons, couvée.*

I am interested to know what you think of *Paradise Lost.* There are admirable beauties in it—passages of a delicious and accomplished preciosity, like that of the Angel and " th' archchemic Sun " ; but beside them are other, more ludicrous passages— that of the Angelic artillery battle, for instance. What a strange idea it is to call it a Christian poem ! Milton was an Aryan, or more exactly, a pagan pure and simple, or at most a Gnostic. His book can console us for the lost poems of Valentine and Basilides. *Paradise Lost* is practically unknown in France. Michelet, with his unhealthy acuteness, remarked that the English often have a very good idea of Satan (Michelet had, too). Thomas de Quincey took up that same remark.

Now that my plans have come to nothing, I shall stay only a short while (two or three days) in Paris.

I have no more news of my *Cantate*, which I sent to Gallimard three weeks ago.

I grasp your hand with affection. My respects to Madame Gide.

P. CLAUDEL.

142.—*Paul Claudel to André Gide*

Paris, 37 Quai d'Anjou [October 1912].

My dear Gide,

I don't understand why the Post Office sent your letter on its travels, but I am all the more glad to have it at last. I've just spent two weeks (except for four days at Villeneuve) in Paris—a busy and harassing time, but filled with very interesting work which taught me a lot. You know that the *Œuvre* is definitely giving *L'Annonce* (without poor Kalff, who is ill) towards the end of this month. I should be delighted to see you at the performance, my dear friend, and I am most grateful to you for giving me your promise in spite of the plans that you had already made. In spite of it all I am glad to be leaving Paris. It's a place that's not made for me. With my weak character I let myself be led on by a crowd of people, and I say things and make promises that I bitterly regret afterwards. I leave to-morrow morning.

P. CLAUDEL.

Gide : *Journal*

19 November 1912.

Went to see Paul Claudel yesterday at his sister's. He receives me with great cordiality. I enter right away the little room he is occupying, which is dominated by a crucifix above the bed.

Paul Claudel is more massive, wider than ever ; he looks as if he were seen in a distorting mirror ; no neck, no forehead ; he looks like a power-hammer. The conversation immediately starts on the subject of Rimbaud, whose complete works in one volume prefaced by Claudel, which the *Mercure* has just published, are on the table.

As I chide him for having, in his study, glossed over the ferocious side of Rimbaud's character, he says he wanted to depict only the

Rimbaud of the *Saison en enfer*, in whom the author of *Les Illumina-tions* was to result. Led, for a moment, to speak of his relations with Verlaine, Claudel, with an absent look, touches a rosary in a bowl on the mantel.

He talks of painting with excess and stupidity. His speech is an unceasing flow that no objection, no interrogation even, stops. Any other opinion than his own has no justification and almost no excuse in his eyes.

The conversation, by a natural slope, reaches matters of religion ; he rises up violently against the group of Catholic politicians of *L'Action Française*, then against Sorel and Péguy, whose " motives he begins to understand better ".

In too great a hurry to get back to my book, I cannot note here all the turns of our conversation.

143.—*Paul Claudel to André Gide*

[Paris], 37 Quai d'Anjou,
8th December 1912.

Dear Friend,

I'm writing to Paris on the off-chance. I'm here myself since Monday. As you can guess, I'm frantically busy. I'd like to see you, but all my afternoons are taken from 2 p.m. onwards, and soon all my evenings will also be taken. Perhaps you could come one morning ? (Let me know in advance.) The perform-ances are to be given on the 20th, 22nd, and 23rd. Of course I shall send you tickets, if you are good enough to overcome, on my behalf, your aversion to the theatre.

I must own that I myself, far from scorning the technical problems of the theatre, am fascinated by them. It's really most absorbing to work on problems of gesture, ensemble, and attitude, and then to watch it all coming alive and taking shape. I don't know what the public will think, but for my part I've already had great satis-faction. All those excellent people are giving of their best— especially the actresses, who are making really terrific efforts. I think that Mad. Frappa will be superb.

I'm not really in the right state of mind to talk of the subjects you mention. But you must realize that young Rivière never claimed to make a *compendium* of Catholic doctrine for the use of those who are outside the Church. He simply set out a point of view which I, for my part, found novel and interesting, although it is always that of a tourist and an amateur. His work does him very great credit. He's on the right road, and I am charmed above all by the tone of simplicity and good faith with which he approaches these great problems.

You must own, too, that it's rather too much to say that Christ has no place in Catholicism. The essence of Catholicism, the infinitely delicate and affecting moment at which it is all summarized, is the Eucharist. The Eucharist is the Real Presence. That means that Christ, for us, is present not only in our thoughts, in our hearts, and in our imagination, but that he is here in flesh and blood, exactly as he was in the days of Galilee, but in a yet more intimate and essential way. It is thanks to the Eucharist that we can really repeat that saying which would otherwise be revolting and unintelligible : " Verily, it is expedient for you that I go away ".

And you feel that yourself. I think that you now believe in Christ the God, and this makes me infinitely happy. That is enough for your salvation. From the moment that you give what you honestly can and act according to the best of your lights, you are part of the spirit of the Church, if not part of its body. But all the same you must feel very well that that is not complete and that, whatever may be the consolations of prayer, you have no *religion* —by which I mean the truly and indubitably objective complement to your interpellation. To speak of religion is to speak of a tie and a restraining influence that are stronger than you [believe].[1] That's what Rivière has ably demonstrated. Those who don't admit the external presence of Christ and don't accept it as a specific dogma must flounder for ever in the marshlands of their own (false) personalities—and how odious at times, how insipid, how insupportable these are ! (Another point well taken by Rivière.) The dogma or objective article of faith is the only thing that can keep us moving forward, the only countersign that keeps us away from the fatal mirages and brings us at last towards something new.

I grasp your hand with great affection,

P. CLAUDEL.

---

[1] The end of this sentence was missing and has been readjusted at the instigation of Paul Claudel.

Young Jahier came to see me in Frankfurt. I was delighted to meet him.

Since you claim that Christ has no place in Catholicism, re-read Book IV of the *Imitation*, that essentially Catholic book.

144.—*Paul Claudel to André Gide*

Frankfurt, 27th December 1912.

Dear Friend,

Here I am, back in Frankfurt, and happy to be among my children and away from those commotions which render sterile both heart and mind.

Last Sunday I made, especially for you, the long journey to Clichy to see the Abbé Fontaine, of whom I had told you. He is the incumbent of Notre-Dame Auxiliatrice. You have to get down at the Porte de Clichy, and then you find, among the cemeteries, a terrible street called Boulevard Victor Hugo, which stretches away for ever to the left. The Abbé Fontaine was Huysmans' last confessor, and now, in the parish which he has inaugurated, he spreads the gospel among a population of railway-men, rag-and-bone men, apaches and prostitutes. He is simple, intelligent, and good. I am sure that he would give you light and good counsel. But you must not imagine that a conversion is ever easy, or that it does not involve sacrifice. The only wisdom in this matter is to respond to the charm of God blindly, with lowered head, as one responds to the appeals of the senses. Don't worry about the things which initially may displease or wound or tear you. For it is written that it is better to enter the Kingdom of God with one eye and one leg than to remain whole and outside it.

I spoke to the Abbé Fontaine of Philippe's horrible *Bubu de Montparnasse*, which impressed me so deeply. He reminded me that Our Lord has said that thieves and prostitutes shall pass before us into the Kingdom of God, and on this subject he told me a wonderful story. He had made the acquaintance of an unfortunate girl who was dying of consumption. Her former lovers and protectors had clubbed together to pay for the room in which she was in her last agonies. On the day when he came to bring her the last sacraments, they were one and all waiting for him, with great respect, cap in hand. The prostitutes who were her neighbours had hung the corridors and the entrance hall with their sheets, which they had ornamented with artificial flowers. The prostitute received the last sacraments with her arms held out like a cross and her face transfigured. She died like a saint.

I grasp your hand,

P. Claudel.

145.—Paul Claudel to André Gide

Frankfurt, 27th January 1913.

Dear Friend,

What an absurd idea ! Of course my feelings for the *N.R.F.* are what they have always been. I like and esteem everybody who works for it. I know too what I owe to this Review which has always treated me perfectly, and I am not a man who forgets a good turn—or, alas, a bad one. I should like nothing better than to send you something, but I really have nothing at all. If I sent the *Revue de Paris* the beginning of my *Cantate*, I admit it was because they offered me tempting financial terms. I didn't want to let pass the Richard Wagner centenary without paying tribute to his memory, but I am deep in some theological work and mustn't lose the thread of it for a single instant.

M. Segalen is the Naval doctor who formerly wrote (under a pseudonym) *Les Immémoriaux*. You can write to him c/o the French Legation, Pekin.

I am going to write to Thibaudet, whose book on Mallarmé is most interesting and, for me, almost tragic. His book explains what Mallarmé said to one of us : " I am a desperate man ". For at bottom Mallarmé was a mystic, and he remained a prisoner behind the cold, bare glass front that he could never break. Why shouldn't the *N.R.F.* print *Un Coup de Dés jamais n'abolira le Hasard* ? You know that I have a proof of it (which I gave to Berthelot, with a covering letter, to avoid any risk of its going astray).

I grasp your hand with affection,

P. Claudel.

146.—*Paul Claudel to André Gide*

Frankfurt, 11th February 1913.

Dear Friend,

Yes, I have got *Leaves of Grass*, but it's either in Paris or in the country and it would be a great business to find it. If I translated anything of Whitman it would be the pieces about the South : " O South, my South " (I forget the title) or that other equally short poem in which he speaks of the singers' voices, tenor and contralto.

I hope that Griffin's translation of the *Threnody for President Lincoln* will not be the one he put into alexandrines (why not in Latin verse ?). That poem is of supreme quality and must not be ruined.

I received your new book, but so far I've only read *Bethsabé*, which is new to me and a lovely thing.

A German, Stefan Zweig, asks me to sell him the manuscript of *L'Annonce faite à Marie* for 500 francs. I asked Gallimard for it, but now it occurs to me that I sent it, through Jacques Rivière, to the Review. Could you have it sent back to me as soon as possible ?

I grasp your hand,

P. CLAUDEL.

147.—*Paul Claudel to André Gide*

Frankfurt, 22nd March 1913.

Dear Friend,

Thank you for your sympathy. No, my poor father did not confess before he died. It makes me full of remorse. Had I come earlier, perhaps I could have persuaded him to do his duty, as he manifestly intended to have done. I hope that God will have given him credit for this good impulse, but I remain in the most terrible uncertainty about his final destiny. It is difficult to endure the thought of Hell, when one is face to face with it, and one's own father's fate is in question. Yet these mysteries are very near to us ; how little separates us from death, and from that moment of terrible

hesitation when the heart stops and the soul takes its departure !
My mother has returned to her traditional faith. As for my sister
Camille, I have just taken her into a nursing home. So you see
that I have been having a bad time.

Yes, the manuscript arrived safely.

Thank you again. I grasp your hand,

P. CLAUDEL.

148.—*Paul Claudel to André Gide*

Hellerau, 22nd September 1913.

No, dear friend, I can't. I am very fond of you, but don't
ask me to take part in any newspaper controversies. They exhaust
one, they exasperate one, and they never do any good. Anyway
I doubt if *Le Temps* will print your correction. You aren't attacked
either directly or indirectly, and so you can't invoke the benefits of
the law. A friendly letter to Lefranc, who edits the *Gazette littéraire*,
and is an acquaintance of mine, would do much more to achieve
your ends. I would readily write to him, if you liked.

Till the 5th, I shall be here, for the performance of *L'Annonce* in
the marvellous theatre of Hellerau. Marie is played by an admirable
actress, " la Dietrich ", who is as wild as a panther.

I am very curious to read your new novel, which will probably
give me fresh cause for melancholy.

I've found some wonderful souls here, a young Jew and an
elderly Polish lady. There is something really amazing in the way
people need God to-day. As soon as they feel themselves in the
presence of a sincere believer and have overcome their timidity,
they tell you things which prove that to be cut off from God is the
cause of profound sorrow among a great many people whom one
supposed to be indifferent. It is a most terrible thing that people
should die of hunger in this way, when there is bread enough for all.

I grasp your hand with affection. Don't bear me a grudge.

P. C.

149.—*Paul Claudel to André Gide*

Hellerau, 29th September 1913.

Dear Friend,

I am writing to-day to Lefranc. The performances of *L'Annonce* will be very beautiful, I think, and will be an important event in Germany. Every single newspaper will be represented. I'd gladly do something for the *N.R.F.*, but I've already promised *Comœdia*. So do try to send Rivière. I assure you that it's of the highest interest—a completely new formula.

I grasp your hand,

P. CLAUDEL.

150.—*Paul Claudel to André Gide*

Frankfurt, 9th October 1913.

Dear Friend,

There's a young Jew from Aix called Darius Milhaud who would like very much to meet you. He has set poems of Jammes and myself to music and would like to do the same with something of yours. He's very gifted—strong, rhythmic, and virile, which is rare among the musicians of to-day. I should be grateful if you could make him welcome.

I grasp your hand,

P. CLAUDEL.

151.—*Paul Claudel to André Gide*

French Consulate-General, Hamburg,
13th November 1913.

Dear Friend,

The *Courrier de la Presse* has sent me Francis Jammes' account of his first visit to me, in 1900, in your company. Jammes says that on this occasion I regarded you with an antipathy which, believe me, I have never felt.   I don't know how he can have come by so strange an idea.

You know that I've been here for a month ?

Hamburg is a town with quite a lot of character, with something tortuous and funereal about it which reminds me of Boston. Above it is a northerly, maritime sky in which tall green steeples rise up like needles of ice.

I grasp your hand,

P. CLAUDEL.

I have just sent *Protée* to Gallimard.

152.—Paul Claudel to André Gide

Hamburg, 17th November 1913.

Dear Friend,

I've just had your letter. As you'll see when you've read the cutting in question, your name is not quoted in Jammes' interview, and as we three are the only people who know that the meeting took place, nobody can identify you as having been Jammes' companion on the visit. For him to make a public correction would not only be useless, but would hinder your own ends by further exciting the malignity of the public, who are always ready to rend anybody whose name is well known. My own private protest was mainly intended to remove the disagreeable impression which you might have been left with after reading *Le Temps*. If you accept my word, let us leave things as they are. The less the papers know of our friendship, the more it will be worth.

You will say that in that case I should never have allowed the story of my conversion (which you have no doubt read) to be made public. Believe me—it caused me great pain. But I was asked to do it by people whom I had not the right to refuse—and there are things more important than one's own modesty.

Speaking of *Le Temps*, Morhardt told me, when I wrote him a friendly letter some weeks ago, that the name of the *N.R.F.* had been omitted in accordance with the " rules of the house " (?). But don't go and write about it !

I haven't got *Leaves of Grass* with me, and you would be very kind if you could send it to me—it's so long since I put my nose inside it ! I'll see what I can do. In any case I don't think that the translation will take very long.

I grasp your hand,

P. CLAUDEL.

Vinohrady is a large suburb, which is really a part of Prague, much as Montmartre is part of Paris or Saint-Gilles of Brussels. The theatre there is very popular, and in fact is more lively than the National Theatre. Prochazka is said to be one of the best Czech writers. I know him slightly.

I beg you to leave the Jammes incident as it stands !

153.—*Paul Claudel to André Gide*

Hamburg, 25th November 1913.

Dear Friend,

For some time the title of your new book, *Les Caves du Vatican*, has been running in my head, and I'm very much afraid, especially when I listen to certain rumours, that it's not yet the book I'm waiting for. I remember that you once asked for permission to take a phrase of mine as your epigraph. I know that I've no way of preventing such a quotation. Still, I must tell you how grieved I should be if my name appeared at the head of a book in which the most venerable person of the Sovereign Pontiff was not treated with the respect and tenderness which a Catholic owes to the Pope. This is a question of appreciation which I leave to your own delicacy of mind.

I wrote to Jammes and I think that the affair is now settled. Perhaps I was wrong to write to you, but I know from experience that anything which is unpleasant for one arrives sooner or later at its destination.

I'm very suspicious of your Rabindranath Tagore. What I have read of his seemed to me rather nauseating, and I so despise that sort of Asiatic !

I grasp your hand,

P. CLAUDEL.

154.—*Paul Claudel to André Gide*

Hamburg, 26th November 1913.

Dear Friend,

Your nice letter came to-day and made me a little sorry about the one I wrote to you yesterday. But you are used to my rough methods. Your suggestion rather surprises me. I can't imagine what effect this broad comedy would have if it were acted. I'd like to ask you for time to think it over and seek the advice of my friends the Berthelots. And then—has the *Vieux-Colombier* troupe got comic actors of its own ? For Protée I should need a strapping fellow with a good load of extra padding. And then isn't the stage too small ? You need space for the Island with its beach of pack-cloth bordered with a flounce of white muslin—and space for a boat to manœuvre on its rollers. And then, finally, *Protée* includes music, with choir and orchestra (Darius Milhaud had already composed it). All that costs a lot of money. Ask Copeau about it, all the same.

As you like *Protée*, do me the pleasure of accepting the manuscript, by way of compensation for the manuscript of *L'Annonce,* which I took away from you.

I grasp your hand with affection,

P. CLAUDEL.

If they gave *Protée*, perhaps we could drop the idea of *L'Échange* for this year ? You know that I haven't very much confidence in it.

———

155.—*Paul Claudel to André Gide*

Hamburg, 2nd December 1913.

Dear Friend,

I was going to write to Daudet, care of you, when your second letter came and I saw that it was already too late. You only left out one thing—his address ; and, as you can imagine I can't write to him c/o *L'Action Française*, whose address, in any case, I also don't know. I'm sorry, because I should have liked to give pleasure to Larbaud and to show him how much I liked his most lively and amusing book. You were misled, by the way. My relations with Léon Daudet don't really exist. I've written to him twice in twenty years, and he's never answered or given me any sign of life. I very much doubt, therefore, if my views would have such weight with him.

I grasp your hand,

P. CLAUDEL.

What does Copeau think about *Protée* ?

156.—*Paul Claudel to Jacques Rivière* [1]

Hamburg, 2nd March 1914.

My dear Rivière,

I have received the *N.R.F.* with my tiny note—adorned, like a good pilgrim of Monsieur Saint Jacques, with a beautiful *coquille* ! *Inconvenable* instead of *inconcevable* ! Please put a correction in the next issue. I really insist on it. [2]

I have been following Gide's novel with mounting discomfort, and finally I was brought to a stop on page 478 by a pederastic passage which throws a sinister light upon certain of our friend's former works. Must I decide once and for all, as I have so far refused to do, that he himself is a participant in these hideous practices ? After *Saül* and *L'Immoraliste* he had no more imprudences to commit. What he has just done must brand him for ever. Doesn't he see that he'll be lost—he himself and all those who are nearest to him ? I wanted to write to him about it, and perhaps I shall. Anyway you can show him this letter, if your heart moves you to do so. Is that why he's so anxious to attribute the same habits to Arthur Rimbaud, and doubtless to Whitman too ?

I grasp your hand,

P. CLAUDEL.

[1] At the request of André Gide, who is anxious that the various elements of his grave difference with Paul Claudel in 1914 should all be represented in this book, we have inserted in the body of the correspondence certain unpublished letters from Paul Claudel to Jacques Rivière, from André Gide to Francis Jammes, and Francis Jammes to André Gide.

[2] This untranslatable passage turns upon a pun on the word *coquille*, which means both *a shell* and *a printer's error*. Claudel alludes to the great Spanish pilgrimage (St. James of Compostella) at which pilgrims are expected to arrive bearing a shell.

157.—*Paul Claudel to André Gide*

Hamburg, 2nd March 1914.

In the name of heaven, Gide, how could you write the passage which I find on page 478 of the last issue of the *N.R.F.* ? Don't you know that after *Saül* and *L'Immoraliste* you cannot commit any further imprudence ? Must I quite make up my mind, as I have never wished to do, that you are yourself a participant in these hideous practices ? Answer me. You owe me an answer. If you remain silent, or if you don't make yourself absolutely clear, I shall know where I stand. If you are not a pederast, why have you so strange a predilection for this sort of subject ? And if you are one, cure yourself, you unhappy man, and do not make a show of these abominations. Consult Madame Gide ; consult the better part of your own heart. Don't you see that you will be lost—you yourself and all those who are nearest to you ? Don't you realize the effect which your books may have upon some unfortunate young people ? It pains me to say these things, but I feel obliged to do so.

Your distressed friend,

P. CLAUDEL.

158.—*André Gide to Paul Claudel*

Florence, 7th March 1914.

What right have you to issue this summons ? In what name do you put these questions ? If it is in the name of friendship, can you suppose for an instant that I should evade them ?

It pains me very much that there should be any misapprehension between us ; but your letter has already done much to create a new one—for, no matter how I take it, and whether I answer or whether I don't, I foresee that you are going to misjudge me. I therefore beg you to consider this only : that I love my wife more than life itself, and I could not forgive any word or action on your part which might endanger her happiness. Now that has been said, I can tell you that for months, for years, I have longed to talk to you—although the tone of your letter makes me despair of receiving any advice from you to-day.

I am speaking now to a friend, as I should speak to a priest, whose binding duty it is to keep my secret before God. I have never felt any desire in the presence of a woman ; and the great sadness of my life is that the most constant, the most enduring, and the keenest of my loves has never been accompanied by any of the things which normally precede love. It seemed, on the contrary, that in my case love prevented me from desiring.

If, after that avowal, you prefer to break with me, you will, I suppose, find it seemly that I should ask you, in the name of those whom you love, to take no matter what pretext—the impropriety of my book, for instance—and not in any way to bring forward what I have revealed to you here. Alone, I should care nothing for the world's contempt ; but I am married.

As for the evil which, you say, is done by my books, I can't believe in it, for I know how many others are stifled, as I am, by lying conventions. And do not infer from this that I commend any particular habits, or even any particular desires ; but I loathe hypocrisy, and I know that some hypocrisies are mortal. I cannot believe that religion leaves on one side all those who are like myself. By what cowardice, since God calls me to speak, should I evade this question in my books ? I did not choose to be so. I can fight against my desires ; I can triumph over them, but I can neither choose the object of those desires, nor can I invent other objects, either to order or in imitation.

Is it really possible that you should despise me, repulse me, after reading this letter ? . . . I have always thought that one day I could speak to you as I have spoken here—even if you did not understand—and that I owed you this confession. Doubtless it is not necessary to understand in order to advise. Yet I do not ask for your advice to-day. I expect only your anger.

I feel that my letter gives you very poor answers to your questions ; but at least you will feel I have not been reticent—except in so far as it is difficult to answer in a few phrases where a whole volume of explanations and the story of my life might not perhaps be enough.

Au revoir. Now it is for you to stretch out your hand to me— if, that is to say, you still consent to extend it.

A. GIDE.

159.—*André Gide to Paul Claudel* [1]

Florence, 8th March 1914.

All the same, Claudel, I can't believe that you would make use of my letter and turn it against me. I am almost ashamed to conceive such an idea, so deeply does it seem to me to wrong you. . . . But I can't beat off the hideous idea that the interrogations in your letter were prompted by somebody else who is waiting for you to pass on my answers ; so that it would now be difficult, almost impossible, for you not to betray me ; for even if you kept silent on the point, that silence would itself be revealing—just as would have been, as you were saying, my own silence.

Since I wrote to you, two years ago, from these same banks of the Arno, I have formed the habit of considering you a little as a priest, and I sometimes let myself be persuaded that God was using you to speak to me. To-day I shall know if this is so, or if you are just a man, like the others. Sometimes I come to wish that you would betray me, for then I should be delivered of this esteem for you, and for all that you represent in my eyes, which so often arrests and embarrasses me.

The extent to which you can misunderstand me—that is what distresses me. Why can I not speak to you, instead of writing ! All the same, I ask you, whom I have always defended, to remember that I have written *La Porte étroite*. . . . And perhaps, after all, this letter of yours, and my answer, will mark an important point in my life. . . . When I asked you once to give me the name of someone to whom I could talk, it was of this that I wanted to speak —for truthfully I tell you that *I do not see how I can resolve this problem* which God has inscribed in my flesh. Do you understand me ? You don't, do you ? And that's why I gave up writing to you two years ago. I realized that I had gone with you as far as was possible ; yet I felt that everything remained to be said—how, I didn't know.

Adieu. Now you can do me great harm, and I am at your mercy.

ANDRÉ GIDE.

[1] André Gide despatched this second letter to Paul Claudel without waiting for an answer to his letter of 7th March 1914.

160.—*Paul Claudel to André Gide*

Hamburg, 9th March 1914.

My poor Gide, I should not have written to you if I were not still your friend. I admit that that passage in the *N.R.F.* came to me as a shock ! But I'm too old a hand to be scandalized by anything, and I don't really know what right I should have to judge anybody. Now that that's been said, I'm going to try to answer you point by point as objectively as I can.

No, you know quite well that the habits of which you tell me are neither permitted, nor excusable, nor avowable. You will have against you both *Revelation* and the natural order of things.

Common logic and decency tell you that man is not an end in himself ; still less so are his pleasures and his private delights. If sexual attraction does not lead to its natural conclusion—that is to say, reproduction—it is irregular and evil. That is the only firm principle. Without it, you abandon yourself to private fantasies. Where will you draw the line ? If one person claims to justify sodomy, another will justify onanism, vampirism, the rape of minors, anthropophagy, etc. There's no reason to stop anywhere.

Revelation also tells us that this particular vice is particularly odious to God. I need not remind you of Sodom, the *morte moriatur* (?), of *Leviticus*, the beginning of the *Epistle to the Romans*, and the *Neque fornicatores, neque adulteri, neque masculorum concubitores*.

That's enough. I deny that the individual has the right to be both judge and defendant in his own case. The devil, pride, and the passion that holds us in its claws—all these are quick to whisper pretexts and excuses in our ear.

You claim to be the victim of a physiological idiosyncrasy. That would be an attenuating circumstance, but it would not constitute a permit or a licence. You are the victim of two things above all : your Protestant heredity, which has accustomed you to look only to yourself for your rules of conduct, and the fascination of æsthetics which lends lustre and interest to the least excusable of actions. In spite of all the doctors I absolutely refuse to believe in physiological determinism. If you have abnormal instincts, the natural uprightness of your nature, allied to your reason, your education and the fear of God, should have given you the means of resistance. Medicine is meant to cure, not to excuse. Alas ! In your case you would have needed a confessor as well.

You ask for my advice. I advise you first of all to do what lies within your power. What lies within your power is to suppress at once that horrible passage in the *N.R.F.* I entreat you to do it for reasons of morality and for reasons of your own personal interest.

For reasons of morality :

You talk of hypocrisy, but there is something infinitely more odious than hypocrisy, and that is cynicism. In these grave questions of the flesh, we are all sinners in greater or less degree, and I must admit to you quite sincerely that, as between you and myself, if I were to make a comparison, it would be to my detriment. But it's one thing to sin, and to be sorry about it, and to know that it's wrong and to wish to do better, and to ask God to give one the strength to do better ; it's quite another thing to believe that one is right to do wrong, and to talk of it, and be proud of it. For in such a case there is not only perversion of the senses, but perversion of judgment and conscience as well.

You also take on yourself responsibility for the souls which you lead astray. Literature can sometimes do a little good, but it also does great harm. The vice of which you speak is spreading wider and wider. It's no small matter when a man like you, with all the weight and charm of your intelligence, your cultivation and your talent, becomes its champion, or simply accustoms the minds of his readers to thoughts from which they should rather turn away in horror. In this respect also, you will have accounts to settle, both in this world and in the next.

For your own personal interest :

I tell you again : *you will be lost.* You will lose all position, you will become an outcast among other outcasts, rejected by humanity. Parisian opinion is more discreet, but it is also more pitiless than that of London. You will cease to count—and you know it. You ask me to keep your letter secret, you beg me not to let your wife suspect the truth. Wretched man ! And at the same time you make public, you display on every wall in Paris, a passage which everybody will interpret as a definitive and official confession. Have no illusions on that subject. At the very least, promise me that the passage will not appear when your novel is published in book form. I beg you, if you set any value on my friendship, to suppress it. Little by little people will forget.

Yes, I shall keep an absolute silence—but it is you who talk, you who make a public show of yourself ! Such a thing has never been seen since pagan times. No writer, not even Wilde, has done it.

I shall not hide from you the fact that when I wrote to you I also wrote to two people : Jammes (a word only), and poor Rivière, to whom you could do so much harm. Poor boy—he trusted you ! As I did. But what have I told them that they have not already learnt from page 478 ?

I've re-read my letter and it seems to me very harsh. Read it coldly, as if it were a doctor's prescription. And above all don't give up hope. There's no such thing as a mortal illness for souls. You can be cured. No, God does not wish for the death of any of his children, he neither hates nor despises you. Each of your faults is merely one more claim upon his compassion. For seven years, as far as I can judge, something has been going on in the best part of yourself ; something is going forward, but I don't know what. But don't tell me that you are satisfied and at peace.

And have no doubt of this : that when everybody else has abandoned you, you will still have me. I know the incomparable worth of a human soul.

I wrote to a third person, too ; but he is a priest. It was the Abbé Fontaine. Now you can go and seek him out. You will not astonish him—be sure of that.

And shall I say that I am almost comforted by the removal of that great load of doubt which has hitherto embarrassed me in our relationship ?

Poor Gide, how much you are to be pitied, and how tragic is your life !

I grasp your hand,

P. Claudel.

I can't now contribute to your *Whitman*. It's impossible.

10th March.

I've just had your second letter. What an absurd idea ! The date alone of my letter shows you that I sent it as soon as I'd read the *N.R.F.*, and, so to say, *ab irato*. I wrote at the same time (i) to Jammes (a simple exclamation), (ii) to Rivière. I think I was absolutely bound to write to Rivière. But you have nobody who is more devoted to you. (iii) I've written since then, under the seal of the confession, to the Abbé Fontaine. Now that that's all said, let me once again be astonished at your apprehensions. Almost everyone, except a few stubborn people like Rivière and myself, knows more or less what to think about you ; and if any doubts remained you've taken care to remove them by your last publication. Only nobody dares to say anything to you. I'm the only one who's brave enough to speak to you brutally, and I'm brave enough because I take so great an interest in your salvation. So don't be astonished, and don't think that I am in any way responsible for the outbreak of a scandal which you may have brought upon yourself. I give you my word of honour that I shall remain silent. I am even returning your letters to you. My poor friend, these are bitter days for you. For my part, your two fine and noble letters give me all the more comfort. You have taken me as your confessor. That is good. If you had said the same things to a priest, you would be absolved, and your sins would be exactly as if they had never been, as it is written in the prophet Joel. I grasp your hand with affection.

P. C.

161.—André Gide to Paul Claudel

16th March 1914.

My dear Claudel,

What will you think of my silence ? . . . I wrote you a very long letter, but I can't make up my mind to send it to you. " Harsh ", your letter ? No ; it would only have been harsh, to me, if I had felt that you were withdrawing your friendship. But how can I answer you without seeming to defend myself (where, in my last two letters, could you find anything resembling an apologia or even an excuse ? I simply told you *how things stand*) or going in deeper than I can honestly go.

Send me the Abbé F.'s address. I am grateful to you for writing to him and making it easy for me to call on him. But persuade yourself, I beg you, not to bear me any grudge if my conversation with him does not lead to the results for which, no doubt, you are hoping. I shall listen respectfully, piously even, to his words. But if the most ardent and constant of loves has never coaxed any response from my flesh, I leave it to you to imagine the effect of his exhortations, his counsels, and his reprimands. (And what, pray, do you mean me to *understand* by the phrase : " in spite of all the doctors, I absolutely refuse to believe in physiological determinism " ?)

I thank you for the sentiments which lead you to ask me (as prudence would likewise do) to suppress a passage from my book ; but I cannot consent to do so. Shall I admit to you that your phrase, " Little by little people will forget ", seems to me shameful. No ; do not ask me either to whitewash or to compromise ; or it will be I who will think less of you.

I can't make out why you felt you had to write to Rivière. I prefer to think that you gave way to an unthinking impulse. I like Rivière, I respect him, and I have the liveliest *reverence* for him. Has there ever been anything in my conversation or my actions that could disquiet him ? No, none at all, it would seem, since you say that he refused to believe anything against me. What absurd or monstrous fancies will he entertain now ? Couldn't you understand that you were compelling me to have it out with him, and to embarrass him with confidences that I should have liked to spare him ?

Au revoir. Be assured that I have never been more
Your friend,
A. GIDE.

162.—*Paul Claudel to André Gide*

Hamburg, 17th March 1914.

My dear Gide,

You will remember with what apprehension and repugnance I allowed you (since you had courteously asked for my permission) to use as the epigraph for a chapter in your new book a passage from *L'Annonce faite à Marie* which, in isolation, has the appearance of heresy. I finally resigned myself to thinking that an epigraph, like a quotation, is beyond my control. Now I find that my Catholic friends are very much shocked by your use of this passage. And I have to take great account of their views. I therefore venture to ask you insistently, and to appeal to your friendship and your sense of delicacy, to expunge this epigraph from the volume which will give the definitive text of your *Caves*.

I grasp your hand with great affection,

P. CLAUDEL.

163.—*Paul Claudel to André Gide*

[After writing letter No. 162 Paul Claudel received, on the same day, letter No. 161 from André Gide.   He at once replied as follows :]

Hamburg, 17th March 1914.

My dear Gide,

The Abbé Fontaine lives at Clichy—6 rue d'Alsace.

You have done a great wrong by inserting in your novel an abominable and scandalous passage.   You do an even greater wrong by retaining this passage instead of cutting it out, *as you are absolutely bound in duty to do*.

I ask you in any case, and in the most formal manner, to expunge my name from a work of this kind.   As you asked for my authority before I knew what kind of a book it was, I have the right to tell you to-day that you no longer have this authority.

And may God, whom you mock, be with you.

P. CLAUDEL.

164.—*André Gide to Paul Claudel*

19th March 1914.

My dear Claudel,

Your two letters, both dated the same day but so different in tone, have arrived together.   I am trying in vain to understand which is the later of the two—the gentle, or the furious one.   It is to your courteous request, and not to your imperative, that I yield in promising to expunge from the book the epigraph which you had originally authorized me to use.   The amusement which

I derived from this unexpected and prodigiously appropriate
epigraph counts for nothing when set beside the displeasure which
it has apparently caused you. I fancy, moreover, that you are not
the sole source of your annoyance, and you have yourself admitted
to me that your Catholic friends have had some part in it. But
you have only to ask : the epigraph shall be suppressed. I seriously
considered whether, in response to your other request, which I was
really sorry not to be able to grant—I mean, the suppression of the
passage which offends you—I should not come to an extreme
decision : that of not allowing the book to appear. (I speak of the
ordinary edition ; as for the editio princeps, which is expensive
and consists of only a few copies, I cannot now disengage myself
from it.)

You know me very little if you think that I should have been
incapable of it. But your letter of to-day—the angry one, I mean
—makes it too clear that you would not think better of me for it ;
that you would attribute the sacrifice to motives of " pride " ;
and that to-morrow the whole thing would have to be begun all
over again. And I thought with some bitterness, and also (forgive
me) with a smile, that I, too, had once asked Jammes to suppress
the very painful and disobliging passage at the beginning of the
article which he sent when Ch. L. Philippe died. But he insisted
on leaving it in, and was indignant that anyone should dare to
touch his prose or dare to ask him to touch it ; and you, then, as a
true friend, declared that he was like St. Jerome.

A. GIDE.

165.—*Francis Jammes to André Gide*

Orthez, 24th March 1914.

My dear Friend,

I find here (my correspondence had not been forwarded for
a month) a book and a translation of yours—about which I shall
write to you soon and at length ; for Rabindranath Tagore is a
great poet and you are a great writer. You say something about
being sorry that you didn't see me again after the Chausson
luncheon. Perhaps it's for the best. Not, by any means, that I

regret having advanced to greet you. The more I am enlightened by God, the more I realize the value of certain things you did for me twenty years ago. The abyss between us has widened, but I am farther than ever from forgetting the forget-me-not which Walter held out to me—the unsullied forget-me-not which you could have offered to your fiancée. Your nerves have got the better of you since then. You wanted to sing the praises of joy, and yet your books, since the *Nourritures*, have been nothing but one long, sickly, rending shudder of nervous excitement. Despite our disagreements, you've had no better friend than I. It's when they aren't there that we stand up most for our friends. I've declared, before people who took my word for the truth, that the ever-increasing rumour about you had no foundation. One evening at Hendaye I told you just what, in my opinion, such rumours meant. At that moment you still understood me. But where do you stand now ? Perhaps, though I don't like to think it, you have completely forgotten your mother's face ; can you no longer see the sad heights of La Roque, where the moonlight played on your fiancée's hair ?

Believe me—I'm not writing in indignation. I'm not writing without having first asked for the guidance of Christ, who is now the very heartbeat of my life. Why should I be indignant ? Is not Mercy available always and to all ? After *Saül*, after the *Immoralist*, after the *Corydon* which seems to exist, this passage on page 478 of the *N.R.F.* could only deal you the final blow. Not only, in your last book, have you made fun of my mother the Church as Voltaire would not, and Rémy de Gourmont would hardly, have dared to do ; but you have disgraced yourself. You have sometimes spoken to me of sinning against the Spirit. Take care that you do not yourself do so. It is the situation of the man who can no longer recover himself, who dies enfolded in his sin— the man whose resistance has become eternal.

In one way it doesn't matter to me how you take this letter. It's not likely that men of my sort will convert men like you, who enjoy the elaborate twists of the mind which it requires a Claudel to follow. But I am intelligent enough to know that my God draws towards him all men of goodwill. So I'm not protesting against the abomination—difficult as it is to defend you to-day—I'm just deeply sorry that you should put weapons into your enemies' hands. What do you want me to say ? Either you may hope in hypocrisy to disguise the truth from me, or you must admit that your conduct as a writer makes one doubt your sanity. Unless, alas ! you own to a truth which I dread—for it was a very touching moment in my life as a friend when I knew that Arthur Fontaine had said " Jammes' word is enough for me ! "

Well, even if what I dread should come to pass, and if you were to say, " Ah ! my poor friend ! " in that voice of yours, I should reply, " Get away from those unwholesome wretches, whose master you were and whose disciple you have become, and cure yourself." You know that leprosy can be cured. Mortify yourself to that end. You must abdicate yourself and become somebody else. Repent. Everything will then revert to normal. True happiness will be yours—for a reputation of that sort is only really fixed in the public mind when it has been established in a court of law.

There is one man who might save you—for if you made sport of his sainthood he would reply to you without impatience. I don't know if he is in Paris at this moment. He is a Dominican, the most eloquent (in our sense) that I have ever come across, the most austere and yet (a strange thing) the one most fitted to hear your story.

Don't think for a moment that I should be surprised if you either don't go to see him or go simply to draw him into your philosophical pastimes. And if I say that even your conversion would not surprise me, it's because I have great faith.

To-morrow morning I shall post this letter on my way to communion, and already my still unsatisfied heart reaches out towards the God who makes it beat. I shall pray for you, my poor friend, for I have felt your weakness, bereft as you are of the God who gives me strength and joy beyond all telling.

I embrace you,

FRANCIS JAMMES.

Father Jean Brisset—you can introduce yourself as my friend if he is there, and if you are unhappy and wish to rid yourself of this nightmare—lives at No. 2 rue de Commailles. Whatever happens, write to me and let me know if I have the right to go on defending you (by saying that your books are merely a matter of paradox and theory) or if I should be silent.

166.—*Francis Jammes to André Gide*

Orthez, 27th March 1914.

My dear Friend,

I have received, read, and instantly burned your letter. If you were moved by my letter, how much was I moved by yours ! Of course, I am too firm a believer to despair of such a situation. It is certain that even if he is thus deprived of certain experiences, man can still raise himself so high that the fugitive pleasures which he renounces are as nothing compared with the love of God. There is no such thing as a complicated situation, and your own is simpler than you or the public believe. If you like—and don't smile—I shall explain you to yourself in a few words.

The sophistry of your letter—there is always a sophistry in your letter and to-day I've spotted it at once—is that you rank the supreme power of Grace lower than the very touching affection of which you speak. If you are to attain to joy, it will not be by the human element in those exhortations which you despise, but by the way in which Grace will work in you through them. You do exactly the opposite by allowing what is evil to work inside you. Not only does it make you blaspheme, but it makes you proclaim for no reason such ideas as will spatter mud upon all that you most respect. Only with all God's help can I read calmly those last phrases in which you assert that those who turned away from you when you read the Gospel are the same as those who would be horrified by all that the Gospel so expressly forbids. There is, in their attitude, a logic of good sense which is my whole philosophy.

Moreover, you doubt the power of Grace because it is so long since you did anything to draw near to it. But you can only draw near to it if you wish to change yourself. But if you are pleased with your present condition (such as you now reveal it to me), then you are mad, because you know that this condition is a deplorable one. It is therefore Pride—that ancient sin which has undone us all—that is destroying you, because it is in you yourself that you place your trust.

You will forgive, dear friend. You will feel the affection that prompts these lines. To continue : I have meditated, long but simply, on your case :

Either you will become mad ;

Or you will be converted ; and, if you become mad it will, I am afraid, be largely your fault. But I still see in you certain broad stretches of lucidity, like the blue in a menacing sky. You can't think that, when I point out the infallible remedy for your soul's disorder, it is from the wretched little human pride of seeing your spirit incline and adhere to some doctrine just because I incline and adhere to it.

Once, in my hearing, you spoke with ironical reproaches of the men who claim to have the Truth in their pockets. Know, my friend, that my heart is not larger than my pocket, and that I believe in the Truth which told me that It was there. That surprises you ; but it was Bossuet who said that " all that is divine must at first astonish human nature, which has sinned and been banished from Heaven ".

You will think that I am still preaching and that I have once again yielded to crying " Wolf, wolf ! ". Yes, my friend, I yielded because I know that you are unhappy and because, alas ! I am no longer surprised to see you draw away from God. Since you are willing to see Father Brisset, so much the better. If he doesn't convert you, he will at least enchant you by his rigid purity and his austere intelligence. There's no reason at all why you shouldn't see him after having written to, or before having met, the priest whom Claudel recommended to you.

I embrace you with all my heart,

JAMMES.

I am asking Father Brisset to write to you, if he is there.

167.—André Gide to Francis Jammes

[The following are sketches for André Gide's reply to letter No. 166. As Jammes destroyed this reply, we do not know which version he finally received.]

[End of March 1914.]

My dear Jammes,

The affectionate tone of your letter encourages me to go on speaking to you. But the conversation between us has one difficult

aspect which has often reduced me to silence when my friendship
for you would have liked to speak out : whereas you yourself
speak to me naturally, you only think that I am speaking naturally
to you when, in point of fact, I am making myself unnatural on
your account. I am exceedingly poor in all those things in which
you are rich ; I have only a small stock of metaphors—and I have
dismissed those few that I had, because they encumbered my
thoughts : my thoughts may not be of much importance, but for
me they represent reality.

Ah ! How strong would my position be, in this debate, if I were
not sensitive to the untruths of your poetry ! How much less
strong would your own position be if you were even a little more
capable of understanding those who are not like yourself : a
Beethoven, a Pascal, a Dostoevsky. But when I hear you speak of
Dostoevsky, for instance, as if he were a madman or a Hottentot,
you will appreciate that I am a little less worried about whatever
you may think of me.

You may be sure that it is not the man of letters, nor above all
the nettled man of letters, who is writing to you. If I had been
going to be nettled I should not have waited for your last letter—
in which, on the contrary, I found nothing but friendship. When
I was sorting my papers the other day I re-read two of your letters :
the one in reply to my *Immoralist* ; the other in reply to certain
" incomprehensions " of mine about your *Existences*. They show
exactly where we stand. My sincerity seems to you an affectation ;
and when I say, to you whom God has given wings, that " to me,
He gave legs instead ", you take it as a mark of pride. . . .

A. G.

My dear Jammes,

I should like to write to you again—even if only in order
that you should not feel that your second letter has found no echo
in my heart—but, however simply I write, you always think, don't
you, that I write as a sophist ? You say so yourself. All the same,
I can't help protesting when you claim to find sophistries in my
last letter. Not for an instant did I suggest that the love of God
would be sure to fail where the love of a human being had failed ;
all I meant was that I doubted that a priest would prove a better
counsellor than love itself ; or that, if I had seen a priest sooner,

I should now be the father of a family. That the love of Christ can sublimate all desires and reabsorb them within itself—that I believe ; I even count on it . . . with the help of age. Nothing else was meant by the passage in my letter which made you so indignant. . . .

A. G.

168.—*Paul Claudel to Jacques Rivière*

Hamburg, 27th March 1914.

Dear Friend,

The programme of the conference is very impressive and I am very sorry not to be able to be present. Give my affectionate thanks to all those who will take part.

You now know everything about X. How providential that you are now a Christian ! You can do a lot of good to him. In my view he is simply an over-nervous person who has let himself go, exaggerated his condition, and poisoned himself with medicine, philosophy, and literature. How fortunate that he has at last unbosomed himself ! Of course a priest would do him most good. Otherwise he would do well to see the best doctor I know of for nervous complaints—Dr. Bucher of Strasbourg, who is really extraordinary. Advise X to see him. If he doesn't take energetic steps about himself he's on the way to a complete " breakdown " (*sic*). He must be given a helping hand, and above all he mustn't be allowed to despair. But you will be a better judge of all that than I. It's a very risky thing to make a diagnosis by correspondence. And I've never known him otherwise than from letters.

In any case, don't take it too badly yourself. We others, we Catholics, are built to walk dry-shod through the Red Sea. *Cadent a latere tuo mille, et decem millia a dextris tuis.*

How's your little daughter ?

I grasp your hand,

P. CLAUDEL.

I shall doubtless spend the last days of Holy Week at the Benedictine Abbey of Maria-Laach, near Cologne.

169.—*Paul Claudel to Jacques Rivière*

Hamburg, 20th April 1914.

My dear Friend,

I am thinking of coming to Paris on 3rd May for the performance of *L'Otage*, which will probably be given on about the 10th. I don't much relish resuming this rôle of theatrical trainer. It always ends in disappointments. Of course I am very glad to accept straight away your kind invitation.

I am very glad to know that your little girl is doing well. You see that God has heard your prayer ! How I should like to see in you a little more confidence, good humour, and filial simplicity ! All that is so simple and so natural—why torment yourself so ? Still, everything will come in its own time. I've no worries on your account.

Yes, I think you can do a lot for Gide, even if only by your own example. As for me, you see what results I've achieved after seven years of correspondence. He wrote me letters which seemed to me to have the ring of sincerity, and yet all the time he was writing the thing which has the title of *Les Caves du Vatican*. (Parenthetically, it has been very disagreeable to me to figure between the same covers as that ignominy.) But there ! I was going to use a bad word which I'd promised myself to avoid, and which doesn't in any case represent what I think. I wasn't disgusted by the book, and I don't despise it ; but my heart is heavy, as if with the weight of something which is chiefly horrifying by reason of its hopelessness. That book is really sinister ; every sentiment in its seems to have been blighted. It has no shape, insignificant events are brought to the foreground and assume a morbid importance, there are stories without any end to them, and the incidents are strung together, or rather follow upon one another, with the absurdity, the languor, and sometimes the obscenity of a nightmare. It's gloomy and, somehow, foreign to humanity. A sad end for a man who promised better things.

I wrote to Gide and begged him to cut out the ignoble passage which shocked me. He made it a point of honour to keep it in. He goes on his way with the obstinacy of a sleepwalker, disguised beneath an evasive exterior. It's a way that won't take him far, poor chap !

I grasp your hand with affection,

P. CLAUDEL.

There's only one book that ever gave me the impression of ghastly desolation which I've tried to depict to you, and that is Voltaire's *Candide*.

Gide : *Journal*

14 June 1914.

This morning, at work at six-thirty, I got fairly well ahead with my notes : but the mail brought me absurd bits of newspaper gossip to which I had to reply for they question my friendship for Claudel. All this because of the epigraph for the third book of the *Caves*, which I had used with his approval and later suppressed at his request.

14 July 1914.

They took me for a rebel (Claudel and Jammes) because I was unable to get—or unwilling to force—myself to that cowardly submission which would have assured my comfort. That is perhaps the most Protestant trait I have in me : my horror of comfort.

———

170.—*Paul Claudel to André Gide*

19 Corso d'Italia, Rome,
14th March 1916.

Dear Gide,

I received your letter and was delighted to have your news. I know that you are going on, in Paris, with the good and useful work that you began there, and I am glad to congratulate you.

As for M. de Unamuno, I only know him from the cutting from *Le Semaine littéraire* which you sent me, but that cutting was enough to make me very suspicious of him. I read there, after all, that he is " a convinced Catholic after the fashion of a Pascal *or* a Bossuet ", and at the same time " tends towards pragmatism ". That, " forgetful of scientific logic, he proceeds by postulates ". That " his Christianity, though Catholic in form, is *marked by the great liberties he takes with tradition,* and has nothing in common with the Thomist Catholicism which is so much in favour at Rome since Leo XIII ". " One must stand by those life-giving truths which are useful to the spirit." His method is " an anti-intellectual vitalism ". In short, this Catholic is a Protestant or, what is worse, a modernist. His doctrine is a résumé of maxims which have been condemned I don't know how many times by Rome and, most recently, by the *Pascendi* Encyclical. So I've nothing in common with him, nor, above all, with that exasperating proposition, which bobs up all down the centuries, that faith and reason have nothing in common and must each rule in its own domain. As for myself, I am purely and simply catholic, that is to say, universal. I see no contradiction between our different faculties and I think that they all find, in the Truth, an object and an employment which harmonize and satisfy them in full measure. God is not made for man ; it's man who is made for God. If, by the way, M. Unamuno is well disposed towards France, I think well of him for it, but he will certainly find other thinkers better qualified than myself to present him to the public.

Thank you for the magnificent photograph of Rimbaud (and for the smaller one which came with it). You could not please me more. We have been living in anguish these last days. It's the supreme crisis.

My greetings to all your associates. I grasp your hand in friendship.

P. CLAUDEL.

Speaking of the sentiments of human love, which ends by giving to our unwittingly tormented race a conscience and a finite personality which we call God, the Rector of Salamanca shows that " *we have God*, IN SOME DEGREE, by establishing a purpose for the world in order to establish a purpose for ourselves and our activity ". It's terrifying.

Gide : *Journal*

Cuverville, Tuesday, March 1916.

Letter from Claudel, whom I had asked if he would write a preface for Unamuno's book that we are to publish in translation. He scents heresy in it : modernism, Protestantism. . . . How

could I be so misled by it ? . . . Decidedly all roads do not lead
to Rome and he alone who keeps his mouth shut can be sure of
staying in the path of orthodoxy. It is better not to enter upon it ;
this is still the best way of not straying.

[Detached pages] February 1918.

I have often said to Claudel :
" What withholds me is not free thought, but the Gospel."
" Withholds you from what ? "
" Why, from entering the Church, of course ! Catholics do not
know the Gospel. And they not only don't know it, they don't
know that they don't know it ; they honestly believe they know it,
so that they continue not to know it.
" It is," Ghéon said to me with the zeal of a neophyte, " the
great error of Protestantism to want to limit revelation to the
Gospels alone, not to understand that God continues to be in direct
relation with listening humanity. The word of God is not confined
to the Gospels, and God continues to explain himself, expressing
himself just as much in the Pope's latest encyclical as in the very
words of Christ ; and the Church does not cease to be divinely
inspired. Seeing an opposition between this and that proves that
one has understood neither one nor the other," he says . . . [. . .]

The idea of bargaining never entered into the religion I knew ;
no, not even the idea of a simple reward. And I recall that this is
precisely what Claudel complained of after reading *La Porte étroite*.
This, according to him, was just where the Protestant error lay ;
he did not consent to see in that very disinterestedness anything
but pride.

171.—*Paul Claudel to André Gide*

Good Friday, 1919.

My best wishes and remembrances, my dear Gide, on the
occasion of this holy festival of Easter, when your friends, dead and
living, are thinking of you.

P CLAUDEL.

172.—*Paul Claudel to André Gide*

French Legation, Copenhagen,
7th August 1920.

Thank you, my dear Gide, for the beautiful book which brings me once again the best part of yourself.

P. CLAUDEL.

Gide :   *Journal*

29 November 1921.

Big article by Massis, in *La Revue universelle*, on (or rather, against) me. Massis sets up against my books a remark by Claudel : " Evil does not compose ". As if it were by lack of composition that my books sinned !

10 September 1922.

It is odd that, in the three convert artists I have known best— Ghéon, Claudel, Jammes—Catholicism brought only an encouragement to pride. Communion infatuates them.

———

173 —*Paul Claudel to André Gide*

Tokyo, 29th July 1923.

My dear Gide,

I am very touched that you should do me the honour of sending me your book on Dostoevsky, which is one of the best you have written. There is something musical in your talent, and you find your way about this difficult score with the ease of a perfect virtuoso. I cannot see that any essential element of this sublime Russian has escaped your notice, although you have not had the time to study Dostoevsky's *art* as it deserves. His way of composing is so accomplished, so interesting by reason of its vast Beethoven-like crescendos, its ennoblement of the technical innovations of Eugène Sue and the other epics of the Bardic school in the age of

Louis Philippe.   In any case you have grasped the fact that
Dostoevsky was neither a barbarian nor a sick man, unless one can
describe as " sickness " the terrible travail of a man (the symbol
and the offering of a whole race and a whole century) in process of
being cured.

This brings me to the only criticism I would make of your book :
that it gives a static and definitive character to a crisis, to the passion
of a man who never stopped changing and who replied to pitiless
interrogations from on high with all the answers and all the subter-
fuges of which the crushed mixture of body and soul is capable. As
you have very ably remarked, when Dostoevsky speaks for himself
(in his *Journal,* and even to a certain extent in his letters, in my
opinion), he talks nothing but nonsense. But when he is on the
tripod, or on the easel, his answers—sly, bizarre, elusive, and
fragmentary, like those which were extracted in ancient times from
men possessed by a devil—those answers simply cannot be taken
at their face value. They are always amended by a certain reserve,
the withdrawal of something fundamental which Dostoevsky
always kept back, and which tormented him to the end. He never
got free of his interrogators, or free of the rack.

This would be the moment to take up in a friendly way your
occasional digs at Catholicism. Dostoevsky's furious anger against
Catholicism is very interesting. It reminds of those convulsions
of the possessed which the Gospel describes : " Son of David,
why dost thou persecute us ? " Neither he nor you seem to have
a good grasp of the Catholic position. Protestants take their stand
by the Gospel, and we take our stand by Jesus Christ, of whom the
Gospel is the evidence, but whose dwelling is the Church. The
Gospel is the memorial of someone who is dead, the Church the
habitation of someone who is alive, and who is with us in all our
earthly transactions. You turn back towards the Christ of history,
whereas we have the living embodiment of an uninterrupted Jesus.
When Dostoevsky dares to put up his melancholy Orthodox
Church (which, by the way, occupies so large a place in his work)
against the Church of God, he lays it open, after all, to some crush-
ing comparisons. On which side do we find a faith that is intrepid
and inflexible ? On which side the examples of heroic renunciation
and impassioned charity ? On which side has the truth always been
affirmed, innocently and precisely, among all the fantasies of self-
esteem and imagination ? All that is not said to depreciate

Dostoevsky, the hero who has rescued the cross from the cloaca of Renan and the marshlands of the nineteenth century. A Christian listens to his weeping, his delirium, his blasphemies, with edification, just as a doctor welcomes the violent fantasies with which an organism finds its way back to health. But we must not be told that a state of paroxysm is a state of repose. Besides, one of the great objects of art is to purge the soul ; and that explains the bad element which is sometimes (but not always) mixed in, as you very ably point out.

I grasp your hand in friendship,

P. CLAUDEL.

Gide : *Journal*

Cuverville, 9 October 1923.

There was waiting for me in Tunis a very beautiful letter from Paul Claudel, which moves me very specially—all the more so since the newspapers were announcing almost his death, or at least, after the catastrophe in Japan, let it be understood that he had probably perished in the earthquake.

21 December 1923.

Jacques Maritain came then Friday morning, 14th December, to the Villa on the stroke of ten, as it had been agreed. [. . .] He declared straight out the purpose of his visit, which I knew, and which was to beg me to suspend the publication of a certain book of which he besought me to recognize with him the danger.

I told him that I had no intention of defending myself but that he must be aware that everything he could think of saying to me about this book I had already said to myself, and that a project that resists the trial of the war, of personal losses, and of all the meditations that ensue, runs the risk of being too deeply anchored in the heart and mind for an intervention like his to hope to change it. He transmitted to me Henri Massis' fear of having, by the provocation of his articles, hastened that publication. I begged him to leave Massis all his fears and regrets and remorse and spoke of the wonderful letter Claudel had written me, about my *Dostoevsky* likewise, in which I felt at least the impulse of a truly Christian thought, which I in nowise recognized in Massis' articles.

174 —*Paul Claudel to André Gide*

Tokyo, 12th January 1924.

My dear Gide,

I have just received your *Numquid et tu . . .* which makes it possible for me to resume our conversation. Despite its ten years' interruption you may be sure that I have never ceased to think of you, and to pray that you will be enlightened once and for all. I feel that in these ten years your path has, all the same, drawn nearer to the humble highway which I am treading. I infer from this moving little book that you now admit the divinity of Christ and have begun to pray. That is something as impressive as the moment when a child first begins to breathe. Your great discovery (and in this you are perfectly right) is that eternal life is not deferred till later but begins here and now, from the very moment that the Kingdom of God is with us, *intra nos*. But the Gospel also says that it works within us like a grain of mustard-seed or a parcel of leaven—that is to say that it doesn't remain inert, that we don't possess it like some inert substance or a piece of capital that is acquired once and for all. It begins growing and working ; somebody is being nourished within us, and within us, at our expense, he carries out his mysterious task of transformation. Of this task, our souls and our bodies are the elements ; and the task ends when we are resurrected entire. The Christian is the man who gives himself over completely to the surreptitious construction of a new life, who asks for nothing but this imposition, who no longer has a life of his own ; but it is Christ who lives in him. Sainthood consists in cutting down the partition, in abolishing oneself, in ceasing to offer any obstacle to the will of God. It is terrifying, painful, and yet at the same time passionately interesting and sweeter than I can describe. It was the Abbé Brémond's book on the French Oratorians, Condren and Bérulle (which formerly I found deeply repellent—almost as much so as the *Imitation*) which made me understand the essential modality of prayer. I never succeeded in meditating according to the method of St. Ignatius. But Condren's method I found easy and congenial from the start. It doesn't consist in any effort of intelligence or memory or imagination, but in abandoning oneself completely, profoundly, and as a son, to the Will which is within us. We have only to listen to Him who is our guide, our doctor, our counsellor, and much else besides. I shouldn't like to write you a " contentious " letter, but I don't think that you can both pray and at the same time retain the attitude of a critic and an epicurean, rejecting one part of the faith and accepting another. You must swallow it all, just as the Jews, when they ate the Lamb of the Passover, consumed even its bones and its intestines with bitter herbs. You must stop pursing your lips at the mention of the miracles. If Christ performed them, he had his reasons ; he wanted to show that nothing on heaven or earth is stronger than love. You must practise Hope, which is a cardinal virtue, and you must not neglect the gifts which are in store for the adult in favour of the occasional spoon-feeding which is the pabulum of little children. If Christ was resurrected, why blame St. Paul, who extends to all Christians, to all the *Christi facti*, their resemblance to their model ? Our resurrection is not entirely in the future. It is also within us, it is beginning, it has already begun. Let us eat and drink, said St. Paul, let us grow fat for the worms, if we do not believe in Christ, if we do not wish to be his meat and his drink. I hope that you will not see all this as a sermon, but as a brotherly effusion. You are certainly in the clutch of Grace, and the surest sign of this is that tenacious preoccupation with the Faith which has marked you for so many years, and which has already wrought in you so many transformations.

I grasp your hand with great affection,

P. C.

———

175.—*André Gide to Paul Claudel*

Auteuil, 04.55 [Paris, May 1925].

I hurried along on receipt of your letter, and am going away in great distress at not having found you.

You will have been given the little book which I left for you. . . . But I am anxious about one thing : hadn't I given it to you already ? In that case please hand it on from me to anyone you like. I am confident that you won't put it into unworthy hands.

I want to see you again and . . . I'm afraid of you, Claudel. I saw Bréal this morning and he told me that he discusses everything with you and makes jokes, and that nothing is more charming than your animation.   But you know that I cannot joke when I am with you.   Our conversation can only be serious, and I am terribly shaken by what you say.   I remember all our conversations perfectly, and I'm still in a sweat of anguish from the excellent letter which you sent me from Japan and which I received at Tunis just when the news of the disaster arrived.   My heart beat like a child's, this morning, when I recognized your writing on the envelope, and I for a moment I didn't dare to open it.   I am more touched than I can tell you by the constancy of your friendship. . . .

I shall come and knock on your door one of these days on the chance of seeing you.   Will you be at home to-morrow at the beginning of the afternoon, towards 2 o'clock ?   Don't answer, if you will.

Yours,

A. G.

[At the foot of this letter, some days after receiving it, Paul Claudel added the following notes :]

Saw Gide on the evening of the 14th.

A long, solemn talk.   He told me that his religious disquietude is at an end, that he enjoys a sort of *felicity*, founded on work and human sympathy.   The *Goethean* side of his character has got the better of the Christian side.   I spoke to him of my Carmelites, of complete understanding, and of the prayer for annihilation.   He appeared deeply interested and disturbed.   He is leaving for French Equatorial Africa with the idea that he perhaps will never return.   His wife.

[Rereading Gide's letter after the publication of the Journal of André Gide in 1939, Claudel added these further lines :]

This letter dates from 1925.   It was my last interview with this unhappy man.   See his *Journal*.

Gide : *Journal*

15 May 1925.

Yesterday evening, call on Claudel.   He has asked me to come and was waiting for me.   At number 80 rue de Passy, an apartment set back and not giving on to the street.   I go through two rooms, the second of which is rather large, and find myself in a third one, still larger, which he uses as a bedroom and workroom.   Open army couch in a corner ; a low bookcase goes around two sides of the room ; many objects, brought back from the Far East, decorate it.

At my ring, Claudel came to meet me and holds out his hand. He seems to have shrunk.   A short, swansdown-lined jacket of coffee-coloured silk makes him look still thicker.   He is enormous and short ; he looks like Ubu.   We sit down in two arm-chairs. He completely fills his.   Mine, a sort of chaise-longue, has such a low back that to be comfortable in it I should have to get too far away from Claudel.   I give up and lean forward.

In the presence of Claudel I am aware only of what I lack ; he dominates me ; he overhangs me ; he has more base and surface, more health, money, genius, power, children, faith, etc., than I. I think only of obeying without a word.

176.—*Paul Claudel to Madame André Gide*

Château de Lutaine par Cellettes (Loir-et-Cher),
20th August 1925.

Madame,

I cannot but have the impression that perhaps you would like to speak to me of a soul which is dear to you, which has been constantly in my thoughts for twenty-five years, and of which God has put the key into your hands.   If I am mistaken, forgive me. If not, I shall be delighted to meet when and where you please, either at Paris or at Cuverville.

Please accept my respectful regards,

PAUL CLAUDEL.

177.—*Madame André Gide to Paul Claudel*

Cuverville, 27th August 1925.

Dear Monsieur Claudel,

Your letter is one more proof of the faithful friendship in God which you retain for my husband ; that friendship has always deeply touched me.

Yes, I am in great anxiety at the long and distant visit to black
Africa which he wished to undertake—but if I had more faith I
should not so torment myself. All those who love André Gide, as
that very noble spirit deserves to be loved, must pray for him. I
pray for him every day—and so do you, do you not?—That, I
think, is how we can best meet one another, and do most for him.

Dear Monsieur Claudel, may I express all my gratitude to you
as a friend—and all my admiration for you as a great writer.

MADELEINE ANDRÉ GIDE.

178.—André Gide to Paul Claudel

Cuverville, 15th June 1926.

My dear Claudel,

On my return from the Chad I learnt from my wife that
you had been kind enough to write to her. She was very touched ;
and now I am touched in my turn and thank you from my heart.
When I think of the constancy of your friendship I find in it a
certain comfort. Sometimes I say to myself rather sadly that I
must see in it only a persistent hope of my conversion ; and I
measure my affection for you by the chagrin that it causes me to
disappoint you. Why aren't all Catholics like you ? You will tell
me that the best are silent. Alas ! There are too many who talk,
and who lie in the name of the Church. Too often, when I read
them, I think : No, we don't love the same God. I can only love
a God of truth. I know that He is your God. But what am I to
think of a tree which bears such *other* fruit ?

Au revoir. Never doubt the depth of my friendship.

ANDRÉ GIDE.

179.—Paul Claudel to André Gide

Chuzenji, 25th July 1926.

My dear Gide,

I was happy to receive your letter yesterday, and to see that
you have returned, apparently in good health, from that African

journey which had filled me with dark foreboding. You have still some way to go ; you are one of those people whose existence has a symbolic value, who realize in its entirety a scheme of life of which others merely sketch the rudiments, and that is, of course, one reason for my interest in you—an interest made up of anxiety, as much as of hope. You are the stake, the protagonist, and the cockpit of a great struggle whose outcome I cannot foresee, but I think that what is best in you will end by opening its wings. You occupy, or rather you constitute in yourself, a strategic position which you must really try to defend on lines other than those which you indicate in your last letter. You don't like Catholics, and you have complaints to lodge against them ! Do you think they've no complaints to lodge against you ? And what is more serious— do you think it isn't true, in the most fundamental sense of the word, that from their point of view you've *gone astray*? That's why they are interested in you. Their interest is not shown in the same way as mine, but it is equally active. I don't know any Catholic who is not preoccupied with you, who doesn't think of you—and in a way (though you mayn't believe it) in which affection is strangely mingled with justified horror. Only they've taken rather too literally the text in the Bible which reads " Knock, and it shall be opened unto you ". Believe me—they would leave you in peace if they didn't feel in their hearts that you are a brother and a captive, and one who is harbouring the Christ whom, for so many years, you have been trying to kill off. You don't know it, but an enormous number of prayers is being offered on your behalf. Still, you are a long way past fifty ; and as for these wretched things, the opinion of Peter and Paul, and the caprices of the senses (a sad lot, whatever they may be) and the displays of the mind, it's high time that they assumed their rightful place in the void ! As old Laotze used to say, " the only thing that I appreciate is the Mother "—meaning the original savour and juice of existence. One must offer one's lips to the very source of creation, instead of being like those orphan piglets who pull at the dugs of a dead sow ! When the Gospel speaks of that man who sold all his belongings in order to buy one unique jewel, it says something which old people know to be true from their experience, and which they understand infinitely better than any young person. It's not that the other belongings were of no worth—they helped, after all, to buy the one that mattered ! But I know now what I grasp tightly in my

hand when I am quite alone. I dare to relax my grip a little.
After forty years, and thanks to the intervention of the two holy
Carmelites of Cholet, the gates of prayer have opened for me.
I am like one of those little ragged men who used to be sent out
on the roads of France to sweep away horse droppings. One
summer day the great gate with its lofty barriers of sheet-iron,
before which he carried out his duties, was no longer shut, but
open. At first he only looked inside ; then he took a few steps
forward on the miraculous gravel, only to run hastily back ; then
he takes a chance and goes as far as the geranium bed, and in the
great silence of the afternoon he hears the sounds of water being
sprayed on the heavenly lawns, and in the distance a river running
with a muffled roar. To-morrow, and the next day, will the gate
still be open ? It will ! And in the end he understands that the
gates have been opened for him.

They are open for you, too. Don't bother about the lodge-
keeper. Just don't look at him, and he won't see you.

I grasp your hand with affection,

P. CLAUDEL.

Please give my best respects to Madame Gide.

Gide : *Journal*

5 March 1929.

I would not swear that at a certain period of my life I was not
very close to being converted. Thank God, a few converts among
my friends took care of this, however. Jammes, or Claudel, or
Ghéon, or Charlie Du Bos will never know how instructive their
example was for me.

30 October 1929.

Finished *Le Soulier de satin.* Staggering. It is hard to imagine
that in another religion Claudel's shortcomings could have developed
as unimpeded as in Catholicism. What a warning ! *A-vertissement,*
as he would say ! And yet I am in no way inclined to consider
myself better than Claudel, and for certain aspects of his character
I maintain a great esteem. But I note with curiosity that not one
of my shortcomings would find encouragement in Catholicism ;

quite the contrary, only my good qualities would, and doubtless the best ones (or so it seems to me this evening)—so that from the effect of Catholicism on Claudel I am quite unable to deduce the effect Catholicism would have on me.

2 November 1930.

Auguste Bréal, on my way through Marseille, tells me of some extraordinary letters from Claudel to Philippe Berthelot, which the latter lent him and which he copied. Letters calling down curses on Goethe, which Bréal promises to read me the next time I come through Marseille. Philippe does not know Goethe well and is ready to judge him according to Claudel (who " cannot be wrong ") —of whom, moreover, he has not read anything in a long time, and this allows him to continue to see in him a superior mind. Claudel has always treated Goethe with an easily sovereign scorn. Oh, how this scorn puts me at ease ! So much voluntary (and instructive) lack of intelligence, that set purpose to reject what cannot be annexed, gives extraordinary encouragement to my resistance, and I am more grateful to them than they could imagine (to Claudel, Massis, etc.) for their rejections.

December 1931.

Claudel. I like him and want him thus, scolding easy, lukewarm Catholics who try to compromise. We can admit him, admire him : he owes it to himself to vomit us. As for me, I would rather be vomited than vomit.

From an Interview given by Paul Claudel to Dominique Arban,
in Combat, 28*th March* 1947

Paul Claudel draws two chairs near together, sits down, and lends ear. Decanted by the years, he no longer looks like a " steam-hammer " or a " coagulated cyclone ". With less blood, less passion, he is a bald-headed, stout, alert old man.

After one or two amiabilities we get down to brass tacks.

" Rimbaud ! I'd rather not speak of him. They've made such a botch of him. I'm disgusted by the way they exploit him. It's so distressing to see such work besmirched. It's like some beauty-spot that's just been discovered ; it's soon one mass of rubbish and sardine-tins, and one just can't go there any more."

" If you know little of the efforts made by those who have assumed the heritage of Rimbaud, perhaps there are other young writers who interest you ? In particular, what is your attitude towards those who, in a universe from which hope has vanished, are founding a system of moral values based on man alone ? "

" Moral values are the commandments of God and the Church. Outside them there are no moral or spiritual values. What our writers have come by seems to me absolutely derisory."

" But their tragedy, their loyalty to . . . "

" That doesn't interest me at all. Let them get out of it as best they can."

My air of bewilderment makes him adopt a gentler tone.

" I am like a turkey-cock, to whom a drake means nothing. It's no part of my rôle as an old fogey to understand all that. Incomprehension is one of the bases of my character."

" Yet this search for a morality which does not transcend man himself is also the work of one of your contemporaries, André Gide."

" Oh, I detest all that ! "

" ? "

" I don't see that Gide has any talent at all."

" His disquiet, or rather, as you would say, his *dis*quiet. . . ."

" You don't think it's all a sham ? "

233

" ! "

" What I still can't understand is his influence. From the artistic and intellectual point of view Gide is nothing. His influence is one of the mysteries with which I am surrounded."

" You once said about him that ' evil never comes to terms '. He admits in his *Journal* that he doesn't quite understand the meaning of this utterance."

" But, in theology, evil does not exist. It is a destructive and purely negative element. Evil is only interesting because it is accompanied by suffering. From that point of view it is incontestably a creative element. Gide gives way to easy temptations, to so-called natural needs—instead of creating a living ambience for his soul. Christianity is a school of energy which teaches us to be heroes."

" If Gide has not been converted . . . "

" It's because he accepted no guide. He offers an appalling example of cowardice and weakness."

" He would not at all like to be defended, but are you not ignoring the courage of his contradictory allegiances—his integrity, in fact ? "

He laughed—a laugh of tranquil contempt.

" All right, I'll give you ' integrity ' if it makes you happy."

He looked at me indulgently.

" Don't think that I bear him ill-will, but you ask me unexpected questions, and I've no time to think them over."

" Really ? "

" I don't want to be controversial. I had a lot to do with Gide when I thought he was profoundly Christian . . . and I knew nothing of his abominable failing . . . "

He turned away, in modesty.

" Yes, up to the day I learnt of that . . . abyss. The police very properly arrest poisoners—but Gide, too, is a poisoner, and I'm not speaking lightly. How many letters have I not received from young men who've gone astray ? At the beginning of their downfall, there's always Gide."

" They come to you in the end ? "

" After a certain time they realize that evil doesn't come to terms, and then they write to me."

" Gide has taught us all the value of integrity in dealing with oneself, and of lucidity in judging the motives of our conduct."

" You think that he really confesses to his true motives ? Mirrors fascinate Gide. His *Journal* is just a long series of poses in front of himself. In the first place, one always poses when one looks at oneself. His *Journal* is, from that point of view, a monument of insincerity."

" But he often speaks of his anxieties on that point. I remember a passage where he says, more or less, " If I haven't kept this *Journal* for some time, it's because the mere fact of keeping it made it less sincere."

" That already is a sort of literary amendment. He dusts himself down with a humming-bird's feathers. The real drama of his existence is never mentioned."

" It's mentioned enough for the reader to sense its importance."

" And as for his gravest and most natural failing, he hardly mentions it."

" But that isn't true. So very often . . . and *Si le grain ne meurt.* . . ."

But did he hear, did he wish to hear ?

" For my part I combat his influence with every weapon I have. What would you ? It's Yes or No."

" And if it's yes *and* no ? "

" Meaningless to me . . . "

NOTES

By

ROBERT MALLET

[For the English edition the following selection has been made from M. Robert Mallet's Notes to the original French edition. Notes of primarily domestic interest have been omitted.]

Letter 1

Paul Claudel occupied the post of French Consul at Foochow from 1899 to 1906. Kuliang, whence this letter was written, was a summer station much frequented by Europeans.

André Gide had sent his two books, published by *Le Mercure de France* in 1899. They were *Le Prométhée mal enchaîné* and *Philoctète, ou le Traité des trois Morales* ; a volume which contained *Le Traité de Narcisse, La Tentative amoureuse,* and *El Hadj.* Gide was thirty in 1899, and Claudel twenty-nine. Both had been enthusiastic visitors to Mallarmé's " Tuesdays " in the years 1891–1895, but it was only in the latter year, and in the apartment of Marcel Schwob, that they had become acquainted with one another.

On 13th December 1907 André Gide noted in his *Journal* : " I find and re-read a letter from Paul Claudel (1899). ' Your mind has no slope,' he said to me. That is just what is needed. No praise is more ' precious ' to me."

Letter 2

Claudel returned to France in May 1900 in order to spend a period of several months' leave. At this time he was uncertain as to whether he should not become a priest ; but after consultation with the Benedictines of Ligugé he was persuaded that his duty was to serve the Church *in the world of his time,* and eventually he returned to China at the beginning of the year 1901.

André Gide recalls having taken a walk across Paris with Paul Claudel in the spring of 1900. " I remember," he notes, " our conversation as we walked by the Seine. Claudel explained to me with great admiration why he considered Jules Renard to be one of the greatest writers of his time. I admit that I was rather surprised that the author of *Tête d'Or* should cherish such an admiration. . . ."

The two books which Gide had given to Claudel were *Paludes* (1895) and *Les Nourritures Terrestres* (1897).

Letter 3

André Gide's lecture on " Influence in Literature " is republished in his *Prétextes.*

At the time of this letter the Boxer Rebellion was causing considerable alarm among the European settlements in China. The Rebellion had been put down by the time Paul Claudel returned to China, but it had a great effect upon his imagination, and the third act of his play *Partage de Midi* takes place in the European quarter of a town that is besieged by the Boxers.

Letter 4

Paul Claudel had been reading Gide's *Prétextes* (1903), a collection of essays, articles, and lectures originally written or delivered between 1898 and 1902.

Here, briefly, is what André Gide says in *Prétextes* about the questions discussed by Claudel in this letter :

" We have known the idolatry of death ; let us prefer the idolatry of life. . . . It is only when the life of a nation declines like an ebbing tide that the art of that nation can cut itself off, or claim to duplicate and repeat the quality of life. To oppose art and life is absurd, because art can only be made out of life. But only where there is a superabundance of life can art have the good fortune to begin. Art is born of excess ; it begins when the act of living cannot of itself express the whole of life. A work of art is a work of distillation ; the artist is his own distiller. It takes an enormous quantity of concentrated life to produce one drop of this delicate spirit."

" You speak of educating the masses ; try it ; if you feel that it's the right job for you, I shall be filled with admiration, for I know that it's not at all the right job for me. . . . Beware of the masses ! If you want to love your neighbour, you must distinguish him from all the others. In the mass, men lose what is most valuable in each of them ; all that they gain, and their only reinforcement, is what they all have in common. . . . The masses respect nothing ; all that is tender, delicate, true and charitable is twisted, broken, and mortified by them ; they form a shifting, witless element, at the mercy of any demagogue ; when they have beauty, it is the beauty of a sea that is beyond control ; when I admire them, I do so from a balcony. . . ."

" Every new genius seems to raise the problem of art in a new guise."

" ' Man proposes and God disposes ' may be true in nature ; but in a work of art the contrary is true : God proposes and man disposes. . . . Cut that phrase in two, take one of its two parts for your text, and you will have the two great heresies of art which are always fighting one another with the object of not understanding that it is only when they are united in mutual compromise that art can be born . . .

" *God proposes :* thence comes naturalism, objectivism.

" *Man disposes :* thence comes a-priorism, idealism.

" *God proposes and Man disposes :* thence comes the work of art." (*Les Limites de l'Art.*)

Of Villiers de l'Isle-Adam, Gide said that " he had no great power of personal invention (being himself the result of an artistic process), but there converged in him a number of divergent influences (false Hegelianism, Wagnerism, Hindu morality, etc.) and there were certain floating (and therefore embarrassing) ideas, which he *worked on*, explored to their limits, and brought to a point of literary perfection, if not of real maturity." (*Quelques livres.*)

Paul Claudel was later to say of Verhaeren that he " mistook perspiration for inspiration ". André Gide, on the contrary, respected Verhaeren, remained faithful to the Belgian poet, and published his work among the early numbers of the *N.R.F.*

Gide's admiration for Nietzsche is summarized in a passage in *Prétextes* :
" Nietzsche, the man of passion, the creator. We all owe him our long-ripened gratitude. But for him, whole generations perhaps would have concerned themselves with timidly insinuating what he has affirmed in his audacious, masterly, demented way. . . . An admirable book ? No. But the preface to admirable books." Paul Claudel, on the other hand, regarded Nietzsche as a most questionable author—if not, indeed, as one best not discussed at all. " His opinion ", he wrote in 1926 in the course of an essay on Wagner, " is about as interesting to me as that of the humblest village schoolmaster. Where poetry is concerned, and in fact where anything else is concerned, the opinion of Nietzsche is exactly and literally zero, zero in figures." (*Figures et Parables*.)

Paul Claudel returned later in the correspondence (cf. letter No. 32) to his opinion of *Eureka*.

Περι Φύσεως is the title of the only book by Heraclitus.

In his account of his conversion, which appeared in the *Revue de la Jeunesse* of 10th October 1913, Paul Claudel describes how, as an adolescent, he accepted the scientific enthusiasms of the late nineteenth century and subscribed to their un-Christian or anti-Christian consequences. And, as he wrote in 1903, at the age of eighteen, " I believed what was believed by most of the so-called cultivated people of the time—I accepted the monistic and mechanistic hypothesis in all its severity. I believed that everything was subject to those ' laws ' and that the world was a rigid network of causes and effects which Science would shortly disentangle to everybody's satisfaction. It all seemed to me very sad and very tedious."

The dialectical poem on which Claudel was engaged was the *Ode aux Muses*. He later composed four other odes, and concluded the series with *Un Processionnal pour saluer le Siècle Nouveau*.

Letter 5

After four years' absence, Paul Claudel returned to France in May 1905 for a long spell of leave.

The poem which he had translated was one by Edgar Allan Poe which had first appeared in the *Fortnightly Review* for February 1904. It is sixteen lines long, dates from the last years of Poe's life, and evokes the unknown Leonania whom Poe's biographers have proved unable to identify.

André Gide's *Journal* : 16th May 1905 (Vol. I.)
(*All passages are from the translation of Justin O'Brien in four volumes.*)

A revised version of *Tête d'Or* was published by the *Mercure de France* in 1901. The play is concerned with a man of exceptional ability who claims to be able to do without God, believes that he has succeeded in doing so and eventually dies a violent death after seeing his fame and his pretensions brought to nothing. The first act, which André Gide so much admired, discloses Simon Agnel in the act of burying, with his own hands, the woman he loved. In the presence of his friend Cébès, he gives a moving description of the anguish with which he faces life, and of the need to rebel which is to make him " Tête d'Or " the conqueror.

Claudel's *Ode aux Muses* had just appeared in the April-May 1905 issue of *Vers et Prose*. It was later reprinted in the volume *Cinq Grandes Odes*.

Letter 6

Franz Blei, a German man of letters, translated *Le Roi Candaule* into German and had it performed in Vienna in 1906 and in Berlin in 1908. André Gide often speaks of Blei in his *Journal* and describes himself as having had " quite good literary relations " with him.

Alfred Vallette was the director of the *Mercure de France* publishing house.

Letter 7

Paludes had been translated into German by Félix Paul Grève, and André Gide wished this translator to have the opportunity of translating Jammes' three novels : *Clara d'Ellébeuse, Almaïde d'Etremont,* and *Pomme d'Anis.*

L'Échange, a play in three acts, was published by the *Mercure de France* in 1901 in a volume called *L'Arbre*, which also contained four other plays by Claudel. André Gide reviewed the book in *L'Ermitage* of December 1901, and said : " No analysis, however detailed, can give any idea of these five plays ; they are like nothing else ever written, and one is astonished that they should exist ; they are alive with a life of their own, a red and violent life that will flabbergast, repel and exasperate most people, but rouse a few others to the wildest enthusiasm . . .".

The play was acted at the *Vieux Colombier* in 1913, in a production by Jacques Copeau, with Charles Dullin in the cast.

L'Ermitage was a literary Review, founded in 1890 by Henri Mazel, who remained its editor until 1896. Édouard Ducoté then took over the editorship until 1904, with Gide and Rémy de Gourmont on the editorial committee. The Review foundered in September 1904, was revived under new management in January 1905, and disappeared definitively in December 1906. Gide wrote for it regularly from 1903 onwards, and Claudel allowed them to print *L'Échange* in July 1905. Others among its contributors were Maurice Denis, Paul Fort, Henri Ghéon, Edmond Jaloux, Francis Jammes, Paul Léautaud, Pierre Louys, Charles Maurras, Robert de Montesquiou, Paul Moréas, Ch. L. Philippe, Albert Samain, P.-J. Toulet, André Suarès, and Paul Valéry.

Letter 8

This letter is written from Villeneuve-sur-Fère, a village in the Aisne, where Claudel was born on 6th August 1868. The eighteenth-century presbytery, in which his childhood was spent, had been built by his great-great-uncle and is still in the possession of his family.

Letter 9

Philippe's *Bubu de Montparnasse* was published in 1901. It is the story of a prostitute who is forced to return to her sordid environment, of which Bubu is the personification, at the moment when she has the chance to re-make her life in the company of a respectable junior office worker.

Claudel takes as a significant example of pagan crime the death of Sejanus and his five-year-old daughter Sejania, who were strangled in prison at Tiberius' instigation.

Renan has always been particularly abhorrent to Claudel, who sees in him the most typical of those who exalted the powers of science at the expense of the mysteries of religion. In 1949 he said to Robert Mallet : " Even before my conversion I never thought him a good writer. I had not, as yet, any sense of religion, but I had a sense of style. He seemed to me nothing more than a man of learning, a technician of religious history. I did not think that he wrote well. It chanced that one day it was he who handed me my prize at the Lycée Louis-le-Grand. In his address to the school he said : " My dear friends, you may have heard it said that I am a great man, but who knows if one day one among you will come and accuse me of spreading poison ? " And Claudel smiled, and said, " Renan didn't know how true it was."

André Gide's *Journal* : 1st December 1905

L'Église habillée de feuilles was a volume of fifty-one religious poems by Francis Jammes. It was later incorporated in his *Clairières dans le Ciel*.

Adrien Mithouard (1864–1919) was the founder of the review *L'Occident* and the author of philosophical essays and several volumes of poetry. He later entered politics and was Chairman of the Municipal Council of Paris during the war of 1914–1918.

Letter 10

André Gide and Paul Claudel met on 30th November 1905 at the apartment of Arthur Fontaine. It was the occasion on which Gide read aloud from Jammes' *L'Église habillée de feuilles*. Gide's reflections on this new meeting have been quoted in the body of this Correspondence. On 5th December Paul Claudel lunched with him, and it was on the evening of that day that this letter was written. The enclosed volume of extracts from the Gospels was the first of a series which Claudel has compiled throughout his life. They include not only texts from the Bible, but also quotations from other sources, maxims and reflections from Claudel's own thought, photographs, press cuttings, and reproductions of paintings. Thus it was that, for example, the notebook of 1905 included a portrait of Keats.

André Gide's *Journal* : 5th December 1905

Le Traité de la Co-naissance du Monde et de soi-même was written at Foochow in 1904. It develops the arguments which should lead Man to take cognisance of where he stands in relation to the whole scheme of Creation : " an image of the creative activity " of God.

The *Ode aux Muses* was begun in 1900 in Paris and finished in 1904 at Foochow. Erato, who personifies lyric and love-poetry, is the last of the Muses to be invoked by the poet.

Both Gide and Claudel had a great admiration for the novels of Conrad, and in 1918 Gide published a translation of *Typhoon*.

Francis Jammes was converted to Catholicism, under the influence of Claudel, in July 1905. Gabriel Frizeau, a friend of Jammes and of Jacques Rivière, had also been converted under the influence of Claudel and his plays.

Letter 11

André Gide at first believed that the portrait of Keats had been inserted in Claudel's notebook as a mark of reprobation. But Claudel has expressly denied this, saying that, on the contrary, he considers Keats " one of the great poets of Humanity, akin in some respects to André Chénier but greatly superior in imaginative power to the French poet ".

Letter 14

André Suarès' *Voici l'Homme* was published in 1906. Suarès (1868–1948) was educated at the *École Normale Supérieure*, and his books include studies of Wagner, Tolstoy, and Shakespeare, volumes of poems and essays, and commentaries upon Péguy, Pascal, and Goethe. The most solitary of writers, Suarès never resigned an iota of his independence. Although the great majority of the public remained indifferent to his work, he captured the esteem, and even the veneration, of an élite of readers ; in 1911, for instance, Gide said of him that " our great-nephews will be astonished by the silence with which our age has surrounded Suarès ".

Letter 15

Paul Claudel was married on 15th March 1906, in Lyons, to Mademoiselle Reine Sainte-Marie-Perrin. The wedding took place in the chapel of the Hospice des Incurables, which had been founded by an ancestor of Mademoiselle Perrin.

Letter 17

Philippe Berthelot (1866–1934) entered the French Foreign Office in 1889 and met Paul Claudel during the course of a period of study in the Far East which lasted from 1902–1904. Returning to the Quai d'Orsay, he became Under-Secretary for Asiatic affairs in 1907 and in 1911 was elevated to the rank of Minister Plenipotentiary. In 1914 he became assistant to the Directeur des Affaires Politiques. After rendering distinguished service during the war and during the preparation of the Treaty of Versailles he became Directeur des Affaires Politiques, Ambassador, and finally Permanent Secretary of the French Foreign Office. He remained an intimate friend of Claudel throughout his life. The problem of religion, which each resolved in his own way, was never raised between them. *Partage de Midi* was dedicated to Philippe and Hélène Berthelot, and in his *Accompagnements* (1949) Claudel published the oration which he delivered at Berthelot's funeral.

Letter 18

Claudel stopped at Pekin on his way to Tientsin where he remained, as Consul, until 1909.

Francis Jammes, Arthur Fontaine, and Jacques Rivière also received copies of Claudel's " Summary ", which had been drawn up at the request of a large number of his friends.

Gide's *Amyntas*, published in 1906, comprises *Mopsus* (April 1894), *Feuilles de Route* (March-April 1896), *De Biskra à Touggourt* (December 1900), and *Le Renoncement au Voyage* (1903–1904).

The passages on which Claudel comments are those in which Gide reverts to his favourite controversy—that of the " uprooting " which he considered a necessary part of the healthy development of every human being. In one passage in *Amyntas* he remarks that " it is not a question of cutting off one's roots : ' *déraciné* ' has never implied that. What is admirable is that the Englishman, like the ancient Roman, takes his roots everywhere with him." In December 1897 Gide had contested the conclusion of Maurice Barreès' famous novel *Les Déracinés*, arguing that to take root once and for all must diminish, rather than enhance, the strength of either an individual or a tree ; and he quoted the example of the poplar, which is the more vigorous for being transplanted in its youth. The controversy was taken up by Charles Maurras, who supported Barrès and accused Gide of advocating that roots should be cut, instead of transplanted. Eventually, in 1916, Maurras admitted the mistake and, in his *L'Étang de Berre*, made amends.

This is the phrase from *Amyntas* in which the two imperfect subjunctives won the admiration of Claudel : " *Dans la foule qui suivait, j'ai reconnu le grand Ashour ; il m'expliqua que ce bouc allait être égorgé dans la nuit pour porter bonheur au village ; auparavant, on le promenait dans les rues, afin que les mauvais esprits des maisons, qui se tiennent au pas des portes,* entrassent *en lui et* disparussent ". (*Feuilles de Route.*)

Letter 21

Arthur Fontaine (1860–1931) was a friend of Claudel, Gide, Valéry, and Jammes.

Ducoté was at this time editor of *L'Ermitage*, to which Copeau (1879–1949) and Ghéon (1875–1943) were contributors.

Marcel Drouin (1870–1943) was a professor of philosophy who married

Jeanne Rondeaux, a sister of Madame André Gide. Gide's *Philoctète* (1899) was dedicated to him. He wrote under the name of Michel Arnauld and was one of the original members of the editorial committee of the *N.R.F.* His *Goethe* was published in 1949 with a preface by André Gide.

A limited edition (150 copies) of *Partage de Midi* had just appeared. In the *Cantique de Mésa* Claudel expresses the exaltation of the repentant sinner who, in the expectation of death, confides himself solemnly to God. The " duo " of the second act occurs when Ysé and Mésa confront one another in the cemetery of Hong Kong and bind themselves by a love-contract which seems to them to set them free from their previous obligations.

André Gide never wrote about *Partage de Midi.*

Letter 22

The Jewish shepherd Amos was a prophet who lived towards the middle of the ninth century B.C., in the time of King Jeroboam.

Letter 23

Claudel's elder daughter (now Madame Roger Méquillet) was born on 21st January 1907. Claudel wrote the *Magnificat*, the third of his *Odes,* in honour of the occasion.

André Gide's *Journal* : 6th February 1907

In his *Prodigal Son* André Gide describes the conversations of the returned prodigal with his father, his mother, his elder brother, and his younger brother. In this way he presents objectively the most diverse, and indeed the most sharply opposed, of opinions.

Letter 25

It was in December 1905 (cf. Gide's *Journal* for 5th December) that Claudel said to Gide that " man's faculties develop continuously until the day of his death ".

Gide's *Le Retour de l'Enfant prodigue* was first published in 1907 in the Review *Vers et Prose.*

Suarès' *Voici l'Homme* is divided into three separate parts : *Retreat in Cornwall, Return to the Desert of Men,* and *On the Destitution of the Sun.* It is a book of heterogeneous impressions, assembled in poetical, rather than logical order ; to Claudel, who prized inspiration above all things, this chaotic procedure was not in itself displeasing ; but to Gide, the amateur of intellectual discipline, the book could only be exasperating.

André Gide's *Journal* : 22nd April 1907

Connaissance de l'Est is a collection of prose poems inspired by the Far East. It was first published in 1900, and a revised and enlarged edition appeared in 1903. Translated by the Benéts in 1914 (O.U.P.).

Letter 26

Paul Claudel hoped to convert Suarès in the end to Catholicism. But Suarès, though deeply and passionately religious by nature, remained faithful to the devotion to art which alone, in his view, could satisfy the desires of those who hungered after God. In 1948, at the age of eighty, he said in the preface to a new edition of *Voici l'Homme* that " to create Beauty is the only real solution ".

Claudel was never sent to Calcutta.

André Gide's *Journal* : 16th May 1907

André Gide was disconcerted by the sentence in Claudel's *Traité de la Co-naissance du Monde et de soi-même* which declares that " a man knows himself by his walk, the spread of his hands, the extent of his reliance upon himself, and the facility (greater or less) with which he uses the instruments which belong to him ". A few pages earlier, the same book affirms of these instruments that they " react to external events with a greater or smaller degree of finesse and fidelity ". As so often in his work, Claudel had followed the inspiration of the moment.

Letter 28

The quarterly *Vers et Prose* was founded in March 1905 by Paul Fort. It lasted till March 1913. It bore on its title-page the following declaration of its aims : " *Défense et Illustration de la Haute Littérature et du Lyrisme en prose et en poésie* ". Its contributors included d'Annunzio, Apollinaire, Barrès, Carco, Colette, Gide, Maurras, and Romains. Claudel contributed to it in 1905–1906.

Letter 29

Gide's *Le Roi Candaule*, a play in three acts, was published in 1901 under the auspices of the *Revue Blanche*. It was produced by Lugné-Poe in May 1901, and the German version by Franz Blei was produced in Vienna in 1906 and in Cracow in 1907. When it was put on in Berlin in January 1908 the audience proved so hostile that it was immediately taken off (cf. Gide's *Journal* for 9th, 13th, and 16th January).

Claudel's two plays were never produced in Germany, but Blei did complete his translation of *Partage de Midi*.

Letter 30

André Ruyters was a young man who divided his time between banking and literature. His *Mauvais Riche* (1907) was a collection of essays with an epigraph from Nietzsche : " the main thing on heaven and earth is to be obedient for a long time and in one and the same direction ". The book is marked by a violent anti-clericalism. Paul Claudel wrote to him to protest against his attempts to besmirch " Christ, the Blessed Virgin, and the saints, who are not, for me, a matter of indifference, like Louis XIV or Othello, but living and familiar realities ". Ruyters bore no grudge against Claudel, and indeed published, in October 1911, an enthusiastic study of his plays.

Letter 31

Frizeau was a friend of Francis Jammes who had been converted to Catholicism under Claudel's influence.

Gide's allusion is to Paul of Tarsus who, even when he was one of Christianity's severest critics, was unwittingly beginning to prepare himself for conversion. Rémy de Gourmont was, of course, openly anti-religious, and Philippe Berthelot, though an intimate friend of Claudel, always declared himself a free-thinker.

In July 1907 Francis Jammes began a correspondence with an unknown young girl, Mlle Ginette Goedorp, who had written to him an admiring letter from her home in the north of France. After two or three letters had been exchanged, Jammes became convinced that Mlle Goedorp had been sent by Providence to become his wife. He wrote to say that he was ready to ask her hand in marriage : she and her mother met him at Pau on 18th August 1907, and they were married in October of the same year. André Gide and his wife were present at the ceremony.

In his *Enfant prodigue* Gide describes how the returned Prodigal incites his younger brother to run away in his turn and says to him finally : " All my hopes go with you. Be strong ; forget us, forget me. May you not come back. . . ." Francis Jammes was scandalized by this, and his long letter of protest caused Gide to review the whole history of his relations with Jammes and Claudel. On 2nd July 1907 he summarized it as follows in a letter to Christian Beck : " Perhaps you don't know that Claudel, after finding in Jammes a lamb that could easily be led back to our Lord, had wished to take me on in my turn ? That is called ' converting ', is it not ? Of course he knew that, with my Protestant heredity and education, it would not be an easy task ; but no matter, he set himself to do it, encouraged to the point of excess by the very lively sympathy with which I regarded his work and the immense respect with which, in consequence, I listened to all that he said. In correspondence, as much as in conversation, we went very deep. Jammes then gave me to understand he was preparing an article, a dithyrambic ' study ', to celebrate my conversion. I realized that there was some risk of a misunderstanding and, being determined not to owe Jammes' praises to an (involuntary but evident) moral compromise, I wrote him a long letter of explanation. After that he suddenly cooled off ; he felt that I was ' escaping '. . . .

" All the same, I understood with every fibre of my being both the *interest* of what Claudel and he wanted me to do, and the reasons why I wasn't going to do it. And I understood how, if I had done it, it could only have been after the fashion of my Prodigal Son who returned home in order to help his younger brother to run away. I therefore wrote this little ' occasional piece ', and put into it all my heart, and all my reason too. I dedicated it to Arthur Fontaine, a friend of Jammes and of myself, who was deeply interested in the ' religious question ', and to whom Jammes dedicated his *Pensée des Jardins* before he went back to Catholicism ; I meant it as a kind of pendant to Jammes' book."

Gide saw Jammes in November 1907 when he went to Pau for the funeral of his brother-in-law Marcel Gilbert.

Antée, a Belgian literary Review, ceased publication in 1908. Claudel had published some of his translations from Patmore in *Antée* in January 1906—before Gide and Viélé-Griffin had tried to re-animate the magazine.

Letter 32

In 1907 the *Mercure de France* organized an enquiry into the " religious question ", in which a great many persons from the worlds of politics, learning and literature were asked for their views on the current and future situations of the Christian religion. Paul Claudel was very impressed by the contribution of George Dumesnil, whose answer may be summarized as follows : " The existence of religious sentiment is bound up with the existence of the religious idea. By ' the religious idea ' I mean an organic system of ideas which is perfectly defined in *concepts* and which therefore truly presents itself as an *idea*. The fashion in contemporary philosophy is to explain the idea in terms of the sentiment, in such a way that the sentiment could exist of itself without the epiphenomenal idea. This explanation, though arguable on an Aristotelian basis, is in general quite false. It is really the idea which supports, attracts, defines, and enhances the sentiment. It is the conscious which makes the subconscious and the unconscious, and the form which holds the substance together. It is the Christian idea which has formed the European way of feeling ; and it is the Catholic idea which has very largely created the thought and the feeling of France." The article went on to say that only by clinging to the Catholic idea could moral and racial disaster be averted.

Georges Dumesnil (1855–1916) was a pupil of the *École Normale supérieure* who eventually became Professor in the University of Grenoble. A fervent Catholic and the author of several volumes of apologetics, Dumesnil founded in 1906 a Quarterly Review of philosophy, law, and politics. *L'Amitié de France* soon counted among its contributors the most gifted of the Catholic intelligentsia : Jammes, Claudel, Mauriac, Louis Bertrand, and many others. Paul Claudel wrote a poem in memory of Dumesnil, which may be found in his *Feuilles de Saints* (1925).

Jacques Rivière (1886–1925) is best known for the great part which he played in the direction of the *Nouvelle Revue Française* at the very summit of its success, but from 1907 onwards he engaged in a correspondence with Claudel which, in itself, is a small classic of its genre, and which resulted in his conversion to Catholicism. His essay on Claudel is reprinted in his *Études* (1912).

Poe's *Eureka* is preceded by the following notice, which was later translated by Baudelaire :

" To the few who love me and whom I love—to those who feel rather
than to those who think—to the dreamers and those who put faith in
dreams as in the only realities—I offer this Book of Truths, not in its
character of Truth-Teller, but for the Beauty that abounds in its Truth—
constituting it true.   To these I present the composition as an Art-Product
alone—let us say as a Romance ; or, if I be not urging too lofty a claim,
as a Poem.

" *What I here propound is true :*   therefore it cannot die : or if by any
means it be now trodden down so that it die, it will rise again to the Life
Everlasting.

" Nevertheless, it is as a poem only that I wish this work to be judged
after I am dead."

It was in the summer of 1905 that Claudel overcame the last hesitations
of Francis Jammes and effected his conversion to Catholicism.   The friendship between the two writers had begun some ten years earlier, but it
was only during a period of leave in France that Claudel was able to
consummate in person the decision which he had long been advocating
in his letters.

Nothing came of Monfort's projected version of *Le Repos du Septième Jour*
—a play in three acts which Claudel had written in China during the
years 1895 and 1896.

Letter 34

André Gide published in the *Grande Revue* for 25th May 1908 a long
article on " Dostoevsky as he appears in his letters ".

Claudel, in quoting from memory, has confused two separate texts :
Epistle to the Hebrews xiii. 8, and *Matthew xxiv. 23.*

In speaking of the nuns of Minsk, Claudel alludes to an episode in the
religious conflicts which caused great strife, and sometimes bloodshed, in
Russia at the beginning of this century.

Dmitri Merejkovsky (*b.* 1865), a disciple of Dostoevsky who concerned
himself with the struggle between paganism and Christianity.   It is to his
Tolstoy and Dostoevsky that Claudel alludes here.

Letter 35

Suarès' study of Ibsen is reprinted in his *Trois Hommes : Pascal, Ibsen,
Dostoevsky* (*N.R.F.*, 1913).   His *Visite à Pascal* appeared in the *Cahiers de la
Quinzaine* for 5th October 1909.

Pascal's letters to Mlle de Roannez were written in 1656, at the time of
the publication of the *Provinciales*.   She was the sister of Pascal's friend the
Duc de Roannez, and Pascal constituted himself, in his letters to her, her
spiritual director.   Fragments from the letters were published in the 1669
edition of the *Pensées*.   Mlle de Roannez, who originally took a vow of
chastity, was later released from her contract in order that she could

marry the Duc de La Feuillade.   It would seem, however, that she did
not achieve tranquillity of mind by this means.

Suarès' attack on Georges de Porto-Riche was reprinted in his *Sur la vie*
(1912).

Letter 36

The poet Emmanuel Signoret (1872–1900) was the author of three
books of poems : *Daphné* (1894), *Vers dorés* (1895), and *La Souffrance des
Eaux* (1898).   In 1908 the *Mercure de France* reprinted his collected poems
with a preface by André Gide.   Among other things, Gide went so far
as to say that he knew no poems in the French language more beautiful
than those of Signoret ; and in his Anthology of French poetry, published
in 1949, he quotes abundantly from Signoret.

An edition of 215 copies of Claudel's *Cinq Grandes Odes* was published in
1910.

Nottker, a Swiss monk of the ninth century A.D., was the author of
rhymed sequences which mark the transition between the traditional Latin
prosody and the assonances of French medieval poetry.   The French
monk Adam de Saint-Victor composed liturgical poems in the twelfth
century, which combine the metrical systems of both Latin and French.
Prudentius, a Latin poet of the fourth century, was the author of allegorical
poems, and notably of a series of *Hymns for the different hours of the day.*

Claudel's Latin quotation is from *Psalms cxiii. 4.*

Claudel never allowed his respect for Pascal the writer to weaken his
suspicion of Pascal the theologian.   He went so far as to say to Jacques
Rivière that he should read " Pascal above all : he is the real apostle
ad exteros for us Frenchmen " ; but he also at one time envisaged the
composition of a tract to be entitled " Against Pascal ".   Gide for his
part (cf. the *Journal* for 9th February 1916) acknowledged the great part
which Pascal had played in his life, and was less disposed to reproach
Pascal for his Jansenism.

Letter 37

The book which Gide had just finished was *La Porte étroite* (*Strait is the
Gate*).   He had had it in mind since 1891, and in 1894 had thought of
calling it *Mort de Mademoiselle Claire.*

Gide first wrote to Suarès on 6th December 1908.   In asking for the
favour of an interview he said that he would readily understand if Suarès
preferred not to see him.   " In any case," he went on, " I want you to
know that you have deepened and ennobled my conception of solitude,
and for this I send you my friendly gratitude."   In his *Feuillets* (1911) he
says of Suarès : " This prodigious writer provokes enthusiasm and re-
pulsion with equal facility ; he makes no attempt to seem bigger or to
talk louder than is natural to him, but neither does he try to belittle or
restrain himself ; the last of his thoughts is amplified by all the echoes
that it awakes in his great cavernous soul ; and sometimes, long after that
soul has launched its cry, Suarès is still talking.   He is never pulled up
short."

Suarès and Gide met for the first time in January 1909. In spite of certain fundamental disagreements (motivated, for instance, by Suarès' indifference to Chopin, or by the divergence between their interpretations of Dostoevsky) they remained friends for many years.

Letter 38

The year 1908 marked the climax of the fashion for gollywogs in France, which was commemorated in the famous " Golliwog's Cake-walk " of Debussy.

Joseph-Louis Lagrange (1736–1813) was the French geometrician who discovered a formula by which one may calculate the successive changes in the dimensions and positions of the orbits of the planets.

The hymns which Claudel mentions in this letter may be found in a volume of religious poems, *Corona benignitatis anni Dei*, which was published by the *N.R.F.* in 1915.

Jean Giraudoux (1882–1944) had begun to attract attention in 1908 by the publication of his *Provinciales*. Jules Romains (*b.* 1885) was known mainly by his three volumes of poems, and one of his new poems had been published in July 1908 in Marinetti's Review *Poesia*. The Futurist leader had been editing this Review since 1904, and had published poems in both French and Italian. Richepin, Cocteau, Larguier, and Tristan Derème were among the oddly assorted names which appeared in its list of contributors. Claudel had said to Marinetti that his review was " the necessary companion " (an echo from Mallarmé) " of the sumptuous cushions of the modern salon ". For his part, Gide had written in his most ironical vein to say that, although he himself had nothing worthy to appear in *Poesia*, the Review had long lain on his table in the country and had found more than one reader among his friends. In his *Feuillets* (1911) he said of Marinetti : " He enjoys a lack of talent which allows him every audacity. . . . He stamps his foot ; he makes the dust fly ; he swears and curses ; he organizes conflicts, cabals, and contradictions from which he himself can emerge triumphant. And yet he's the most charming man in the world, with the exception of d'Annunzio. . . . He came to see me some ten years ago and made himself so incredibly amiable that I had to leave at once for the country ; if I'd seen him again it would have been all up with me ; I should have thought him a genius."

Jammes' *Alexandre de Ruchenfleur* was later reprinted in the volume entitled *Rayons de Miel*. It is a story in verse, and is concerned with an elderly landowner whose life comes to an honourable end in the serenity of the Catholic faith.

Letter 39

Paul Claudel had sent to the *Occident* the manuscript of his *Cinq Grandes Odes*, which they published in book form in 1910.

The Review *Occident* was founded in 1901 and ran until July 1914. Both Gide and Claudel contributed to it from 1902 onwards. They also wrote for Paul Fort's *Vers et Prose*, which existed from 1905 to 1913. But from 1908 onwards the grand object of all their occasional writing was the newly founded *Nouvelle Revue Française*. This Review (probably the most distinguished in French literary history) published its first number on 15th November 1908. This proved a false start, however, in that the editorial committee was violently divided by an article by Léon Bocquet, of which the title (*Contre Mallarmé*) was in itself enough to alienate both André Gide and Jean Schlumberger. They therefore dissociated themselves from Eugène Montfort, the original director of the *N.R.F.*, who for his part went back to his own publication, *Marges*. The *N.R.F.* resumed publication on 1st February 1909, with an editorial committee composed of Jacques Copeau, Jean Schlumberger, and André Ruyters. André Gide's rôle was that of a discreet but powerful adviser. From the first, the character of the Review was based on Gide's belief that " there are no problems in art to which the work of art is not a sufficient solution ". Writers of every sort were welcome in the *N.R.F.*, provided only that the element of art was present in their work. The " marriage of modernity and traditionalism " (as it was called in the *Mercure de France* in 1911) was the great aim of the *N.R.F.* ; and it was effected with undiminished success for more than forty years.

Ch.-L. Philippe's *Charles Blanchard* appeared in the *N.R.F.* in February 1910.

Jules Romains' book of poems was called *La Vie unanime*, and was published in 1908.

Letter 40

The *N.R.F.* for April 1909 contains Claudel's *Hymne du Saint-Sacrement*.
For Claudel's hatred of Flaubert, France, the Goncourts, Renan, Taine, and Zola, cf. the oration with which François Mauriac welcomed his illustrious elder to membership of the Académie Française on 13th March 1947.

Letter 41

Claudel's *Jeune Fille Violaine* was published, in revised form, in 1901, under the collective title *L'Arbre*. When asked if permission could not be granted for a stage production, Gide wrote to Jammes for his opinion, and said, among other things, that " perhaps after all it's a very bad idea. Those who liked Claudel will find in it only a pleasant opportunity of applauding him ; the rest will think it simply grotesque, and the performance will not earn him a single new reader." Jammes agreed ; and so, as will appear, did Claudel. The play later served as the point of departure for *L'Annonce faite à Marie*.

Letter 42

Alphonse Séché's *Le Nouveau Théâtre d'Art* gave afternoon performances of avant-garde plays at the *Théâtre du Palais Royal*. H. R. Lenormand (*b.* 1882), whose own early work had been given there, persuaded Séché to attempt to perform Claudel's play ; and Mlle Kalff, who later became

Mme Lenormand, was a fanatical enthusiast for Claudel and had given many recitals of passages from his works. Claudel remained grateful to her for her passionate advocacy of his work, and in 1912 he invited her to take the part of Violaine in the *L'Annonce faite à Marie*—an invitation which she had to refuse for reasons of health.

Fragments of *Partage de Midi* were acted at the *Théâtre Gymnase* in 1916, on the occasion of a Franco-Belgian charity performance. Jacques Copeau produced them, and Eve Francis, who played Ysé, has described the production in her book of reminiscences *Temps héroïques*. The first complete performance was given on 16th December 1948 at the *Théâtre Marigny* with Jean-Louis Barrault, Edwige Feuillère, Pierre Brasseur, and Jacques Dacqmine, the Company which visited London in 1951.

The Chinese expression " *Maski !* " is the equivalent of the Russian " *Nitchevo* "—" It can't be helped ".

Alissa's Journal in *Strait is the Gate* is perhaps the most important part of the book. It includes her famous appeal to God : " O Lord ! Preserve me from the happiness that I had thought to reach too soon ! Teach me to postpone my happiness, to thrust it away until I find it in you."

André Gide had met Jacques Rivière at the house of André Lhote in 1909. Rivière had submitted an article on Suarès which was published in the *N.R.F.* in April 1909, and thenceforward he became ever more closely associated with the Review ; at the time of his death in 1925 he was its editor. Though supremely influenced by Claudel, he always retained great admiration for Gide. (On this subject, cf. his correspondence with Alain Fournier, published by the *N.R.F.*) Gide, as always, resented any suggestion that he had tried to impose his own views on Rivière, and went out of his way to say, in his memorial tribute, that " what he most appreciated, in his relations with me, was, I think, that he realized through them the strength of his capacity to differ. Certainly I always encouraged him to see the matter in this way." Claudel has written of Rivière both in the preface to his posthumous *A la trace de Dieu* . . . (*N.R.F.* 1925) and in a memorial poem which is reprinted in his *Feuilles de Saints* (*N.R.F.* 1925). For Rivière in general, cf. the special double number of the *N.R.F.* which was devoted to him in 1925.

Letter 45

Gide spent a week at the monastery of Monte Cassino in 1909. Adelberto Grestnitch, a Dutch monk whom Gide had met in Rome through the intermediacy of Maurice Denis, had made it possible for Gide to stay in an ordinary monk's cell and to take his meals in the refectory. His reminiscences of the visit may be found in the preface to his *Notes sur Chopin* (*L'Arche*, 1948) which he dedicated to Father Adelberto Grestnitch.

Letter 46

Gide's *Strait is the Gate* is the story of Alissa, a young girl of mystical, devotional nature, who renounces Jérôme, whom she loves, in favour of her sister Juliette, who also loves Jérôme but is not loved by him. Alissa, free to devote herself to her aged and ailing father, sees her father die and her sister given in marriage to someone other than Jérôme. Jérôme sees no possible remaining objection to his marriage with Alissa, but she prefers to remain faithful to her mystical solitude, and eventually dies, serene and triumphant, leaving Jérôme disconsolate. In her free acceptance of torments which not only concern herself, but also afflict her innocent admirer, Paul Claudel sees a problem of conscience which, in his view, is not satisfactorily resolved in Christian terms.

Letter 47

Jammes' *Lettre à Paul Claudel, consul,* is a poem of eighty-two alexandrines, written at Bucy-le-Long in May 1909. It appeared in the *N.R.F.* for 1st July 1909.

Letter 48

Claudel's open letter to the *N.R.F.* was primarily concerned with the shortcomings of French printing and publishing ; but it also contained some virulent and irrelevant attacks upon contemporary authors, which removed it from the plane of rational controversy and made it impossible for the *N.R.F.* (cf. *Letter* 51) to print it.

Letter 49

Claudel eventually admitted that Anna de Noailles had a certain lyrical sensibility, but he never forgave her the quality of verbal gush which Gide later describes as " lyrical inflation ". As for Barrès, he saw in him a great publicist, rather than a novelist, and a man of doubtful spiritual standing (cf. the notes to *Letter* 98).

Letter 50

The *Homoousios* is an expression from Catholic theology which designates, in the mystery of the Holy Trinity, the common possession by the Father and the Son of one identical divine nature. The term was defined at the Council of Nicaea in A.D. 325. It was violently opposed by the Aryan heresy which divided the Church during the greater part of the fourth century ; its principal defender was St. Athanasius, Bishop of Alexandria.

The formula " *Filioque* " expresses the belief that, in the Holy Trinity, the Holy Spirit enjoys eternal life by the common action of the Father and the Son (*qui ex Patre Filioque procedit*). It was added to the faith in Spain, between the fifth and sixth centuries, and was accepted in Rome by Pope Benedict VIII (1012–1024) at the instigation of the Emperor Henry II. The *Homoousios* controversy has been settled for centuries and persists only in a certain tendency to deny the full divinity of Jesus Christ ; but the *Filioque* controversy, on the contrary, still divides the Roman

Catholic Church from the Eastern Churches, although the Eastern Churches were allowed by the Council of Florence (1438–1445) to omit the formula on condition that they share the same faith. The Mass still retains, in the *Credo*, these two words, with all their weight of history and doctrine.

Monsignor Pierre Batiffol (1861–1929), Rector of the Catholic Faculty of Toulouse, is the author of many works on theology and religious history. Claudel especially admired his *Études d'histoire et de théologie positives*.

The new work which Paul Claudel proposed to send to the *N.R.F.* was a hymn to St. Peter, St. Paul, and St. James, which was eventually published in that Review for 1st December 1909.

Letter 52

The edition of which Claudel complains is that of Banville's *Princesses*, which was published in 1904 with twenty-four etchings by Rochegrosse. André Gide shared his displeasure at the mishandling of Banville—of whom he said in his *Feuillets* : " I am excessively fond of this delicate, charming, and perspicacious spirit, so full of poetic malice. At times, he is almost Ariel."

Letter 54

Paul Claudel lived at No. 7 rue La Trémoille during his long stay in Paris in 1909.

It appears from Gide's *Journal* that he entertained Claudel at his house on 7th November 1909, and dined with Claudel two days later.

Letter 55

Charles-Louis Philippe (1874–1909) was born at Cérilly in the Allier, and was the son of a shoemaker. He left his native province in the hope of becoming a Polytechnicien, failed, and was forced to accept the most modest of functions as an employee of the city of Paris. In his books he aims to express the experience and suffering of ordinary people ; himself naturally plebeian, he wrote in an instinctively flawless style which has caused his books to endure long beyond his own lifetime. During the last decade of his life André Gide was on excellent terms with Philippe and did his best to further his career. Their acquaintance, which began when they were both contributors to *L'Hermitage*, came to an end when Philippe died of typhoid fever at the age of thirty-five. Gide, Léon-Paul Fargue, Valery Larbaud, Jacques Copeau, Marcel Ray, Chanvin, Guillaumin were among the few who attended Philippe's funeral at Cérilly. Gide and Léautaud have published accounts of the death and funeral of Philippe ; both should be read by all those who are interested in the curiosa of French literary history. The memorial number of the *N.R.F.*, devoted entirely to Philippe, was published on 15th February 1910, and included essays or poems by Claudel, Charles Guérin, Michel Arnauld, Anna de Noailles, Marguerite Audoux, and Philippe himself.

Émile Guillaumin (*b.* 1870) had known Philippe as a child, was a neighbour of his in the Allier, and was the author of a number of books inspired by rural life in the Bourbonnais.

Marcel Ray, a graduate of the *École Normale*, and a future Minister Plenipotentiary, had also known Philippe as a child. He had contributed critical articles to several Reviews ; it was he who apprised Claudel of Philippe's death.

In 1906 Philippe began to prepare a novel which was to be more or less an account of the life of his father, the shoemaker of Cérilly. After four years, however, he had completed only a part of what he had intended to be one of his most substantial books, and even this part did not satisfy him. Whereas he had meant to show " Charles Blanchard " at the time of his unhappy early youth, he had sketched out a quite different piece of work in which the main figure was happy and high-spirited. The *N.R.F.* later published both versions with a preface by Gide, and the first version was published in book form by the *N.R.F.* in 1913, with a preface by Léon-Paul Fargue.

Letter 56

Paul Claudel remained at Prague, as French Consul, until he was appointed to Frankfurt in 1911.

Philippe's *Croquignole* was a novel, published in December 1906. It describes the fate of a minor employee who, after leading an insignificant life, inherits 40,000 francs, squanders it, and commits suicide.

Marcel Schwob (1867–1905) had been a friend and admirer of Claudel. Francis Jammes in his *Mémoires* describes the meal which he had with Schwob and Claudel in 1900. Schwob was already gravely ill, and, according to Jammes, he " drank in, as if they had been the waters of Grace, the words of Claudel, who was promising him a life of eternal bliss ".

The manuscript of *Partage de Midi* which Claudel gave to Philippe, has never been recovered.

Letter 57

La Mère et l'Enfant was the title of an autobiographical essay by Philippe which was reprinted by the *N.R.F.* in 1911.

Paul Claudel's poem on Philippe's death was published in the *N.R.F.* special number of 15th February 1910, and later formed part of his *Corona Benignitatis Anni Dei*.

Letter 60

In the January 1910 issue of the *N.R.F.* André Gide published a long commentary of Balzac's little-known *Cathérine de Médicis*. In his enthusiasm for the Queen's political sense, Balzac proves, or tries to prove, that the massacre of St. Bartholomew's Eve was a stroke of political genius, and rich in desirable consequences. Gide quotes in this connection an article in which Charles Maurras had recently argued that Calvin (whose centenary the Protestants were then celebrating) was the initiator of " an event from which civilization in general, and French unity in particular, had long suffered and were suffering still. We can no longer excuse either the separation from Rome, or those long rebellions which have produced, from the sixteenth century onwards, all the ideas which have undermined our unity : liberalism, parliamentarianism, republicanism, democracy, romanticism, and one might even say Dreyfusism. . . .''

André Gide criticizes the attitude of Balzac, which finds its prolongation in Maurras, and ends by saying, " I admire this train of thought in M. Maurras precisely because he is not a Catholic and because, although he admirably seizes the political justification of the Catholic organization and the Catholic hierarchy, yet the basic feeling, the very essence of Christian devotion, escapes him almost completely. I am less pleased that some of those politicians should invoke the name of Christ. There is a painful misunderstanding in that."

Paul Claudel had heard *Tannhäuser* in Vienna. He still holds to his great admiration for this opera, and said in 1949 that " where the Christian and the sensual elements are mingled, everything is made for my delight ".

Letter 61

On the same day that he wrote this letter, Claudel wrote to Rivière and once again expressed himself very forcibly on the subject of the career of letters. " There is no worse career," he said, " than that of the writer who has to live by his pen. You are compelled to write with your eyes on your patron, the public, and to give him not what you like, but what he likes—and God knows whether or not his taste is lofty and delicate ! Ah ! I don't know that the life of a cobbler is not better than the life of an X. . . . I always remember the tragic appearance of Verlaine and Villiers de l'Isle Adam, with the remains of their talent hanging about them like the last hairs of a moth-eaten old fur. It's not honourable to try to live off one's soul and to sell it to the people ; whence the contempt, partly legitimate, that people have always felt for actors and artistes." (*Correspondance Rivière-Claudel*, Plon, 1926, pp. 195–196.)

In his next letter Claudel apologized for the violence of his language, and shortly afterwards he procured Rivière a post as philosophy teacher at the Collège St.-Stanislas.

Letter 62

Gide sent to Claudel a copy of Péguy's *Mystère de la Charité de Jeanne d'Arc*, published in 1910 by the *Cahiers de la Quinzaine*. Péguy had not dared to send it himself to Claudel, because he knew that Claudel was far from being a wholehearted admirer of him and his work. For his part Gide was a veteran enthusiast for Péguy, and in March 1910 he said of the new book that " nothing, since Claudel's *L'Arbre*, had impressed me so much ".

Scantrel was one of the pseudonyms of André Suarès, whose articles from the *Grande Revue* had just been printed in book form.

The play on which Claudel was at work was *L'Otage*.

Letter 63

The phrase of Anna de Noailles, which Claudel admired, could roughly be translated as follows : " Above you stands your splendid mother, who distributes life like a mountain whence torrents, vineyards, flocks, and herds come down into the valley ".

Marguerite Audoux was the great literary sensation of 1910. She was born in the Nivernais, and was abandoned by her parents as a child. Some local farmers took charge of her, and eventually she came to Paris as a young girl and set up as a dressmaker. She then met Charles-Louis Philippe in a tea-shop. He formed the highest opinion of her gifts as a writer, but it was only after his death that her *Chaland de la Reine* (a collection of nine stories) was published. Her great success, however, was with *Marie-Claire*, which was prefaced and championed by Octave Mirbeau. Alain Fournier wrote of it, in the *N.R.F.* for November 1910, that " the literature of the last thirty years has perhaps not produced a lovelier poem of the life of the heart than this *Marie-Claire*, of which the action takes place among the peasants of the Sologne ".

In Gide's notes on the death and funeral of Philippe he referred to the sacristan of the church as the " deacon " ; it is to this that Claudel refers.

Lugné-Poe (1869–1931) is considered by Claudel to be the pioneer of dramatic art in the early twentieth century ; and he was the first person who ever thought of putting any of Claudel's plays on the stage. André Gide, whose *Roi Candaule* was produced by Lugné-Poe in 1901, agrees entirely with Claudel's estimate.

Letter 64

Jammes' *Le Triomphe de la Vie* had appeared in 1902. It included a verse satire called *Existences* which did not command the admiration of Jammes' usual supporters. The author was very much annoyed by the fact that neither Gide nor Philippe could applaud it.

The *Correspondance Francis Jammes-André Gide* (Gallimard 1948) contains the full text of the exchanges between Gide and Jammes on the occasion of the Philippe memorial number of the *N.R.F.* The friendship between Gide and Jammes never really recovered from this incident ; and when Gide made the friendly gesture of sending Jammes a copy of Péguy's new *Jeanne d'Arc* Jammes preferred not to acknowledge it.

Jacques-Émile Blanche (1861–1948) left many portraits which are of value to the literary and social historian—among them those of Debussy, Barrès, Valéry, Proust, Gide, Cocteau, and Poulenc. In his reminiscences he speaks of Gide in his youth as " a pale young Huguenot with dark flat hair, who claims to be timid but is really a man of authority ".

Claudel's letter about Péguy's *Mystère de la Charité de Jeanne d'Arc* was forwarded to Péguy and has unfortunately been lost. Perhaps it is worth saying that it is Claudel who, in his *Jeanne au bûcher*, has written the greatest account of the death of St. Joan. Her triumphant march towards Rheims has also been treated with the utmost magnificence in *L'Annonce faite à Marie*.

André Gide compares Péguy's conversion to that of Saul of Tarsus who was changed, almost miraculously, into the apostle Paul, the corner-stone of Christendom.

Letter 65

It was in 1909 that Claudel discovered Chesterton's *Orthodoxy* and became its foremost supporter in France. The *N.R.F.* published his translation of a chapter from it in August 1910.

Claudel alludes to the quarrel of St. Jerome and Rufinus, whose friendship was destroyed, in the fourth century, by an incompatibility of views on the Origenist question.

Letter 66

Napoléon Landais (1803–1852) was a lexicographer and man of letters whose novels (written under the name of Eugène de Massy) are now completely forgotten, but whose *Dictionary of French Dictionaries* (1833) and *Grammar of French Grammars* (1843) are still often consulted. *L'Occident* had reprinted an essay of his on the reform of orthography.

Henri Fabre (1823–1915) was the author of many works of popular science. His nickname of " the Virgil of the insect world " derives above all from his *Souvenirs entomologiques* (1879–1889).

Letter 67

Claudel's *Magnificat* appeared in the May 1910 issue of the *N.R.F.*

Letter 68

Valery Larbaud's long essay on Patmore appeared in the *N.R.F.* for September and October 1911.

Conrad's *Nigger of the Narcissus*, translated by Robert d'Humières, was published by the *Mercure de France* in 1910.

The poet Saint Léger-Léger, whose real name is Alexis Léger, was born in 1889. The son of a creole lawyer, he was brought to Pau after the disaster in Martinique ; at Pau he met Jammes, who at once recommended him to Claudel. At the age of twenty-one he began to publish his prose poems in the *N.R.F.* He later entered the French Foreign Office and attained a high rank in the service. His poems (one of which, *Anabasis*, has been translated by T. S. Eliot) have in general been published under the name of Saint-John Perse.

Letter 69

In one of his letters to Jacques Rivière (*Correspondance Claudel-Rivière*, Plon, 1926, p. 177) Claudel comments as follows on his discovery of Chesterton's *Orthodoxy* : " I have lately found many passages of wit and merit in the work of this whimsical Englishman. He shows that the truth of Christianity differs from all the doctrines in that its wisdom does not consist in a certain mediocre neutrality, but in the extremest possible development of apparently contradictory feelings (joy and penitence, pride and humility, love and renunciation, etc.). . . . I believe that I have myself, in my time, applied this theory of ' perpendicular verities ' in the domain of morality. *Quantum potes, tantum aude.* For the great blason of Art and of Christian civilization is that which made Europe into something other than that stupid ' Empire of the Middle Way.' "

In 1910 Valery Larbaud profited by a journey to London to make the acquaintance of Chesterton. He sent Claudel the following account : " . . . I am the only one of his sponsors in France who has seen him. He told me that he found your translation admirable—' better than the original ' (he meant it, he is too ingenuous to feign modesty). . . . He kept us (a young Anglican priest and myself) nearly half an hour in the bathroom, before taking tea, in order to tell us in ten different ways that everything he had written now seemed to him bad, that of course he had moments of enthusiasm in which he thought his books really excellent and comparable to the greatest things in English literature, but that on the whole, looking at it in cold blood and from every angle, his work didn't amount to much. I told him about you ; I said (and I believe it) that you are the best of our poets and only comparable to the greatest poets of other nations : to Cervantes, Dante, and Shakespeare. But he seemed to be abstracted, and I wonder if he even heard what I said. . . . I feel that like all men of genius he has remained a child. . . . He does a great deal for the truth by questioning the real value of the central ideas of our time." (Cf. Jean-Aubry's *Valery Larbaud: sa vie et son œuvre,* Editions du Rocher, 1949, p. 171).

Henri Lavedan (1859–1940) wrote weekly articles on Parisian life for *L'Illustration.* Eleven volumes of these were reprinted, under the titles *Bon an, mal an* (5 vols.) and *Les Grandes Heures* (6 vols.).

Letter 70

Rémy de Gourmont (1858–1915) was one of the first to discover André Gide and Paul Claudel. As early as 1891, in reviewing the *Cahiers d'André Walter,* he said of Gide that he was intellectually and spiritually a descendant of Goethe. In 1896 he went further : " if anyone deserves to be famous," he wrote, " Gide does—for the Master of our souls has ordained that, in this exceptional being, originality of talent should be allied to originality of spirit. So rare a being deserves to be talked of." (*Premier livre des Masques, Mercure de France,* 1896.) After reading *Tête d'Or* he wrote with the same perceptive enthusiasm of Claudel : " As we make our way into this vast genius, our feet resound upon slabs of marble, and echo answers to echo. . . . He has the gift of tragedy, and in his puissance he has all the virtues of a great dramatic poet." (*Deuxième livre des Masques, Mercure de France,* 1898.)

But neither Gide nor Claudel felt bound, in gratitude for these eulogies, to conceal the fact that in general they thought very badly of Gourmont. His generally sceptical turn of mind was nauseous to them. In 1905, and again in 1910, Gide published articles which spoke unsparingly of Gourmont. Here are a few sentences from the second of these articles. " I find in M. de Gourmont that fatal propensity (which Voltaire also had) to regard as stupid or hypocritical everything which betokens lofty aspirations, reverence, or piety. . . . Like the encyclopaedists, M. de Gourmont does not understand or admit or want to admit that free-thinking has not a monopoly of intelligence, or religion a monopoly of stupidity. . . . Scepticism may sometimes be the beginning of wisdom ; but it is often the end of art. His hatred of modesty (which M. de Gourmont calls a Christian invention) has taught him the hatred of Christianity. The hatred of Christianity has taught him the love of Science. I very much suspect that he only loves Science so much in order that he may hate Religion the more. . . ." " No, no, you know as well as I do, Rémy de Gourmont, that religions are not all ' ugly ' or ' stupid ' ; it is merely that people (and you above all) sometimes make them so. Note carefully what Renan said : ' There are many delicate spirits who prefer to believe, rather than to disbelieve in bad taste '."

Letter 73

Jules Romains had just published *Un être en marche*. With René Arcos, Georges Duhamel, and Charles Vildrac he had founded the Unanimist Group, whose purpose was to attach the individual to an organized " expression of unanimous collective life ". " We feel," said Romains, " a religious sentiment before the life which surrounds us and is greater than any one of us. We wish to render this sentiment in poetry which is immediate—that is to say by the direct, unadorned, and unfarded expression of reality as we see it."

Not only did the hatter launch a hat named after Claudel, but one of the photographers of Prague gained for him a considerable notoriety by displaying a photograph in which Claudel, in full diplomatic uniform, had a hallucinatory resemblance to Napoleon.

Letter 75

The *N.R.F.* did not, in the end, publish Chesterton's *Orthodoxy*.
Blei's reference is to *Les Caves du Vatican* which was published in 1914.

Letter 77

In 1903 Gide made the acquaintance of Dominique Dupouey, a young naval officer who was deeply influenced by *Les Nourritures Terrestres*. He gradually reverted, however, to the faith of his childhood ; and when he was killed in action, while leading a company of Marines in action on the Yser front in April 1915, he was mourned as a saint by all who had known or served with him. Gide later wrote a preface for his *Lettres (N.R.F.)*. He never met Claudel, but maintained a correspondence with him.

Letter 78

L'Otage, signed Paul C., appeared in three numbers of the *N.R.F.*
(December 1910, January 1911, February 1911).

The *Revue Indépendante*, which Claudel applauds for its aggressiveness,
was supported from 1890 to 1896 by the publisher Albert Savine. Its
contributors included Paul Adam, Barbey d'Aurevilly, the Goncourts,
Villiers de l'Isle Adam, Anatole France, Zola, and Heredia.

Letter 79

In his *Notre Jeunesse* Péguy describes the disturbing effect of the Dreyfus
case on the minds of those who were young at the time.

The other book mentioned by Claudel is not by Péguy but by Paul
Milliet, and its real title is *Une famille de républicains fouriéristes, les Milliet*.
It had appeared in Péguy's *Cahiers de la Quinzaine*.

Romain Rolland has stated that Péguy was an admirer of Claudel
from 1910 onwards ; for his part Claudel had a greater regard for the
personality of Péguy than for his work. Gide, on the contrary, who never
lost an opportunity of praising Péguy, was scorned by Péguy as a dangerous
dilettante.

The volume of Philippe's stories was *Dans la petite Ville* (Editions
Fasquelle).

Letter 80

The writer Lucien Jean had been Ch.-L. Philippe's best friend. They
had worked together in the same office, and on the little Review *L'Enclos*.
Philippe said of him that " his intelligence is clear, deep, and humane.
Many a time he has been my guide and support. There is light within
him." His *Parmi les Hommes* was published by the *Mercure de France* in 1910.

André Gide's attack on Rémy de Gourmont provoked, in May 1910,
a violent riposte from Eugéne Montfort, the original director of the *N.R.F.*
Montfort accused Gide of literary opportunism, and of fomenting the
fashions of the moment. " This soi-disant immoralist, this soi-disant
Nietzschean," he said, " is a man with a horror of scepticism . . . and
his revolt against Gourmont is the revolt of the puritan, the Bible-eating
Protestant, against Voltaire. . . . What shocks him is that Gourmont's
immoralists have done away with sin. But M. Gide wants to be a sinner,
he wants to have laws for the pleasure of transgressing them. . . . What
is annoying is that his attacks on Gourmont-Voltaire are attacks on the
spirit of France." André Ruyters took up the defence of Gide in the
N.R.F., and in their number for July 1910 Gide himself replied : " I
tried to show in my article to what extent the negative scepticism of Rémy
de Gourmont was fateful to art. As for M. Montfort's suggestion that
Calvinism may be ' equally ruinous ' to a work of art, I claim that it
may well be much worse. I don't know that one could imagine a line
of thought more contrary to art (and to my work in particular), and more
hostile to it, than Calvinism. . . . M. de Gourmont may well write on
that subject, at M. Montfort's suggestion, but his article will not be against

me. . . . M. Montfort must allow me to say that the idea of sin as a titilla-
tion, and of sacrilege and satanism as they were envisaged by Barbey
d'Aurevilly, and sometimes by Rémy de Gourmont, could not be farther
from Protestantism. Nor does that make them any the nearer to me. I
certainly cannot conceive, as the Calvinists do, of a morality that is independent of psychology ; but to conceive of psychology in mechanistic
terms, and to claim to take no account of the moral quality of human
actions, or of their inner reverberation—that is what leads us straight to
the picaresque. . . . My article was in no way an apologia for Calvinist
morality, but simply and solely a protest against those who propose, in
religion and politics, to impose unity upon us by force."

Letter 82

From 1910 onwards the *N.R.F.* became Paul Claudel's principal publisher. The *Mercure de France* retained the plays written between 1890 and
1900, and they also published in 1948 a new edition of *Partage de Midi*.

Letter 83

It was only in 1928 that the first collection of Claudel's essays (*Positions
et Propositions*) was published by the *N.R.F.* A second volume, *Figures et
Paraboles*, appeared in 1936.
Contragentes was the title of a work of apologetics by St. Thomas Aquinas.

Letter 85

L'Otage is concerned with the sacrifice of a young girl of noble lineage
who, in the time of the First Empire, saves the Pope at the price of her
marriage to the son of her parents' bailiff.

Letter 86

L'Art Libre was a little Review, published at Lyons, which devoted its
number of July-September 1910 to Claudel. It bore the ironical epigraph :
" I have not the honour of M. Paul Claudel's acquaintance. Émile
Faguet." Rivière's article was entitled *Les Œuvres lyriques de Claudel*. The
articles by Rivière which Claudel had admired in the *N.R.F.* were doubtless the review of Suarès' *Bouclier du Zodiaque* (April 1909) and the *Introduction à une métaphysique du Rêve* (November 1909).
Paul Claudel confirmed in 1949 that he had never much cared for
anything but the *Mémoires* of Chateaubriand. Like Gide, he was elsewhere
repelled by the pomposity and over-elaboration of this author's style.
Léon Brunschvicg, Professor of the History of Philosophy at the Sorbonne, had foreseen that strictures such as those of Claudel might well be
aimed at his edition of the *Pensées*. He had therefore written the following
" notice " :

" The publication of these fragments raises a problem which cannot be satisfactorily resolved. The modern editor is equally unable either (i) to put himself in Pascal's place in order to reconstitute in arbitrary style a book that was never finished or (ii) to print a chaos of incoherent notes whose disorder would make them both inaccessible and unintelligible. . . . The only remaining course is to take the fragments for what they are ; to follow Pascal's indications with scruple and circumspection, though with no illusion as to the objective value of one's work ; to arrange the fragments coherently, to bring out their logical continuity, and to illuminate them by their inner coherence. Thanks to this arrangement, Pascal can become his own interpreter." (*Pensées de Pascal*, Hachette, 1897.)

Havet's edition of the *Pensées* was published by Dezobry in 1852. Until it was superseded by Brunschvicg, it was the edition most generally consulted in France. Claudel derisively spells Havet as Navet (a turnip).

Pope Pius X had just published his decree " *Quam Singulari* ", in which he reminded Roman Catholics that children were allowed, and indeed obliged, to receive communion before reaching the age of reason.

Louis Massignon, who later became a professor at the Collège de France, was the author of many remarkable volumes of oriental studies. He was converted to Catholicism after studying the life of a Moslem who was burnt at the stake, towards the year A.D. 1000, for going over to Catholicism.

Junius was the collective name of several writers who contributed occasional articles to the *Écho de Paris*. René Bazin was one of them.

Letter 87

Edmond Biré's edition of Chateaubriand's *Mémoires d'Outre-Tombe* was published by Garnier in 1900.

Letter 88

Claudel was to spend part of his leave in his father-in-law's château at Hostel, in the region of Valromey. His *Cantate à trois voix* was written there in 1912, and is saturated in the noble landscape of the area.

The rumour that Pascal had finally broken with Port Royal was started by the Abbé Beurier, who had discussed the matter with Pascal not long before his death. As to whether Pascal had really retracted, no solid evidence has ever been forthcoming ; but in 1909 the Abbé Brémond published a long article in which he inclined to support the Abbé Beurier's theory.

The modernist heresy was developed towards the end of the nineteenth century and was the counterpart of Pragmatism in philosophy. Pope Pius X formally condemned it in 1907. The modernists kept to the traditional phraseology of religious life, but based their beliefs on historical criticism rather than on any transcendental interpretation. For them, Christ was merely the man who had had the most perfect religious experience, and they attached only a symbolical validity to Biblical legend. Their leader in France was Alfred Loisy.

Letter 90

The suggested coat-of-arms of the Coûfontaines was not reproduced in *L'Otage*, but Claudel gives a minute account of it in his stage directions for the first act : " Prominently displayed is the Coûfontaine escutcheon ; two clasped hands, gules, on a field of gold, a drawn sword, argent, between Sun and Moon, and the motto or cry, ' *Coûfontaine Adsum* '."

Letter 91

The monument to Charles-Louis Philippe (a bust by Antoine Bourdelle) was inaugurated in the cemetery of Cérilly on 25th September 1911.

André Gide's lecture does not refer to the " redoubtable influence " of Claudel. It speaks of Claudel as one of the influences (others being Michelet, Dostoevsky, and Nietzsche) which Philippe had undergone. " It was in the penultimate period of his life that he hearkened to Claudel, whose strong and self-confident voice impressed Philippe, as it was later to impress many others among us. It may seem paradoxical that this influence, this wholly Catholic influence of Claudel, should have had the same effect as the influence of Nietzsche. But in Claudel, as in Nietzsche, he found an exultant and strengthening virtue . . . that of the joy, the exaltation, the wild health of those who suffer and are sick, that superior health that must be won and re-won—all that he had already learnt from Nietzsche. . . . The example of Claudel had deeply impressed more than one of us. Nothing is more contagious than melancholy, nothing more convincing than joy. Philippe felt within himself an urgent need of happiness. What could be the secret of Claudel's overflowing happiness ? At that precise moment, Philippe was very near to becoming a Catholic. ' What's the use of resisting ? ' he wrote to me. ' You know that we'll all come to it in the end.' On this delicate point I am not required to give my private opinion. Those who were nearest to Philippe in his last days consider that he had mastered Claudel's influence and had at last come out on the other side. . . . You will realize, as well as I, that we are dealing with something stronger, more important, and more terrible than the influence of an individual writer. Behind Claudel was hidden, or rather was not hidden, the Church. I think I can suggest quite objectively that where this last influence was concerned Philippe decided, after having listened to it for a long time, that victory lay in not giving way. What remained to him was that he understood all the comfort, the dignity, the strength and the nobility of the refuge that was proposed to him ; he could never again be a Voltairean (if, in fact, he had ever been one) ; and yet it seemed to him that, by turning away, he was re-conquering himself."

André Gide had written a eulogy of Baudelaire in reply to an article in which Émile Faguet had said that Baudelaire was a poet of the second rank. " A book needs deep qualities," Gide replied, " if it is to survive. It is these secret qualities which make it at first seem rather uncertain, uneasy, mysterious, disquieting to those who claim to know at a glance ' what the author meant to say ', enigmatic perhaps and even (let's out with the dreadful word) unhealthy ! What made the work of Baudelaire seem disquieting and unhealthy to his contemporaries is precisely what has kept it young and poignant for us to-day."

Letter 92

Tolstoy died on 7th November 1910 at the age of eighty. He had abandoned his home some ten days earlier in order to find refuge in the house of some humble friends ; but he fell ill en route and died at Astapovo.

Letter 94

The Academician René Bazin was the father-in-law of one of the brothers of Madame Paul Claudel.

The slogan quoted by Claudel (*Toujours à mieux*) was that of the firm of Amieux in Nantes which was famous for its tinned fish and vegetables.

The definitive version of *La Jeune Fille Violaine* was published in November 1911 by the *Mercure de France*. The " destinies of the Coûfontaines in the nineteenth century " were the subject of two later plays by Claudel : *Le Pain dur* (1913–1914) and *Le Père humilié* (1916).

Letter 95

Elémir Bourges (1852–1925) was one of Claudel's best friends. Claudel considered him, in fact, one of the most delicate and honourable natures of his time, and he regretted that his gifts as a writer were not such as could make this clear to a wide public. In his *Accompagnements* (*N.R.F.*, 1949) he devotes many pages to Bourges, who was the author of, among other things, *Le Crépuscule des Dieux* (1884), *L'Enfant qui revient* (1903) and an immensely long poem (one of the longest in modern literature) *La Nef* (1904).

The book of Marguerite Audoux which Claudel found insipid was her autobiographical novel *Marie-Claire*.

Letter 96

The character of Turelure in *L'Otage* represents an aspect of Claudel's thought which, by reason of its rough manner and prosaic good sense, is more approachable than the sublimities of (for instance) his heroine Sygne de Coûfontaine.

Letter 97

The Life and Adventures of a Young Man of Toggenburg was the autobiography of Ulrich Braecker, a Swiss, who was born in 1735 in the canton of St. Gall. It tells of his adventures in the Prussian Army, and of his desertion and subsequent return to Switzerland. The poet Adolf Wildbrandt had reprinted the book in 1910.

Letter 98

Maurice Barrès and Paul Claudel were never on very good terms. Temperamental differences between them were too great to be overcome ; and although Barrès liked to see himself as the patron of rising young writers, and had indeed asked Claudel to give him some facts about himself for a forthcoming article, the article was never written. Claudel had, indeed, done his best to sabotage the project by dilating upon his enthusiasm for Rimbaud—an author whom Barrès could not abide.

Letter 99

From October 1910 onwards Marcel Rivière was the publisher of the *N.R.F.* and of all books published with its imprint.

Letter 100

Gide's *Isabelle* appeared in the *N.R.F.* during the first three months of 1911.

Jean Schlumberger, to whom Gide's *Symphonie Pastorale* was later dedicated, had just published a volume of poems with frontispiece by Maurice Denis. His *Éveils* (*N.R.F.* 1950) contains a great deal of information about the early years of the *N.R.F.*

Letter 102

Maurice Berteaux, whom Claudel considered as a personal enemy, was a radical-socialist. Minister of War in 1911, he died of an accident in the following year.

Letter 104

In the *N.R.F.* for March 1911, Schlumberger had attacked those translations (notably of Ibsen, Tolstoy, and Dostoevsky) in which the thought, as much as the style, of important writers was grossly abused.

Chapter 2 of the first book of Tacitus' Histories appealed to Claudel because it showed the decomposition of the Roman Empire, in which the general picture of intrigue and treachery was occasionally lightened (in Claudel's view) by evidence of divine intervention. Émile Combes (1835–1921) was a politician who had been Minister of Education and Minister of Fine Arts in the Bourgeois cabinet. In June 1902 he took over the leadership of the Government from Waldeck-Rousseau, and himself became Minister of the Interior. He introduced measures for the separation of Church and State and the dissolution of state-run Roman Catholic schools. Briand and others of his successors followed the same policy, which for Claudel remained associated with the name of its originator.

Isabelle is the story of a young girl, the last heiress of a noble family, who lives alone with her parents on the family property. She becomes

Letter 122

...ul Reboux had reviewed *L'Otage* in the *Journal* in terms of the greatest
...empt both for Claudel and for his admirers. " An invincible boredom,"
...oncluded, " is exhaled by this flat and pretentious volume." Jacques
...au replied in the *N.R.F.* that it was not the first occasion on which
...oux had professed to be bored by anything that was not conceived in
...s of popular entertainment. " A Mallarmé and a Claudel," he con-
...ed in his turn, " have the power to forbid certain intruders to enter
... domain."
...he isolated " I " in Claudel's translation appears at the beginning of
...nore's poem *Winter*.
...he reference to *Virgile travesti* is, of course, to Scarron's parody of the
...ing of the *Aeneid*.

Letter 123

...audel had just been appointed consul at Frankfurt-on-Main, where
...emained until his appointment to Hamburg in 1913.
...he *Mercure de France* for November 1911 contained a very severe criti-
..., by Henry D. Davray, of Claudel's versions of poems by Patmore.
...se, in his opinion, were inexact in detail and inapposite in tone. " One
...d have to be unusually good-natured," he concluded, " to be content
... so defective a rendering." As usual, Claudel's admirers rallied to
...upport, and Valery Larbaud was able to adduce the admiration of
...nore's son Francis, who had written to express his complete satisfac-
...with the translations. Davray was not discomfited, however, and said
..., although Francis Patmore had no apparent qualifications to express
...opinion in the matter, he was delighted that the versions had found
...ny rate *one* contented reader. Gide, for his part, had written to ask
...baud if the original English could possibly be as fine as certain passages
...he French.
...adame Gide's second sister had recently been converted to Catholicism.
...heotokos signifies " the mother of God ". The expression was laid
...n and authorized by the Council of Ephesus in A.D. 431 against the
...osition of Nestorius who wished the Virgin to have only the style of
...istokos, or " mother of Christ ". Claudel identifies the Virgin Mary
... the Church, because they both were given the mission of giving God
...he world.

Letter 124

...arbaud's essay on Patmore, and Claudel's translations from his poems,
...e united by the *N.R.F.* in book form in 1912.
...lthough Gide's parents were both Protestant, and he himself was
...ught up as a Protestant, yet his maternal grandfather, Edouard Ron-
...ux, was the last of a long line of Catholics.
...aterne Berrichon, the husband of Rimbaud's sister Isabelle, devoted
...ch of his life to the cult of his brother-in-law's memory. The *Mercure*
...*France* had acquired the exclusive right of publishing all Rimbaud's

pregnant in the course of a secret liaison, and is turned out of the house
immediately after the birth of her son, whom her parents insist on keeping
at home. When she in her turn inherits the house from her father she
immediately sells it and abandons her son to the care of an old servant.

Letter 105

The translations mentioned by André Gide are those of Calderon by
Hinard (1869) and Lope de Vega by Baret (1879). The later translation
of Calderon's religious plays was by Léo Rouanet (1898).

Letter 106

Gide's *Nouveaux Prétextes*, dedicated to Paul Desjardins, was a collection
of lectures and articles, many of which are eloquent of Gide's determination
that morality should be a department of æsthetics, and that in any case
moral questions should not be allowed to spill over into the problems of
art.
Mallarmé's article on the *Passion* is reprinted under the title of *Catholicisme*
on page 392 of the Pléiade edition (1945) of his complete works.
Arvède Barine was the pseudonym of Mme Charles Vincent, who wrote
on literary subjects for a number of reviews.
Téodor de Wyzéwa (1862–1917) was the author of many works of
criticism—more especially on art and music.
The Review *Indépendance* ran from March 1911 to May 1913 and, like
the *N.R.F.*, was published by Marcel Rivière. René Benjamin, Vincent
d'Indy, Paul Jamot, Georges Sorel, and the brothers Tharaud were on
its editorial committee. Ostensibly quite neutral in its opinions, it soon
took a sharp turn to the right. Georges Sorel (1847–1922) had made
himself known by his celebrated *Apologie de la Violence* (1908) ; but he
too had turned sharply to the right, and in 1910 was in sympathy with
the monarchist *Action Française*. This phase was quickly over, however,
and Sorel was soon one of the first Frenchmen to salute the rise of Bol-
shevism in Russia. An anti-parliamentary syndicalist, a disciple of Bergson,
Nietzsche, Marx, and Proudhon, and a convinced anti-intellectual pessi-
mist, Sorel founded his beliefs on the supremacy of violence and the power
of the general strike.

Letter 107

The Belgian monarchist Review *Les Guêpes* had devoted a special number
to Boileau. Claudel, Barrès, Bordeaux, Bazin, Lemaître, and others sent
short messages of appreciation. Claudel's own letter saluted Boileau as a
master of the essential forms and expressions of the French language.
Unfortunately these authentic tributes were followed by a group of awkward
parodies in which various other authors were supposed to have answered
the same enquiry. Jammes was among those who were held up to ridicule
in this way, and Claudel was quick to take offence on his behalf.

Letter 108

Relations between Jammes and Gide had taken a turn for the better in February 1911. Jammes had sent a short letter of friendly greeting, and Gide had telegraphed his appreciation, and a correspondence followed ; but the reconciliation was never much more than formal.

Letter 109

When *Tête d'Or* and *La Ville* were re-issued in 1911, Claudel subjected them to meticulous revision—as, indeed, has always been his custom when reprinting his work.

Proudhon's *De la Justice dans la Révolution et dans l'Eglise* (1858) had prompted Claudel to write the essay on Justice which is reprinted in his *Positions et Propositions* ; it is essentially a protest against the deformation of the truths of Christianity and the substitution of profane for sacred Justice.

Letter 110

Marcel Rivière ceased to be the publisher of the *N.R.F.* in 1910, and a limited company was formed. Gaston Gallimard was then, and is still, its managing director. For the time being Jacques Copeau and Jacques Rivière continued as director and secretary of the Review.

Letter 111

Paul Claudel wrote a short commentary for the extract from d'Ablancourt's *Tacitus*, and here is an essential passage from it : " Nothing is more difficult, or less appreciated, than a good translation. Translation is the school in which all of the great writers of the past were formed. This extract from d'Ablancourt is of value in itself ; to my ear, at least, he has created some of the fullest and most perfect music that our language has ever known. It fulfils exactly my idea of a good translation which, though it should be exact, must not be servile ; on the contrary it should be infinitely sensitive to the *values* of the original—should be, in a word, a veritable transubstantiation. . . . I feel that our compatriot has acquitted himself with the finest of taste. He could never have rivalled the strength and concision of Tacitus' Latin ; he had to transpose, in accordance with the genius of his own language ; and he has done it so perfectly that here and there his version even seems to me to excel the original. . . ."

Tono Bungay and *The New Machiavelli* had appeared in 1908 and 1911 respectively.

Pierre Lasserre (1867-1931) was the author of books on Nietzsche, Romanticism, and the *Christian Crisis*. He wrote a long review of *L'Otage* in the *Action Française* on 7th May 1911. It was by no means entirely favourable, and many of Claudel's friends were affronted by much of what was said in it ; but Claudel was delighted, and did not begrudge Lasserre his frankness. Gide's *Journal* for 7th May 1912 reveals that

Lasserre had intended to speak still more severely, by many of his young readers who warned him t constitute, in their eyes, an irrecoverable blunder.

Letter 113

Claudel had been won over to Patmore by *Th* translated several of the poems from this volume. the same time, was preparing to write a long stud impressed by these translations and wrote to Cla to the text of the original all the dignity of the F

Letter 115

La Mère et l'Enfant was an autobiographical s which the *N.R.F.* reprinted in 1911.

André Gide visited Larbaud in London in July see (among others) Arthur Symons and Joseph C

Letter 118

On 21st July 1901, a monument by Berrichon t in the station square at Charleville. The origina cerned itself with this project included Felix F Ghil, Pierre Louys, Jean Moréas, Laurent Tailha Verhaeren. Neither Gide nor Claudel took part. Nothing came of Claudel's proposed series of se

Letter 119

Philippe's *Croquignole* tells the story of a minor squandering an unexpected legacy, commits suici he finds himself as poor as before. Claudel disl more because Philippe shows it to have been a lor his lecture on Philippe, Gide had said that he f re-discover in *Croquignole* the impatient and glutton I have traced for you as it developed, slowly at fir

André Gide never visited Claudel in Prague.

Letter 120

Coventry Patmore (1823-1896), one of the fin was an Anglican who became converted to Cathol though attracted by such a sequence of events, co never read anything of Patmore except the *Un Positions et Propositions* he reprints his impressions o extended French view of Patmore, cf. Valery L (*N.R.F.*).

works, but the *N.R.F.* had hoped that it might be possible for Berrichon to break away from them on the grounds that the *Mercure* had also published Rémy de Gourmont's attack on Rimbaud. In the course of this, Gourmont had said that Rimbaud was " often obscure, bizarre, and absurd. Completely insincere, womanish (if not girlish) in his nature, instinctively malicious and even ferocious, Rimbaud's talent is of the kind which interests but does not please." He also said that many pages in his work had the kind of beauty that one would experience before a fine case of syphilis. The " Censeur " of the *Mercure* assured Berrichon that the article would be modified before it appeared in book form, and Berrichon took advantage of the general *détente* to publish an article in which he attempted to explain away the journey of Rimbaud and Verlaine to Belgium. When Gourmont next published a book of essays he did, in effect, modify his original strictures ; but he also seized the chance to ask " how anybody could believe that Verlaine and Rimbaud had hidden themselves away in hotels for no other reason than to sing matins and convert M. Claudel ? "

Letter 125

Gide's article on Gautier, in the *N.R.F.* for 1st December 1911, contained the following salient passages : " I do not at all reproach Gautier for his doctrine of ' art for art's sake ' ; in fact I see no other reason for existence ; but I do blame him for having reduced art to the expression of such trifles. . . . I am grateful to him for having denounced utilitarian art, but I can't forgive him for regarding all thought as utilitarian—or else for having known nothing at all about it. . . . Nor do I reproach him for having wanted to create only things of beauty ; but merely for having failed so signally to achieve them. . . . I don't reproach him for being immoral, but on the contrary for having made immorality even stupider and more tedious than virtue. Yes, I reproach that immorality for being so feeble a resource. His indulgence is nothing but apathy."

Claudel agreed, of course, with this judgment. Pierre Grassou, whom he compares to Gautier, is a character from Balzac's *Cousine Bette, Cousin Pons*, and *La Rabouilleuse*. A painter, a member of the Institut, and a typical fake " great man ", he is meant to show how the mass of mediocrities can push one of their number forward to the highest honours.

It was after reading Rimbaud that the eighteen-year-old Claudel felt himself turning back towards the Church, and he has always admitted to the profound and fundamental effect of this perusal. Gide, too, felt able to say to Berrichon in 1911 that *Les Illuminations* had been " my viaticum, and almost my only nourishment, during the month of convalescence which was the most important month of my life."

It was Mgr. Baudrillart who preached, on 3rd November 1911, in the Carmelite Church, the sermon which is based upon the argument of Claudel's *Magnificat*.

The exact quotation from Rimbaud's *Adieu* in *Un Saison en Enfer*, is as follows : " *L'automne déjà !—Mais pourquoi regretter un éternel soleil, si nous sommes engagés à la découverte de la clarté divine,—loin des gens qui meurent sur les saisons.*"

Letter 126

At the end of Act I of *L'Annonce faite à Marie*, Anne Vercors, the elderly owner of a large farm, decides to leave his property and his people and go to Jerusalem with the Crusaders. He takes care, however, to hide his emotion, and leaves with no more fuss than if he were simply going out to the fields.

André Gide here alludes to yet another violent controversy. *L'Indépendance*, under the spiritual ægis of Georges Sorel and pursuing its habitual policy, had published in November 1911 an attack upon Paul Desjardins. Desjardins was one of the last great European free-thinkers, and he used his disaffected Cistercian Abbey of Pontigny as a sort of clearing-house for intellectuals of every shade of opinion. He meant it to be a place at which contacts could be made and sympathies aroused without any ulterior motive. Sorel's Review preferred to call it a sump of anti-religious activity, the more noxious for being situated on what should strictly have been Church land. A month later Copeau replied in the *N.R.F.* " The article ", he said, " is not a piece of healthy polemic. It is not written in good pamphleteer's ink. In place of eloquence, a mediocre malignity suffuses its pages. . . . And when we reach the last line of the last page, we must admit that our anger, which had seemed strong enough, is appeased, and even momentarily discouraged, when we see that it is only signed : Jean Variot." Variot challenged Copeau to a duel, but Copeau did not consider the matter of sufficient importance, and Variot had finally to content himself with the publication of the relevant letters in the *N.R.F.* for 1st January 1912.

After the publication of Ch.-L. Philippe's *Lettres de Jeunesse*, Sorel accused Philippe, in *L'Indépendance*, of having exploited the socialist cause in the interests of his own personal success. " It is appalling to think ", he concluded, " that such feeble-minded phrase-makers may soon, thanks to the march of Democracy, be called upon to regenerate the homeland of Pascal."

These controversies affected the relations of Gide and Claudel, in so far as Gide remained for many years a faithful supporter of Desjardins' *Entretiens de Pontigny* and regarded these assemblies as immensely stimulating. Claudel for his part was always suspicious of them ; on the other hand, he admired Philippe and was sorry that Sorel should express himself so wildly.

Letter 127

Under Western Eyes was published in 1911.

Bazin's *Davidée Birot* (1912) is the edifying story of a young country schoolmistress.

Péguy had a particular hatred for certain university professors, whom he regarded as traitors to the true image of French greatness. His especial enemies, in this context, were Lavisse, Langlois, and Lanson, and his *Cahiers de la Quinzaine* contain large-scale attacks upon them all.

Letter 128

There was never a definitive quarrel between Gide and Péguy, but Péguy took care to detach himself from Gide's influence, and is reported to have said in 1911 that he had " broken with André Gide because he detested his dilettantism ".

André Gide's *Journal* : January 1912

Gide profited by a short journey in Switzerland to make a series of reflections upon his position as a man of over forty, his intellectual possibilities, and so forth.

Letter 129

Nothing came of Gide's projected visit to Frankfurt.
Rivière's long essay on Gide is reprinted in his *Études* (*N.R.F.*).

Letter 132

Valery Larbaud was the son of a Catholic father and a Protestant mother. He was brought up as a Protestant and his conversion to Catholicism was inspired by his many friends in English Catholic circles. Claudel had no part in it, but when he was apprised of the event by André Gide he instantly wrote to congratulate Larbaud, and added : " Let us hope that poor Gide's turn will come soon. He looks very unhappy and tormented to me—though he has never really unburdened himself or offered to go deeply into these matters ".

The German pastor Theodor Harnack (1817–1889) was well known for his works of exegesis, and more especially for such volumes of Protestant apologia as his *Fundamental Beliefs of the Lutheran Church*.

Vladimir Soloviev was a late nineteenth-century Russian Orthodox philosopher. His works include *The Justification of Good*, and *The Crisis of Occidental Philosophy*.

Newman's *Essay on the Development of Christian Doctrine* is the book to which Claudel means to refer.

Letter 133

Claudel's Latin quotations in this letter are, respectively, from *Luke* x. 42, *John* xi. 33 and 38, and *Mark* xiv. 33.

Paterne Berrichon gave Claudel two family photographs of Rimbaud in early youth. Together with a sketch of Rimbaud by Forain, and a drawing of him on his death-bed by Isabelle Rimbaud, these now hang on the walls of Claudel's apartment in Paris.

The quotation, *Factum, non genitum*, is taken, or rather inverted, from the *Credo* (*Genitum non factum consubstantialem patri*).

Letter 134

Leconte de Lisle's translations from the Greek are : *Anacreontic Odes* (1861), *Iliad* (1866), *Odyssey* (1867), and works by *Hesiod* (1869), *Sophocles* (1877), and *Euripides* (1885).

André Gide's *Journal* : 8th May 1912

It appears from Gide's *Journal* that during his visit to Italy in the late spring of 1912 he had an important exchange of letters with Claudel ; but, as on many other occasions, only Claudel's letters have survived.

Letter 135

The poem on which Claudel was engaged was his *Cantate à trois voix* : *Cette heure qui est entre le Printemps et l'Été*.

In June 1912 the *N.R.F.* had printed a translation of some of Keats' letters to Fanny Brawne. The text of these was somewhat man-handled by the *N.R.F.*'s Belgian printers.

Gide's new book was *Les Caves du Vatican* which, in the event, fully justified Claudel's apprehensions.

Letter 137

Suarès eventually gave up the idea of writing on Rimbaud in the *N.R.F.*, and Claudel's long essay appeared in the Review for 1st October 1912. It was reprinted as the preface to Rimbaud's collected poems (*Mercure de France*, 1916) and in Claudel's *Positions et Propositions*. It is famous for its presentation of Rimbaud as an unacknowledged and unacknowledging mystic. " His life ", Claudel asserts, " was a misunderstanding, a vain attempt to escape from the voice which by turns attracts him and casts him away, the voice which he refuses to recognize. . . ."

During Claudel's pilgrimage to the Rimbaud country he was received at Roche, near Attigny, the birthplace of Rimbaud's mother. In his article he speaks of what he saw there : " As I lay down my pen, I see once again the country that was his : the pure black Meuse, the old fortress of Mézières pinned between the severe hills, and Charleville in its valley of resounding furnaces. (It is there that he lies at rest, in a little girl's white grave.) Then that region of the Ardennes, with its meagre harvests, its little groups of slate roofs, and always on the horizon the legendary line of the forests. It is spring-country . . . the blue-green Aisne encumbered with waterlilies and long yellow reeds. And then Voucq station, and the sad canal, bordered with poplars and stretching as far as the eye can follow. It was there that, one dark evening, on his return from Marseilles, the amputated Rimbaud stood waiting for the cab which would take him back to his mother. Then, at Roche, the big house of mouldered stone with its high peasant roof and the date—1791—above the door, the granary where he wrote his last book, the fireplace (with the crucifix above) where he burnt his manuscripts, and the bed where he lay ill. And I handled the yellowing papers, the drawings, the photographs— among them that most tragic one in which Rimbaud is seen as black as any negro, bare-headed and bare-footed, in the costume of the convicts he once admired, on the banks of a river in Ethiopia—the blacklead portraits, and the letter from Isabelle Rimbaud which describes her brother's last days in hospital at Marseilles."

In 1949, Claudel announced exultantly that, after his visit to Roche, a letter from Berrichon had informed him of the discovery of a radiant cross carved with the point of a knife in the underside of the worktable in the attic where Rimbaud had written *Une Saison en Enfer*.

Letter 138

L'Indépendance never lost a chance of making fun of what it called " the Pontigny talking-shop " ; but Gide remained faithful to it, and was there, in fact, when the last Entretien was broken up in September 1939 by the outbreak of war.

Copeau followed up his lecture on *L'Échange* by a production of the play at the *Vieux-Colombier* in November 1913.

Letter 139

Lugné-Poe, though disappointed in his hopes of putting on *Partage de Midi*, produced *L'Annonce faite à Marie* in 1912 and *L'Otage* in 1914.

Paris-Midi for 10th July 1912 carried a paragraph about the article which Barrès had intended to write about Claudel. The literary columnist revealed that Claudel had long since furnished Barrès with the necessary information, and spoke of the astonishment which was generally felt at Barrès' failure to produce the tribute in question.

Letter 140

Since the end of 1911, Gide has ceased writing for the Reviews in order to concentrate on *Les Caves du Vatican*. His isolation was such as to provoke a rumour that he no longer took any hand in the affairs of the *N.R.F.* ; but this he formally denied in January 1913.

Claudel's theological studies were embodied in an article called *La Physique de l'Eucharistie*, which was published in June 1913 by the *Revue de la Jeunesse*.

Marie Kalff, whose enthusiasm for Claudel's work will be familiar to readers of this Correspondence, had given a series of recitals from his plays in Holland during the winter of 1911–1912, and in April 1912 she organized a matinee at the *Théâtre Michel* in Paris at which she, Charles Dullin, and Edouard de Max read scenes from *L'Arbre*.

Manet's portrait of Madame Manet belongs to the Berlin Art Gallery.

Letter 141

The Great Schism lasted from 1378 until 1417. It was not a Schism in the strict sense, since none of the conflicting parties denied the authority of the Holy See. There was, however, great uncertainty as to who should be Pope, and at one time Rome, Avignon, and Pisa all had their rival candidates. The Schism was finally settled when Martin V was accepted as Pope by all Roman Catholic countries.

Claudel applies to Gide the famous line from Mallarmé's *Tombeau d'Edgar Poe* : " *Tel qu'en lui-même enfin l'éternité le change* ".

He later quotes from *Perrette et le pot au lait*, a propos of the involuntary defection of Marie Kalff. The exclamation " *Adieu veau* " is, of course, a pun on the English equivalent of " *Veau* "—calf, *i.e.*, and Kalff.

The admired passages from *Paradise Lost* are those which begin respectively at Book III, line 622, and Book VI, line 568. ·

Valentinus and Basilides were heretical philosophers of the second century A.D., who taught respectively in Rome and at Alexandria. Both were representatives of Gnosticism—a line of thought by which the origin of the world, the problem of evil, and the Christian mysteries themselves were all given a purely philosophical explanation.

In his little-known *La Sorcière*, Michelet alludes to the " sense of Satan " which, in his view, the English possess, instinctively, to a greater degree than any other people. He holds that Satan, the master of the world, personifies all those revolutionary truths which begin by being considered as dangerous and end by imposing their fecundity upon the whole world.

It would seem unlikely that de Quincey could have taken anything from *La Sorcière*, since the book was published in 1862 and de Quincey died in 1859.

Letter 143

André Gide was present at the first performance of *L'Annonce* on 20th December 1912.

Jacques Rivière's essay *De la Foi* in the *N.R.F.* for 1st November 1912 was divided into three parts : *Eulogy of Faith, Reasons for Belief,* and *The Difficulty of Belief.* These titles summarize his state of mind at the time, which was still too hesitant to please Claudel.

Book IV of the *Imitation* is called " De Sacramento " and deals with the Eucharist.

Letter 144

It was through Louis Massignon that Claudel met the Abbé Daniel Fontaine, to whom Huysmans had bequeathed his library. The Abbé had founded a little magazine, *La Voix de Clichy*, in order to reply to the virulent attacks of a free-thinking chemist who had come to live in his parish. Both Claudel and Mauriac contributed to this magazine. The Abbé Fontaine was the incumbent of Saint-Antoine-des-Quinze-Vingts when he died in 1921. Claudel wrote a poem in his memory which ends with these lines :

Et je crois que demain je serai avec toi dans le Paradis
Tenant le pan de ta robe sacerdotale dans ma main, simplement parce que tu
  me l'as promis.

The poem appears in *Feuilles de Saints* (*N.R.F.* 1925).

The quotation from the *Gospel according to St Matthew* is a paraphrase
of verses 8 and 9 of chapter xviii.

Letter 145

As Claudel had given his *Cantate à trois voix* to the *Revue de Paris* instead
of the *N.R.F.*, Gide wrote to ask if he had any grievance against the *N.R.F.*
Claudel's answer does not reveal the underlying cause of his defection,
which was that he was displeased with an article in which Henri Ghéon,
an intimate associate of Gide and of other members of the *N.R.F.* editorial
committee, had teased Jammes for his recent assertion that books based
on belief in God had a nobility and a natural radiance that belonged to
them alone. Claudel then wrote to Jammes (on 4th October 1912) and
said : " I was very displeased by the last number of the *N.R.F.* After
many a tergiversation they have made clear their attitude ; and, if it
should be confirmed, it is one which would lead me to a tacit separation
from them, despite all the kindnesses I have received from them. Must
we witness the re-appearance of all those old catchwords about ' Art
First ' and ' Art for Art's Sake ' ? Besides, Gheon's article does not represent your point of view fairly." Claudel went on to support Jammes'
point of view, and ended by saying : " Nothing can be beautiful unless
it is necessary, and nothing is necessary unless it serves the glory of God."

When Claudel's *Cantate* appeared in the *Revue de Paris* it was prefaced
by an editorial note which, by its cautious and ingratiating tone, showed
that he was by no means accepted among the great public as an important
writer.

In 1926, at Tokyo, Claudel at last completed his long-planned essay on
Wagner (cf. *Figures et Paraboles*, *N.R.F.*, 1936). In this he stresses (dis-
covers, indeed) the Christian aspect of Wagner, and declares that Wagner
made a tremendous effort of faith in order to proclaim his beliefs at the
very moment when a blind belief in material progress was possessing his
countrymen. " Alone on the Bayreuth hill, above a Germany that was
killing itself with gold and good living, Richard Wagner declared his belief
in the sacramental forms of Christ."

Victor Segalen (1878–1919) had met Claudel in 1907. By profession
a Naval doctor, he was at the same time a writer and an archæologist, who
had also published poems and impressions of the Far East. In his enthusiasm for Claudel he had the audacity in 1915 to devise a variant of *Le
Repos du Septième Jour*, and at the same time to apprise Claudel that he
was basically anti-Catholic. Claudel's superb reply is published, together
with much other interesting matter, in the special Segalen number of
Cahiers du Sud (1st issue, 1948).

In 1912 Albert Thibaudet (1875–1941) published his first book of
literary criticism, *La Poésie de Stéphane Mallarmé*.

Mallarmé's *Un Coup de Dés* had so far appeared only in a magazine

(*Cosmopolis*, 1897). André Gide had admired the poem immoderately from the start, and Claudel's suggestion could not have been other than welcome to him. As he had written to Mallarmé in May 1897 : " The last lines chilled me with an emotion very similar to that which one feels after a Beethoven symphony (of course, I'm not teaching you anything by saying this) . . . and the pacified grandeur of the final phrase is like the perfect concord of the last bar. That is admirable " (cf. Mondor, *Vie de Mallarmé*, *N.R.F.*, 1946).

Mallarmé had given a proof of *Un Coup de Dés* to Claudel, and another to Valéry. The *N.R.F.* published the poem in 1914.

Letter 146

André Gide was preparing a collective translation of a selection from Whitman's works. He had asked Claudel to translate certain poems from *Leaves of Grass*, but Claudel later, in March 1914, backed out of the agreement, in consequence of his grave differences with Gide. The volume eventually appeared in 1918, with translations by Gide, Larbaud, Schlumberger, Laforgue, Louis Fabulet, and Francis Viélé-Griffin. The translation by Viélé-Griffin to which Claudel refers was not included.

Letter 147

Claudel's father died on 2nd March 1913.
André Gide had just returned the manuscript of *L'Annonce* to Claudel.

Letter 148

Le Temps had announced in error that Claudel's *Cinq grandes Odes* had been published by the *Mercure de France* and not by the *N.R.F.* André Gide wrote to the editor of *Le Temps* and asked for a correction to be inserted in their next issue. He also remarked that *Le Temps* had always been noticeably less well disposed towards the *N.R.F.* than towards certain other publishers.

Claudel was staying at Hellerau, a small town near Dresden, where Wolf Dohrn and Alexander Salzmann had founded a school of theatrical production analogous in some respects to Copeau's *Vieux-Colombier*. *L'Annonce faite à Marie* was one of their first productions. It had been transposed not merely into German but into a German setting and a given point in German history. The *N.R.F.* for 1st September 1913 includes some notes by Claudel on the theatre of Hellerau.

Letter 149

Abel Lefranc, editor of *Le Temps'* literary supplement, was a specialist in the literature of the Renaissance who later became a Professor at the *Collège de France*.

Comœdia published, in October 1913, a report by Claudel on the productions at Hellerau.

Letter 150

In 1908 Darius Milhaud, then a very young man, came to visit Francis Jammes at Orthez, and played over to him some settings of his poems. Jammes gave him a volume of Claudel to read in the train, and Milhaud was fired by this to begin the long series of collaborations with Claudel which includes the *Oresteia*, the *Choephorei*, the *Agamemnon*, the ballet *L'Homme et son Désir*, the *Eumenides*, and many settings of individual poems, odes, and cantatas. When, in 1917, Claudel was appointed French Ambassador in Brazil, he took Milhaud with him on his staff. On the return journey, a mechanical breakdown caused them to be fifty-three days at sea between Rio de Janeiro and New York, and they filled in the time by preparing a new musical setting and a new translation of the Psalms. Milhaud has also set part of Gide's *La Porte étroite* to music.

Letter 151

Claudel had just been appointed Consul-General at Hamburg, where he remained until the outbreak of war.

In October 1913 Jammes gave an interview to *Le Temps* in which he did, in effect, attribute to Claudel certain remarks which do not show any great tenderness towards Gide. As, however, Gide was not named in the interview, it could only be by a process of divination that any reader could identify Gide as the third person in the party. Though pressed by Gide to insert a correction, Jammes never did so ; and Claudel, as appears from the next letter, came in the end to regret that he had ever raised the matter.

Protée is a satirical play in two acts which Claudel wrote in 1913. He had formed the idea while meditating on the possible character of the lost play by Aeschylus which bears the same name, and which formed a pendant to the *Oresteia*.

Letter 152

Claudel's story of his conversion had just appeared in the *Revue de la Jeunesse*, at the request of the Dominican Père Barge, who was then its editor.

Prochazka (1869–1925) was a Czech critic and translator who at one time edited the *Moderni Revue* in Prague and lost no opportunity of expressing his admiration for French literature.

Letter 153

André Gide did not consider that Claudel was justified in his anxieties ; when *Les Caves du Vatican* appeared in the *N.R.F.* (January-April 1914) he retained, at the beginning of Book III, the epigraph which he had taken from *L'Annonce faite à Marie*.

André Gide greatly admired Tagore, who had just (in 1913) been awarded the Nobel Prize ; and his translation of the *Gitanjali* was published by the *N.R.F.* In 1922 he translated the two-act comedy *Amal et la Lettre du Roi*.

Letter 154

Copeau had asked Gide to ask Claudel if he might produce *Protée* at the *Vieux-Colombier*. Nothing came of this plan, but Milhaud's incidental music was published in 1922, and the play was at last produced in 1933 at Courtrai, in Belgium. It was also produced, in 1947, in Switzerland and Holland.

Letter 155

Gide had asked Claudel to suggest to Léon Daudet that he might review Valery Larbaud's *Complete Works of A. O. Barnabooth* (*N.R.F.*, 1913). Claudel and Daudet had been at school together. From 1890 to 1892 they often met, in company with Barbusse, Renard, and Marcel Schwob, at the Restaurant d'Harcourt. Although their opinions diverged ever more widely, they remained on excellent terms, and Daudet usually reviewed Claudel's books editorially in *L'Action Française*. Eventually, however, Claudel broke entirely with the paper, after Maurras had made a violent attack in its columns upon Philippe Berthelot. During the war he became still more strongly opposed to it, and in 1918 he wrote an article for *L'Aube* in which he detailed the grievous harm which, in his opinion, *L'Action Française* had done to France. Daudet none the less remained a firm admirer of Claudel's work.

Gide only once came into direct contact with Léon Daudet ; and that was during the war, when the monarchist leader was in charge of a counter-espionage department, and Gide had to report to him the existence of an espionage cell in a house not far from his own in Paris. Daudet, who always tried to keep art quite separate from politics, was a staunch defender of Gide's merits as a writer, and in 1923 he went so far as to defend Gide actively in the *L'Action Française*, at a time when he was under heavy fire from Henri Béraud, and to describe Gide as a writer " of terrible penetration ". And later he said : " Even if M. Gide were to steal my boots while I was asleep in the train, or to pour aconite into my soup, or to proclaim the superiority of democracy over all other forms of government —even then I should still consider him a man of great talent. And then we have a great admiration in common : for Dostoevsky. I put Dostoevsky high above Tolstoy, and high above all those who criticize Dostoevsky. So I say to myself that if, as is probable, M. Gide and I meet in Purgatory, we shall talk of Dostoevsky."

Letter 156

The passage from *Les Caves du Vatican* which so horrified Claudel is that in which the young Lafcadio is travelling by train from Rome to Naples, at the beginning of Book V. It leads up to the famous moment at which, in his search for the *acte gratuit*, Lafcadio pushes Fleurissoire out of the window. It was not this, however, which offended Claudel, but the homosexual daydream which immediately precedes the entrance of Fleurissoire into the compartment. Claudel wrote letters of stupefaction not only to Rivière, but also to Jammes and to the Abbé Fontaine.

Letter 158

It was during a fortnight's visit to Florence that Gide received Claudel's first letter of commination.

Letter 160

The Biblical references for Claudel's warnings and objurgations are : *Genesis* xix. ; *Leviticus* xx 13 ; *Romans* i. 27 ; *I Corinthians* vi. 9–10.

Letter 162

The epigraph which Gide had wished to place at the beginning of Book III of the *Caves* was drawn from the Prologue to *L'Annonce faite à Marie*. In this, Violaine says : " But of which Pope are you speaking, and of which King ? For there are two of them, and we don't know which is the right one."

Letter 164

The *editio princeps* of *Les Caves du Vatican* was in two volumes and was limited to 550 copies, with a Frontispiece by P.-A. Laurens. It did not bear Gide's name, simply *Sotie par l'auteur de " Paludes ".* The first commercial edition, which appeared later in 1914, was in one volume and did bear the author's name.

Claudel was always fond of quoting the example of St. Jerome who, though quite content to endure fifteen years of mortifications in the desert, came out like a roaring lion when he heard that an obscure rhetorician called Rufinus had made fun of his books (cf. Letter 64 of this Correspondence).

Letter 165

The letters between Jammes and Gide which appear in this book have not been published before.

When Jammes came to Paris in February 1914 to give a lecture on religious poetry, André Gide took great pains to show his sympathy for the author of the *Georgiques Chrétiennes*. With Henry Bordeaux and François Mauriac, he sat on the platform at Jammes' lecture, and in the following week Madame Chausson, the widow of the composer, gave a formal reception for Jammes at which Gide was present.

Jammes recalls in his letter the fact that Gide had helped with the expenses of publishing *Un Jour* (*Mercure de France*, 1895). Gide, Mallarmé, and Henri de Régnier had in fact been among the earliest and most efficacious supporters of Jammes.

Letter 167

For earlier disputes between Gide and Jammes, cf. the *Correspondance Francis Jammes-André Gide* (*N.R.F.*, 1948), pp. 184-201.

Letter 168

" X " in this letter is, of course, André Gide. The manuscript shows that Claudel had first written Gide's name and then effaced it with an X. The Latin quotation in this letter is from *Psalm* 90.

Letter 169

Claudel lunched with Rivière during the time which he spent in Paris in connection with the production of *L'Otage*, which was first given in the Salle Malakoff in May 1914. Rivière had been disquieted by his small daughter's refusal to eat—this explains Claudel's little homily.

Letter 170

Claudel had been sent to Rome on an economic mission, but in 1917 he left Rome for Rio de Janeiro, with the rank of Minister Plenipotentiary. During his stay in Rome he had constantly to return to the Quai D'Orsay for consultations, and he met there Paul Morand, who confided to his diary his impressions of Claudel's personality. " How surprised I was ! " he noted. " He's a thick-set man, with neither neck nor wrists. A ready-made tie, hideous spectacles, and very untidy. If he knew what *Connaissance de l'Est* has meant to me ! And *L'Arbre* to Giraudoux ! There's nothing dominating about him at first sight, except his striking way of first masticating his phrases and then spitting them out with a sort of exasperated authority. . . . When I asked him if he would soon return to Rome as commercial attaché, he suddenly came alive ; the thought of it put him in a good humour and for the first time he lit up. ' Ah, yes ! The sun,' he said. When Claudel speaks to you he is so abrupt that you feel as if he had slapped your face."

From 1914–1916 André Gide took a leading and onerous part in the Foyer Franco-Belge, a charitable organization which concerned itself with the lot of those whose homes had been overrun by the Germans.

Miguel de Unamuno (*b.* 1864) was a Professor of Greek who became Rector of Salamanca in 1914. A philosopher, a poet, a novelist, and a pamphleteer, he was just beginning to be known in France. His profound but highly personal Catholicism was not of a kind which could appeal to Claudel.

The *Pascendi* Encyclical was that in which (cf. *Letter* 88) the Pope condemned Modernism in all its forms.

Gide had sent Claudel two copies of a rare photograph of Rimbaud.

The " great crisis " of which Claudel speaks is the German offensive against Verdun.

Letter 172

Gide had sent Claudel his new *Symphonie Pastorale*. From 1919 to 1921 Claudel was French Minister Plenipotentiary in Copenhagen.

André Gide's *Journal* : 29th November 1921

After the appearance of Gide's *Morceaux Choisis* (*N.R.F.*, 1921) Henri Massis published a long article in the *Revue Universelle* with the object of warning his more youthful readers of the hazards of reading Gide. " The teaching of André Gide, and what he calls his influence," said Massis, " amount to no more than this : that he stirs up every element of disquiet in the reader's mind, brings it to the reader's notice, half-sympathizes with it, and then runs away as soon as the problems become really urgent." Massis also took up Claudel's assertion that " Evil admits of no compromise ". " That ", he said, " explains the whole failure of Gide and his art." Gide, for his part, admired Claudel's remark, but suggested to Massis that the enduring quality of his work (which was then already beyond question) might perhaps prove that Massis was over-sanguine in his dismissal of Gide's art. Even in 1937 (cf. his *Journal* for 26th June) Gide was still baffled by the exact significance of Claudel's phrase. In 1943, when prefacing his stage version of *Le Soulier de Satin*, Claudel spoke of the letter which he had always meant to write to Gide to prove to him that " *Le bien compose et le mal ne compose pas* ". Those who are interested in this controversy will find Massis' final word in his *André Gide à Marcel Proust* (Lardanchet, 1948).

Letter 173

Claudel was French Ambassador in Tokyo from 1921 to 1927. Gide had sent him his book on *Dostoevsky* (Plon, 1923), which particularly interested Claudel, in that Dostoevsky (with Homer, Virgil, Aeschylus, Shakespeare, and Rimbaud) is one of the few authors to whose influence he has ever admitted. When he accused Gide, however, of scoring off the Catholic Church, he was in reality referring only to those passages where Gide had spoken impartially of the Russian Orthodox Church. This in itself, to so ferocious a partisan as Claudel, was an act of indefensible criticism. The idea of art as a purge for the spirit was dear to both Claudel and Gide. " If I had not written my *Prométhée*," Gide wrote to Jammes in 1902, " my *Candaule* would have been cluttered up with it ; and if I had not written my *Immoralist* I might myself have become one. I purge myself." The great Tokyo earthquake of September 1923 destroyed a great part of Claudel's archives, and with them many of Gide's letters.

André Gide's *Journal* : 21st December 1923

Jacques Maritain (*b.* 1883) had already become well known for his studies of Aquinas, Bloy, Bergson, and Psichari, and above all for his *Art et Scholastique* (1920).
The book which he hoped to persuade Gide to suppress was *Corydon*, which is essentially an attempt to present homosexuality as normal, natural, and sanctioned alike by nature and by history. In 1911 twenty-one copies of an early version had been printed, with the title of *C.R.D.N.*, but no

mention of either the author's or the publisher's name. In 1920 an enlarged version was printed in an edition of twenty-five private copies, with the title of *Corydon : Quatre Dialogues Socratiques*, but again no mention of either author or publisher. Finally in 1924 the *N.R.F.* brought out an ordinary edition of 5500 copies with Gide's name on the cover.

Letter 174

Numquid et tu . . . ? is a title drawn from the *Gospel according to St. John*, vii. 52. The book consists of notes written, 1916 and 1919, during a period of acute religious disquietude. It is dedicated to Charles du Bos, who later persuaded Gide to publish it. It now figures in the Pléiade edition of the *Journal*.

Claudel especially admired Gide's elucidation of the idea of eternal life. " One of the gravest misunderstandings of the spirit of Christ," Gide had written, " comes from the confusion, so common in the minds of Christians, between future life and eternal life. There is nothing of futurity in the eternal life that Christ offers, and in which all his teaching invites us to share. It is not on the far side of death that it awaits us ; and, indeed, if we do not attain to it at once there is no hope that we shall ever attain it. . . . ' Verily, verily I say unto you ', Christ repeats everywhere, ' he that heareth my word . . . HATH (not *will have* but *already has*) EVERLASTING LIFE."

In 1936 Paul Claudel collected his religious essays and published them under the title of *Toi qui es-tu ?* (*N.R.F.*). This title is evidently intended to echo Gide's *Numquid et tu . . . ?*

The Abbé Henri Brémond (1865–1933) published an immense history of religious sentiment in France from the end of the wars of religion to our own time. Volume III deals exhaustively with Bérulle and Condren. Claudel speaks again of his admiration for this book in *Positions et Propositions*.

The *Spiritual Exercises* of St. Ignatius Loyola define five methods of prayer. The best known is that in which memory, intelligence, and will-power are all brought into play , after the use of the mind in meditation. The will is led freely, and with the help of grace, to subject itself to God. Condren's " French school " of spirituality conceives of prayer as essentially an act of adoration ; man is urged towards active contemplation of the divine mysteries and, under the influence of the Holy Spirit, comes to cleave to them with all his being.

Letter 175

In 1925 Claudel spent several months' leave in France. He then returned to Japan, and in 1927 was appointed ambassador to Washington. He ended his diplomatic career as Ambassador in Brussels (1933–1936).

Auguste Bréal was an intimate friend of Berthelot, through whom he came to know Claudel. He and Gide had been together at the *École Alsacienne*.

Claudel's detestation of Goethe was a minor cause of his progressive estrangement from Gide. Goethe and Nietzsche were equally vital to Gide, equally repellent to Claudel. In the essay in which he describes Nietzsche as " a zero ", Claudel remarks : " I shall only affirm, modestly but firmly, that Goethe has been, with Kant and Luther, one of the three evil geniuses of Germany."

Claudel's Carmelites were two nuns from the convent of Cholet whom he had met in 1925 on board the ship which was taking him home to France. Through them he learnt the mysteries of the Carmelites and was astonished afresh by the enormous power of prayer, and particularly of that sort of prayer in which the supplicant annihilates himself by ceasing to offer any obstacle to the will of God. In 1901 he had met another Carmelite, on his way back from China, and had heard from her of the saintly conduct of Sister Theresa of Lisieux. By a strange coincidence, St. Theresa had heard the call of God for the second time on 25th December 1886, the day on which Claudel himself had returned to the faith in Notre Dame.

Two months after his interview with Claudel, Gide left for Equatorial Africa, and remained there till June 1926. Accompanied by the film director, Marc Allegret, he travelled up the Congo and the Oubangui to Lake Chad, and thence to the coast at Douala by way of the Cameroons. Two books, *Le Voyage au Congo* and *Le Retour du Tchad*, contain a minutious account of their journey which, despite all reasonable precautions, was bound to be difficult and dangerous. Both Gide and Allegret were seriously ill with fever at various times ; but as Keats said in the phrase which Gide used as an epigraph for *Le Voyage au Congo* : " Better be imprudent moveables than prudent fixtures ".

Letter 176

In the summer of 1925 Claudel rented the Château de Lutaine in the Loir-et-Cher as a retreat for himself and his family. He later published the *Conversations dans le Loir-et-Cher* (*N.R.F.*, 1929) which were written at this time.

Letter 179

Laotze was a Taoist ascetic of the seventh century B.C. who has since become one of the most popular figures of Chinese legend. Claudel's quotation is from the Tao-toe-king, a work of mystical philosophy which is attributed to Laotze.

André Gide's *Journal* : 5th March 1929

Charles du Bos, author of *Le Dialogue avec André Gide*, was a graduate of Balliol College, Oxford, and both his many excellent books of criticism and his *Journal* (now in process of complete publication) display a rare understanding of English, as well as of French literature.

André Gide's *Journal* : 30th October 1929

Claudel's *Soulier de Satin* is the dream of a conscience which is tempted equally by the path of evil and the path of good. Fortunately, Dona Prouhèze, the protagonist of this struggle, has entrusted the Virgin with one of her slippers as an earnest of her good faith, and she can never tread the path of sin without limping. In this way she is eventually steered on to the path of virtue which, as everyone knows, is also that of renunciation.

The play was begun in Paris in May 1919 and finished in Tokyo in December 1924. It was published in 1929 by the *N.R.F.*, and in 1944 Claudel published a new stage version of the play, which he had devised in collaboration with Jean-Louis Barrault. This version is now in the repertory of the *Comédie Française,* and has incidental music by Honegger and scenery and costumes by Lucien Coutaud. Paul Claudel has written a new preface in which he contests Gide's epigram : " It is not with good sentiments that good literature is made " ; and he also returns to the theme that " *le bien compose et le mal ne compose pas* ".

December 1931

L'Annonce faite à Marie was to have been produced by Louis Jouvet in 1931, but Paul Claudel withdrew his permission after learning that Jouvet had produced a play by Roger Martin du Gard, *La Taciturne,* in which the plot turned upon certain abnormal passions, both male and female.

Paul Claudel's Interview with a Reporter from *Combat,* March 1947.

In March 1947 *Combat,* then edited by Albert Camus, sent Mlle Arban to interview Claudel with the object of discovering his views on the aspirations of the younger generation of writers. She had intended to keep to this theme, but having incidentally introduced Gide's name into the conversation, she found that the interview was developing its own momentum. It was published under the heading : " Monsieur Claudel answers some unexpected questions ".

INDEX OF PERSONS

The division between Text and Notes is indicated by a colon

INDEX OF TITLES

Books, articles, essays and lectures, with date of publication, or first appearance in print

I. PAUL CLAUDEL

II. ANDRÉ GIDE